THE HOMESCHOOL CHOICE

CRITICAL PERSPECTIVES ON YOUTH
General Editors: Amy L. Best, Lorena Garcia, and Jessica K. Taft

Fast-Food Kids: French Fries, Lunch Lines, and Social Ties
Amy L. Best

White Kids: Growing Up with Privilege in a Racially Divided America
Margaret A. Hagerman

Growing Up Queer: Kids and the Remaking of LGBTQ Identity
Mary Robertson

The Kids Are in Charge: Activism and Power in Peru's Movement of Working Children
Jessica K. Taft

Coming of Age in Iran: Poverty and the Struggle for Dignity
Manata Hashemi

The World Is Our Classroom: Extreme Parenting and the Rise of Worldschooling
Jennie Germann Molz

The Homeschool Choice: Parents and the Privatization of Education
Kate Henley Averett

The Homeschool Choice

Parents and the Privatization of Education

Kate Henley Averett

NEW YORK
NEW YORK UNIVERSITY PRESS

NEW YORK UNIVERSITY PRESS
New York
www.nyupress.org

© 2021 by New York University
All rights reserved

References to Internet websites (URLs) were accurate at the time of writing. Neither the author nor New York University Press is responsible for URLs that may have expired or changed since the manuscript was prepared.

Library of Congress Cataloging-in-Publication Data
Names: Averett, Kate Henley, author.
Title: The homeschool choice : parents and the privatization of education / Kate Henley Averett.
Other titles: The home school choice
Description: New York : New York University Press, [2021] |
Series: Critical perspectives on youth | Includes bibliographical references and index.
Identifiers: LCCN 2020035723 (print) | LCCN 2020035724 (ebook) |
ISBN 9781479882786 (cloth) | ISBN 9781479891610 (paperback) |
ISBN 9781479801664 (ebook other) | ISBN 9781479820689 (ebook)
Subjects: LCSH: Home schooling—Social aspects—United States. | Privatization in education—United States. | Gender identity in education—United States.
Classification: LCC LC40 .A94 2021 (print) | LCC LC40 (ebook) | DDC 371.04/2—dc23
LC record available at https://lccn.loc.gov/2020035723
LC ebook record available at https://lccn.loc.gov/2020035724

New York University Press books are printed on acid-free paper, and their binding materials are chosen for strength and durability. We strive to use environmentally responsible suppliers and materials to the greatest extent possible in publishing our books.

Manufactured in the United States of America

10 9 8 7 6 5 4 3 2 1

Also available as an ebook

For Sanden, for everything,

And in memory of Charlie Long and Blondie and Charlie Brownfield

CONTENTS

Introduction — 1

1. Homeschooling in the United States: A Brief Overview — 17

2. What Is Childhood? Contrasting Views of Childhood Gender and Sexuality — 29

3. Educating the Unique Child — 59

4. Views of Education: What Do Children Need out of an Education, and Who Should Provide It? — 89

5. Giving Up on Government — 114

6. Motherhood and the Gendered Labor of Homeschooling — 142

Conclusion: Is Homeschooling a Problem? — 177

Acknowledgments — 191

Appendix: Methodology — 195

Notes — 219

Bibliography — 237

Index — 251

About the Author — 257

Introduction

Sharon Bennett, Maura Harrington, and Alma Garcia all homeschool their children. On the surface, they have little else in common. Sharon, a fundamentalist Christian, turned to homeschooling because she saw public schools as hostile to her family's religious beliefs, especially when it came to issues like sexuality, where she thought the schools overreached by teaching children too much. In contrast, Maura, a self-identified feminist, homeschooled in part because she felt public schools were not doing *enough* to foster healthy sexual development in students, especially girls. And Alma had quite a few critiques of her own local school district and how they handled her son's learning disability—a frustrating experience that led her to homeschool both of her children—but she considered herself a great supporter of public schools in general.

Sharon Bennett lived in the suburbs about half an hour north of Austin, Texas, in a single-family home with her husband and sixteen-year-old son, Luke. I began my interview with her by telling her I wanted to learn about how people make the decision to homeschool. She replied, without hesitation, "Well I know for us, [it's because] we are a Christian family." She recalled how, when Luke was just a toddler, "that's what I felt God calling me to do, was to homeschool." Later, when I asked her what she saw as the main advantage of homeschooling over public schooling, she said, without hesitation, that it was educating her son in a Christian environment. "You can't really do that with the public schools," she mused. "It's almost like there's everything *but* Christianity. I mean, they can teach all of these other things, but if you want to bring the Bible into it, you can't." Recounting some recent drama in a neighboring school district about teaching gay- and lesbian-inclusive sex-education content in the high school, she reflected nostalgically on an imagined public school of the past, saying that "years and years ago, probably fifty years ago, back before they took prayer out of school, you used to be able to talk about God, or pray in school, or have your Bible—those were things that you could do." She paused, then added wistfully, "and they've changed all of that, so culturally it's gotten so different."

Unlike Sharon, Maura Harrington—who lived on a narrow dirt road in a small town in the Texas Hill Country with her husband and her twelve-year-old daughter, Merri—said she homeschools, at least in part, for "feminist reasons." She and her husband were especially concerned about some of the ways in which girls are treated in society, particularly about how they are socialized to objectify themselves starting at a young age. She explained to me, "We had concerns about the way that it seems like girls are being sexualized younger, and younger, and younger. And we wanted her to keep her sense of being, looking out through her own eyes at the world rather than thinking about how she appears to other people. Because that seems to be a large part of that process, is the turning of the gaze, instead of through her own eyes, thinking about how she appears to others. That was a big concern for us." I asked her if she feels as though homeschooling has helped in this regard, and she said, "Yeah, I do think so. I don't know if it's entirely homeschooling or what it is, but she is still, you know, very much—although she's [physically] developed, and she looks like a teenager at this point, she is very much still looking out of her own eyes. I'm pleased about that." Homeschooling allowed Maura to keep Merri in a peer environment with far less pressure to fit in. It also afforded her the opportunity to talk in some depth with her daughter about her perspective on feminism; she even bought Merri a feminist reader and discussed some of the essays with her.

In contrast to both Sharon and Maura, Alma Garcia spoke in largely positive terms about public education. Alma lived in southeast Austin with her husband, Joe, and their sons, Matthew, age fifteen, and Andrew, age thirteen. Alma and Joe were each the first in their family to attend college, and they both came from large, tight-knit, Mexican American families who felt strongly about the importance of public education. Despite being raised in this context, however, Alma began homeschooling her sons shortly after Matthew began middle school. Alma had been very involved at Matthew's elementary school, in part because Matthew was diagnosed with Attention Deficit Disorder (ADD), but she found herself being shut out once he began middle school. Describing the relationship between parents and the school as "a great divide," Alma recounted, "If I had a question or a concern, the answer that I continuously got was, 'Well we've already discussed that with your child.' Well, I'm not asking you to discuss it with my child, I'm asking you to discuss it with me." Alma had an increasingly hard time accessing Matthew's teachers to find out how concepts were being taught, which made it next to impossible for her to help Matthew when he was struggling with his homework. After a particularly frustrating day of meeting with a team of Matthew's teachers and administrators, Alma reached her breaking point. "I thought, 'Wait a second. They don't want me involved. This is not the way to teach a kid. Why am I here?' And we never went back."

How did these three women, with their contrasting perspectives on public schools, all end up homeschooling? In a climate of deep political polarization, an outside observer might not expect that Sharon, Maura, and Alma would be able to find common ground about much of anything. Why do they all agree on homeschooling?

Sharon, Maura, and Alma are three of the forty-six homeschooling parents whom I interviewed for this book, and their children are among the almost two million US children who are currently homeschooled.[1] Between August 2013 and May 2016, I conducted a survey of over six hundred homeschooling parents, interviewed forty-six of those parents, and attended five homeschooling conferences and conventions across the state of Texas. I did this research in response to what I saw as a fascinating paradox: that parents with varying stances in terms of politics and religiosity—and particularly, with distinct perspectives on childhood gender and sexuality—could all come to the same practice of homeschooling their children. When I was growing up, the only families I knew who homeschooled were conservative Christians, like Sharon Bennett and her family, who held strong beliefs about sex, marriage, and the "traditional" (heterosexual) family. But a few years before beginning this research, I began to notice an interesting trend: people on social media, who were self-identified liberals and progressives, feminists, and queer parents, talking about homeschooling, often in discussions about the negative experiences of LGBTQ+ youth in schools or critiques of abstinence-only sex education. In such an adamantly politically divided society, especially about topics related to sexuality and gender, how do these parents find themselves in similar positions, opting to homeschool their children? I suspected that parents with different views might have very different motivations for homeschooling, and I wanted to know: what are these motivations?

In the chapters that follow, I show that parents' motivations for homeschooling are, in fact, quite varied. Some parents' motivations, like Sharon's and Maura's, are grounded in an incompatibility between the parent's understanding of what schooling and childhood *should* look like, and how public-school students experience schooling and childhood. These parents can find a misalignment between their ideals and the practices of schools from more conservative or more progressive perspectives. Nowhere are these political differences more evident than in their critiques of gender and sexuality in American public schools. One critique sees schools as overly sexual spaces that are a threat to the sexual innocence of children. Parents who feel this way—largely, but not entirely, conservative and religious parents—see homeschooling as a way to protect their children from the influence of peers, the school curriculum, and a perceived broader liberal agenda in public schools. The other critique sees schools as promoting a narrow understanding of gender and sexuality, in which the heterosexual and/or traditionally gendered space of the school forces children to adhere to a model of gender and sexuality that is, at best, constraining and, at worst, dangerous. The parents who express this critique tend to see homeschooling as a way to avoid the forced conforming of their children to a narrow expression of gender and sexuality.

For other parents, like Alma, motivations for homeschooling are grounded less in an ideological critique of education than in specific negative experiences with public schools. I spoke with many parents over the course of this research who recounted stories of long, drawn-out conflicts with their children's public (and, in a few cases, private) schools that they came to see as unresolvable. These included conflicts over the quality of education; over accommodation for disabilities, special needs, health issues, and giftedness; and over the handling of bullying and peer conflict. Many of these parents had never considered homeschooling before, but they came to see it as their only choice when they felt their children's schools were not able to offer what their children needed.

The existence of ideological diversity in the homeschooling community is, of course, not new. In his groundbreaking 2001 book on the

American homeschooling movement, sociologist Mitchell L. Stevens details the ways in which liberal and conservative forces have shaped modern homeschooling from the beginning.[2] However, in the two decades since Stevens's book was published, this diversity has increased, as religion is no longer the most-cited motivation for parents' decision to homeschool. In more recent years, it has not been ideological critiques of public education at all but rather concerns about the environment of these schools that have been the most-cited motivation of these parents.[3]

Other things about the homeschooling movement have changed in the last two decades as well, including a near doubling in the number of homeschooled students, as well as changes in the broader context of public education in the United States. For this reason, the scope of this book extends far beyond the answer to *why* parents homeschool. Rather, I use the narratives of homeschooling parents to understand the rising popularity of homeschooling and what this trend indicates about broader cultural beliefs about childhood, parenting, and education. Contemporary homeschooling gives us insight into three important areas of social concern: (1) the shifting relationships among the state, public schools, and families, especially in light of the increased privatization of both education and social reproduction, (2) changing beliefs about childhood gender and sexuality, and (3) the implications of intensive mothering for children's education and for gender inequality more broadly.

In *The Homeschool Choice*, I demonstrate that these three theoretical conversations—about school choice, childhood gender and sexuality, and intensive mothering—are not, in fact, separate conversations, but that, in the context of homeschooling, they are intimately linked. I show that beliefs about childhood, particularly as they pertain to gender and sexuality, are central to parents' narratives about why they choose to homeschool. I argue that this is due to the fact that school choice is presented as a free-market solution to moral and religious debates about gender and sexuality, such as debates about teaching sex education and LGBT-inclusive content in schools. In these debates, parents—particularly mothers, who are seen as responsible for their children's education as well as their moral upbringing—are framed as consumers of educational services, who can opt out of the public school system if it comes into conflict with their beliefs about, for example, the acceptability of same-sex relationships or the existence and normalization of transgender identities.

School Choice and the Privatization of Education

Education in the United States is moving away from the common-school model of education and toward a marketplace or "school-choice" model.[4] In the common-school model, the ideal is that all children be provided with a similar educational experience, grounded in preparing them to engage in a democratic society. Under the school-choice model, however, it is theorized that the quality of education for all students will increase if schools are forced to compete with each other in order to continually offer a better "product" to children and parents, who are understood as the consumers of educational services.[5]

The rise in both the popularity and the acceptability of homeschooling has occurred in tandem with the rise of the rhetoric of school choice, where homeschooling is one of the many educational choices that should be available to parents and children. The school-choice model is itself part of a larger trend toward the privatization of public education and other public services—what scholars have come to call the "neoliberalization" of public education.[6] Neoliberalism refers to a broad set of global economic policies focused on competition, market discipline, and fiscal austerity.[7] Privatization of what were previously public services—including education—is one of the hallmark practices of neoliberalism. While the privatization of public education is most often associated with the emergence of privately run (and for-profit) public charter schools or voucher programs that allow children to attend private schools using public funding, homeschooling is arguably the most radical manifestation of this trend, in which education moves into the private realm of the family home. Just a few decades ago, homeschooling was considered a deviant practice, but the privatization of education has helped to legitimize it.[8]

How are neoliberal education reforms affecting families? The narratives I present in this book give us a rich understanding of how parents make decisions about their children's education under the school-choice model, revealing the ways in which parents navigate the rhetoric of school choice and the corresponding changes in education. The decisions that parents make around homeschooling help illuminate the changing relationships among the family, the state, and public schools, and the stories I present in this book highlight how trust in, and reliance upon, public services are changing, and what this means for families.

Childhood Gender and Sexuality

Homeschooling also provides a window into contemporary changes in the meaning of childhood in general, and of childhood gender and sexuality specifically. Understandings of childhood are historically and culturally situated. At least in the West, the very concept of childhood, as distinct from both infancy and adulthood, only emerged beginning in the fifteenth century.[9] In *Pricing the Priceless Child*, sociologist Viviana Zelizer argues that the movement to end child labor and move children from factories and into schools through compulsory education laws was largely an ideological dispute between two opposing views of children: the "sacred child," who is in a special part of life and in need of nurturing and protection from adults, and the "productive child," who can contribute to the family economically like any other family member. Ultimately, the sacred child won, and compulsory education is now the norm in the United States.[10] The concept of childhood as a distinct, special stage of life has thus always been intimately linked to ideas about the role of public schools in children's lives. Recent changes in the provision of education, and particularly beliefs about the *purpose* of this education, beg the question of whether our societal beliefs about childhood have also changed. Homeschooling offers fresh insights into the ways in which dominant beliefs about childhood are shifting alongside these shifts in education.

Debates about what is "sacred" about childhood often revolve around gender and sexuality. Are children innocent and asexual, and in need of protection from sexuality, or are they sexual beings who can and do exercise agency? These debates have deeper roots, and more far-reaching consequences, beyond how we understand childhood. They are really debates about sexuality more broadly; the concept of "childhood" serves as a container within which society expresses anxieties about sex, gender, and sexuality.[11] As the narratives of Sharon and Maura at the start of this chapter indicate, debates about childhood gender and sexuality are central to competing framings of homeschooling in the United States. These narratives are a microcosm of broader societal anxieties about gender and sexuality.

Institutional context matters to how children experience and understand gender and sexuality,[12] and education is one context in which childhood gender and sexuality are especially salient.[13] The environment of the school—and the perceptions of that environment by parents—are highly gendered,[14] and academic instruction in public schools contains both explicit and implicit lessons about gender and sexuality.[15] Parental concerns about peer influence at school tend to be formulated in racialized, classed, gendered, and sexualized terms: that is, parents construct racial, class, and gendered "others" as potentially dangerous influences on their own (assumed-to-be) innocent, impressionable children.[16] In this book, I explore the ways in which homeschooling parents' critiques of public education are tied to their beliefs about childhood gender and sexuality. How are the homeschool environments they create themselves gendered and sexualized spaces? And how do homeschooling parents resist—or reproduce—popular notions of gendered childhoods?

Mothering and Gender Inequality

Cultural beliefs about childhood are intimately tied to beliefs about what it means to be a good parent, and more specifically, how to be a good mother. Parenting the "sacred child" requires the investment of money and time, particularly on the part of the mother, and it requires that parents take a protectionist stance toward their children, as the sacred child holds an emotional value greater than any other.[17]

The investment of time and money into raising children is the hallmark of what Sharon Hays dubbed the "ideology of intensive mothering," which, she argued in the 1990s, had become the dominant way of thinking about parenting in the United States.[18] Intensive mothering functions as an ideology insofar as it orients the behavior of mothers in certain ways.[19] Though this ideology is adapted and resisted by individual women, all mothers in the United States are aware of it, and it shapes how they think about, feel about, and experience motherhood.[20] Intensive mothering requires that mothers be both economically productive and highly invested in caring for their children, and this creates tension for many women as they strive to achieve the ideal of the working mom who "does it all."[21] The ideology of intensive mothering remains central to the experiences of most American mothers today, whether or not they are able to come close to attaining its ideals. As sociologist Jennifer Lois has argued, the fact that mothers perform the vast majority of homeschooling labor supports this claim.[22]

However, since Hays first conceptualized the ideology of intensive mothering, the cultural rhetoric of neoliberalism, with its "buzzwords" of "efficiency" and "individual responsibility," has crept into our thinking about parenting. Parenting under neoliberalism is marked by the need for mothers to manage their children's lives. This trend is informed by two primary beliefs: the first, consistent with the ideology of intensive mothering, is that parents must rely on expert advice in caring for their children; and the second is that implementing this advice is an individual, private decision.[23] As "expert advice" on child rearing has proliferated, parents—particularly mothers—are faced with an onslaught of contradictory advice on how to best raise their children. But it is seen as their responsibility—not the responsibility of the "experts"—to sift through this competing advice and make individual decisions about what is best for their children.[24] Thus, mothers are required to be the ultimate experts on their own individual children—even when this means going against certain expert advice, as is the case with mothers who choose not to vaccinate their children.[25] This is certainly the case with homeschooling, as "expert advice" advocating both for *and* against homeschooling abounds. An understanding of how mothers make the decision to homeschool, and how they understand the gendered nature of this decision, is thus central to understanding gender inequality in the era of neoliberal motherhood.

The Study

I carried out the research for this project between August 2013 and May 2016. During this time, I conducted a survey of over six hundred homeschooling parents, interviewed forty-six of those parents, and attended five homeschooling conferences and conventions across the state of Texas. The parents I surveyed came from all over the state and represented a wide range of political stances, religious affiliations, and motivations for homeschooling. The survey asked about homeschooling experiences and approaches, motivations for homeschooling, and political and social views, including, for example, views on same-sex marriage, abortion, school prayer, and sex education.

More than half of the parents who responded to my survey said that they were interested in being interviewed for the project as well. Out of these parents, I carefully chose a diverse sample to interview in person. The purpose of these interviews was to elicit the narratives of homeschool parents about how and why they made the decision to homeschool, their homeschooling approaches, and the advantages and disadvantages they see to homeschooling compared to traditional public schooling.[26] I selected interview respondents in such a way as to collect as diverse a sample as possible. I was particularly interested in having a representation of various political views (conservative, moderate, and liberal) and degrees of religiosity, and thus attempted to initiate contact with roughly equal numbers of conservative and liberal, and religious and nonreligious, respondents: of the forty-four focal interviewees, one quarter (eleven respondents) identified as politically moderate, while 39% (seventeen respondents) identified as conservative or very conservative, and 36% (sixteen respondents) identified as liberal or very liberal. Half of the sample identified as not very or not at all religious, and the other half as somewhat or very religious.

I also engaged in participant observation at various homeschooling conferences and conventions throughout the period I was carrying out this research. I attended five such events between August 2013 and April 2015: three large, explicitly fundamentalist Christian homeschooling conferences, one small Catholic homeschooling conference, and one small conference of unschoolers—those who engage in "child-led" homeschooling. At these conferences, I acted as a participant observer in order to understand the narratives of homeschooling families as part of a larger set of discourses (collective ways of thinking and talking about a subject that help to organize social life).[27] I participated as a regular registrant, attending various talks, workshops, and special events/performances, and "window shopping" among the vendor areas. Attending these events helped me to contextualize the experiences of the parents I interviewed within the broader homeschooling culture.

Why Texas?

In many ways, Texas is an ideal place to study homeschooling. Despite its reputation as a deeply conservative state, Texas is, in fact, a large, diverse state with a wide range of political perspectives represented. While there is a massive religious infrastructure in place in Texas (as in much of the United States) to support homeschooling, there are also plenty of resources available to support nonreligious homeschoolers. In fact, I learned during this research that some consider the capital city of Austin to be one of the epicenters of progressive, "alternative" education in the United States—a trend that includes "unschooling," or child-led homeschooling.

Texas is also a great place to study homeschooling because it is relatively easy to homeschool in the state. Regulation of home education in the United States—like regulation of education in general—occurs at the state and local levels.[28] There is a great deal of variation in homeschooling regulations across different states.[29] Currently, Texas is considered one of the least restrictive states in the United States in which to homeschool, with the Home School Legal Defense Association, a conservative homeschool advocacy group, calling Texas "a model state in upholding parental rights."[30] The Texas courts have ruled (and the Texas Supreme Court has unanimously upheld this ruling) that homeschools in the state of Texas are considered private schools, and thus are subject to the same (lack of) regulation as any other private school in the state.[31] If a parent in Texas wants to homeschool, they simply need to withdraw their child from school with a note explaining that they will be homeschooling—or, if the child has not started school yet, they simply do not need to enroll the child.

Because these structural constraints on homeschooling vary by state, Texas serves as an ideal case for studying parents' motivations for homeschooling. Extrapolating from national numbers, I estimate that the number of homeschooled children in Texas could exceed two hundred thousand—and I suspect the number is actually much higher.[32] With Texas having far fewer hoops for parents to jump through to withdraw a child from public school than most other states, and a lack of strict curriculum requirements or testing, it would make sense that parents who are *considering* homeschooling in Texas may be more likely to actually begin homeschooling than parents considering homeschooling in other states. Thus, Texas is an ideal location for this study because there is a wide variation in parents' motivations to homeschool, including those whose motivations are not based on strong ideological or religious commitments.

Roadmap of the Book

In the chapters that follow, I examine the discourses about childhood, education, government, and parenting that homeschooling parents draw on in discussing their motivations for homeschooling. In other words, rather than just look at the motivations themselves, I take a deeper dive into the ideals they express about children, families, education, and the state in order to highlight some of the prominent differences, as well as the points of convergence, among parents who may have homeschooling, but little else, in common.

Homeschooling is a social movement that has served as a container for multiple, competing ideological perspectives, and that has grown in both popularity and diversity in the last decade. In chapter 1, I discuss the history and present state of homeschooling in the United States in order to contextualize the narratives of the parents featured in the remainder of the book. I first provide a brief history of the modern homeschooling movement, highlighting the ways in which both conservative and progressive education critiques have driven the movement. I then discuss the current state of homeschooling, including the legal status and regulation of homeschooling, the spectrum of homeschooling instruction approaches, and research findings about the outcomes of homeschooling, as well as about demographic trends in the kinds of people who homeschool.

In chapters 2 and 3, I ask how homeschooling parents understand who children are and what childhood is, and interrogate how these understandings impact their decision to homeschool. In chapter 2, I examine two different critiques of gender and sexuality in American public schools that arose both in my interviews with parents and in the homeschooling conferences I attended. First, some parents critique schools as overly sexual spaces that are a threat to the sexual innocence of children and see homeschooling as a way of protecting their children. Second, some parents argue that schools promote a narrow understanding of gender and sexuality that is heterosexual and traditionally gendered, and this understanding ends up constraining, and even hurting, children. I argue that these two critiques correspond to two competing ideologies of childhood: one that views children as "in process," or as developing toward selfhood, and the other that views children as already selves, capable of exercising agency and autonomy. These two ideologies of childhood result in different homeschooling practices, highlighting how the homeschooling experience can be very different for children depending on their parents' ideological standpoint.

The competing ideologies of childhood that I discuss in chapter 2 were not the only ideologies of childhood that I came across in my research. Whether they understand children as innocent people-in-development or as already agentic, autonomous people, the parents I interviewed almost universally talked about their children as unique. In chapter 3, I examine this ideology of the unique child, arguing that it has taken hold as one of the dominant ideologies of childhood in the United States. Examining how homeschooling parents utilize this discourse of unique children demonstrates the ways in which this ideology leads parents to prioritize their own children's needs over the needs of other children. I demonstrate that parents talk about homeschooling as a practice that allows them to tailor children's education to their unique temperaments, aptitudes, interests, and other needs, and furthermore, that it does this in a way that is just not feasible in public-school classrooms.

In chapters 4 and 5, I look more closely at parents' perceptions of public education. In chapter 4, I show that these parents believe that children need certain things out of their educational experiences, but they do not always see children—their own and others—getting these things from public schools. The parents I interviewed use the logic and rhetoric of the school-choice movement to talk about their search for alternative options to their local public schools when they see an incompatibility between what they think their children need out of their education and what schools are providing. The school choice model has, ironically, resulted in increased standardization of schools, with a corresponding decrease in individual and collective efficacy of teachers to advocate for their students. I argue that these twin trends, when combined with the increased pressure for mothers to manage the individual needs of their children, effectively pit motherhood and public schools against each other. Mothers feel forced to take an oppositional stance toward public school to ensure that their children's needs are met. When these needs are not met, the responsibility falls on the mother, not the school, to find an alternative solution. I argue that these narratives reveal how some mothers feel pushed into homeschooling, seeing it as a "choice" that they were forced into when faced with a lack of alternatives.

In chapter 5, I look at how parents view public schools as an extension of the state, complete with political agendas that parents often dislike. Given the political diversity of the parents I interviewed, it should come as no surprise that the substance of their critiques of the political agendas present in schools varied. Parents also critiqued the inefficiency of the state in running public schools, with some critiquing the overall lack of funding for education and others criticizing what they see as poor prioritization with respect to what that funding goes to. Parents also expressed a profound disappointment with federal education reforms, using these as an example of general government incompetence. In short, even when their assessment of what children needed from education varied, there was a common sentiment among these parents that the government would not, or could not, provide that education.

Mothers do the majority of the day-to-day homeschooling labor in most families. In chapter 6, I examine the way motherhood was framed at the conferences I attended, as well as how the parents I interviewed understand their roles as mothers, in order to understand why homeschooling is so overwhelmingly seen as women's work. Some mothers explained their assumption of homeschooling work in essentialist terms, describing it as something at which women are naturally better—or, for some, divinely ordained to be better. Other mothers, however, described homeschooling as an extension of the general work of mothering. This was particularly true for those parents who practiced attachment parenting. And some mothers articulated the gendered division of labor in their own, and other, homeschooling families as being a reflection of a larger society with pervasive gender inequality, in which men's higher earnings, women's and men's gendered skill development, and the accountability that mothers, but not fathers, face for their parenting decisions all push women toward being the primary homeschooling parent. I argue that these explanations are all best understood in the context of the ideology of intensive mothering and the neoliberal mandate that mothers exercise managerial control over their children's lives—or be held accountable if they do not. These ideologies work together to constrain mothers' actions to their own family, because they feel that any work they may want to undertake to make social change at a larger level would mean sacrificing the well-being of their own children. In other words, I argue that the demands of neoliberal mothering depoliticize these women.

In the book's conclusion, I turn to an ongoing question among critics of homeschooling: is homeschooling a problem? I discuss how I see this research contributing to larger debates about homeschooling regulation. I argue that, because this book demonstrates that homeschooling is one case of the larger phenomenon of school choice, rather than asking whether homeschooling is a problem, it is more appropriate to ask whether school choice is a problem. I demonstrate that, because school choice more broadly reinforces social inequalities along the lines of gender, sexuality, race, class, and age, we should see school choice—and the encroachment of neoliberalism into education, family, and childhood—as a social problem.

The Homeschool Choice is a book about how American families have responded to increasing polarization around issues of gender and sexuality, in an era of privatization. It offers a window into how parents feel both empowered and constrained by recent changes in education policy motivated by the ethos of school choice. The narratives of homeschooling parents illuminate the changing relationships among the family, the state, and public schools under a neoliberal policy model, and the infiltration of neoliberal beliefs into our broader cultural ideologies of childhood, education, motherhood, and the state. These accounts highlight how trust in, and reliance upon, public services are changing, and what this means for the changing burdens families face as the state divests from public education.

1

Homeschooling in the United States

A Brief Overview

Many homeschoolers are quick to remark that homeschooling is a centuries-old practice: George Washington, Abraham Lincoln, and Thomas Edison were some of the most popular "famous homeschoolers" I heard mentioned over the course of my fieldwork.[1] However, this narrative is only partially true, as home-based education was, for many early Americans, the only option available. The modern homeschooling movement, however, in which homeschooling serves as a self-conscious alternative to public schools, began in the United States in the 1960s.[2] From the early part of the twentieth century, when compulsory education laws became widespread, the idea that children would attend public (or, for some, private) schools was largely unquestioned by Americans, and homeschooling was practically unheard of.[3] How did the practice come to be taken up by hundreds, thousands, and eventually hundreds of thousands of American families? In this chapter, I briefly discuss the origins and growth of the modern homeschooling movement, followed by a discussion of what homeschooling in the United States looks like today, including current homeschooling regulations, recent changes and trends in the kinds of people who homeschool, and some of the common forms of homeschooling instruction.

The Emergence of the Modern Homeschooling Movement

Though the homeschooling movement's growth is largely credited to the practice being taken up by fundamentalist Christians, the movement itself originated in the work of progressive education reformers, most notably John Holt.[4] Holt, a public school teacher who had grown disillusioned with the school system, published several notable works in the 1960s that scrutinized public schools and promoted the idea of "deschooling," or letting children learn apart from institutionalized schools.[5] These progressive reformers believed that education should be flexible and should cater to the needs of the individual child—something they did not see happening in public schools. They were also concerned that public schools ended up quashing children's innate curiosity, and argued that children would learn most of what they need to know if left in charge of their own education. This critique was part of a larger critique in the 1960s of institutions in general, which many on the Left saw as being conservative, overly bureaucratic, and designed to maintain the status quo of racial, gender, and class inequalities. In this vein, education reformers argued that schools were preparing students for routinized, industrial careers rather than to be independent thinkers.[6] This system may have served the interests of elites, but, education reformers argued, it certainly did not serve the interests of most children.

At around the same time, homeschooling also began to be advocated and practiced by some in the religious Right. Seventh Day Adventists Raymond and Dorothy Moore are generally credited with being the first conservative Christians in the United States to publicly advocate for homeschooling. The Moores were critical both of the secular nature of education and of the way a formal curriculum was being pushed onto children at younger and younger ages.[7] They became frequent guests on James Dobson's *Focus on the Family* radio show, and Dobson's endorsement of homeschooling is credited with its rapid growth among conservative Evangelical Christians.[8]

For many conservative Christians, homeschooling was a way for their families to resist what they saw as the increasing encroachment of secular culture into their—and their children's—lives.[9] The US Supreme Court rulings in the early 1960s that ended the practices of school prayer and Bible reading in public schools played an important role in catalyzing the religious Right against public schools (and continue, to this day, to motivate some parents—more than a few of the parents I interviewed brought up the end of school prayer as an important turning point in what they saw as the downward spiral of American public education).[10] Some research has also suggested that school desegregation played a role in the rise of homeschooling among the religious Right, and that early Christian homeschooling can be understood as a form of "white flight" from integrated school districts.[11]

In the early decades of the modern homeschooling movement, there was a fair amount of cooperation between progressives and conservative religious homeschoolers. While they had somewhat different motivations for advocating homeschooling, movement leaders such as John Holt, on the left, and Raymond and Dorothy Moore, on the right, had in common their belief in the importance of child-centered pedagogical approaches.[12] However, historians of the movement argue that, as the religious Right gained broad political momentum and an increasing number of conservative Protestants took up the practice of homeschooling in the 1980s, religious homeschoolers increasingly critiqued these pedagogical approaches, and thus began distancing themselves from the secular wing of the homeschooling movement.[13] Scholars point to the founding in 1983 of the Home School Legal Defense Association (HSLDA), an explicitly (fundamentalist) Christian organization, as one of the pivotal moments in the eventual division of the movement.[14] This trend away from cooperation between the two wings was further cemented by the legislative success of the movement.

Controversy and Legalization

Even as homeschooling was being established as an alternative to public schooling during the 1970s and 1980s, the practice was still illegal in most states. Despite their very different political and religious orientations, the religious Right and the progressive education reformers of the Left worked together to mobilize politically to get pro-homeschooling legislation passed in each state. Scholars note that several US Supreme Court cases pertaining to parental rights paved the way for the success of homeschoolers' legislative efforts, including *Meyers v. Nebraska* (1923) and *Pierce v. Society of Seven Sisters* (1925), which established parents' fundamental authority over their children's upbringing, including their education, and *Wisconsin v. Yoder* (1972), which argued that, in certain cases, parents' religious freedom could trump compulsory education laws.[15]

Homeschoolers took a two-pronged approach of litigation and lobbying—targeting both the courts and state legislatures—in almost all states, in order both to make homeschooling legal and, once it was legal, to attempt to strip away some of the more obtrusive regulation of the practice. This effort was quite successful; by 1993, homeschooling was legal—with varying degrees of regulation—in all fifty US states.[16] In Texas, where I carried out the research for this book, the legality of homeschooling was decided in 1987 via the *Leeper v. Arlington Independent School District* class action case, which ruled that homeschools count as private schools under Texas law. The decision was appealed by the state twice but was upheld both times, in 1991 by a district appeals court and in 1994 by the Texas Supreme Court.[17] (Interestingly, Texas is one of the only states where litigation, rather than lobbying the state legislature, was the primary means of achieving legality of homeschooling.)[18] Once this legislative agenda was accomplished in every state, there was less need for cooperation between the left and right wings of the movement, and from this point, the movement became quite bifurcated.[19]

Current Homeschooling Regulations

Over the course of just a few decades, then, homeschooling in the United States went from being a deviant, often illegal, practice to one that is increasingly normalized.[20] Homeschooling is now seen by many as an acceptable alternative to public education; however, because homeschooling, like all other forms of education, is overseen by states rather than the federal government, the degree of regulation of homeschooling varies widely across the United States.

Texas falls on the less-regulated side of the spectrum—while a handful of states are *as* unregulated, none are *more* unregulated.[21] Homeschool parents are not required to register with the state, and because homeschools are considered private schools under Texas law, they are subject to the same (lack of) regulation as other private schools.[22] Many of the homeschoolers I spoke with over the course of my research took great pride in Texas's lack of regulation. I even acquired a bit of "conference swag" at one of the Texas Home School Coalition conferences that I attended that allowed me to partake in the national "bragging rights" of the state's homeschoolers: a bright red, reusable shopping bag emblazoned with the Texas flag and the words "I homeschool in Texas, where people are FREE."

On the other end of the spectrum, with high levels of regulation, are states like New York. Parents who homeschool in New York must submit a yearly notice of intent to their local school district superintendent, submit a yearly "Individualized Home Instruction Plan," file quarterly reports on the child's progress, including grades or narrative evaluations for each subject, and assess the child through standardized tests (yearly in grades 1–3 and 9–12, and every other year in grades 4–8).[23] Other states fall somewhere between the two, requiring registration with the state and/or some form of assessment or reporting, though few states require quite as rigorous reporting as New York.[24]

Homeschoolers themselves are far from being of one mind about the question of state regulation of homeschooling, and what the "right" degree of regulation should be.[25] While some of the parents I interviewed expressed concern about the lack of oversight of homeschooling in Texas, others—including parents on both the political Right and the political Left—expressed a deep appreciation for being able to homeschool without the government telling them what to do. This debate has occasionally reached the mainstream, often arising when cases of child abuse by homeschooling parents make headlines. It is important to note that while there is no evidence that homeschooling families are more likely to abuse their children, some critics argue that homeschooling—particularly in states with little to no oversight—is a tool that abusive parents can use to hide abuse from the outside world through limiting their children's interactions with institutions and adults who are mandated reporters.[26]

Homeschooling Instruction

Homeschool instruction is itself a spectrum. On one end is what many refer to as the "school-at-home" model, in which things look pretty similar to a public school, just with far fewer students and (usually) mom in the place of the teacher.[27] Some families I interviewed who follow this model have a dedicated "school room" or school space (a table, a desk or two) within a room. These families usually follow a structured, purchased, comprehensive curriculum, and while children may "work ahead" in some subjects (for example, by completing two grade levels of math in a single year), their parents usually keep track of the grade level at which they are currently working in each subject. These families often have a regular daily schedule for "doing school," such that school time and play time are kept separate.[28]

On the other end of the spectrum is unschooling, or "child-led" learning, in which children follow their own inclinations to learn about the world, primarily (at least for younger children) through play and exploration. Unschooling parents may put opportunities (books, musical instruments, other instructional materials) into their children's environment to encourage them toward certain topics—a practice some of the parents I interviewed referred to as "strewing"—but the choice of what to do is the child's. In unschooling, the line between learning, play, and the rest of life is blurry, if not completely nonexistent.[29] In states where there is greater regulation of homeschooling, such as requiring the submission of specific curricula and other materials, unschooling can be much more difficult to do. Several of the unschooling parents I interviewed wondered aloud to me how parents in more restrictive states manage, and noted that they appreciated not having to force their children to fit into somebody else's predetermined idea of what education should look like.

Though unschoolers tend to avoid prepackaged curricula, this does not necessarily mean that unschoolers avoid any kind of curricular materials or activities that outsiders might see as more "traditional" forms of learning. Several of the unschooling parents I interviewed talked about their children's use of online resources like Khan Academy and YouTube tutorials to learn any number of subjects, like math or coding. Others talked about their children being fascinated by science and picking up science textbooks at the library and reading them cover to cover. Several also took part in weekly homeschool co-ops, in which a group of families gathers weekly and parents volunteer to teach classes on topics of interest to the children. Several unschoolers with high school–age children told me that their children were taking or were planning to take classes at local community colleges as part of Texas's "dual enrollment" program, in which high school students can take a certain number of credits, for free, at community colleges and receive high school credit. Some did this in order to prepare for college, while others did it in order to learn something that was harder to pick up independently, such as Japanese language.

In between these two ends of the spectrum are a variety of other practices and approaches. Some of these approaches, such as Classical education and the Charlotte Mason method, are centered on specific educational philosophies. Classical education, which a few of the Christian homeschooling families I interviewed used, centers on what is called the "trivium" of grammar, logic, and rhetoric, each of which corresponds to a developmental stage and segment of a child's schooling (elementary, middle, and high school). In the Classical approach, children are exposed to many of the same topics (e.g., history) over the course of their education, but with a different focus at each stage: memorizing facts as elementary schoolers, analyzing and critiquing the logic of arguments in middle school, and effectively communicating arguments in high school.[30] The Charlotte Mason method, which a couple of the families I interviewed had used when their children were younger, centers on the use of literature to teach subjects such as language arts, history, and geography. It emphasizes the importance of journal keeping, creative play, and time spent in nature as important components of children's intellectual development.[31] Other homeschoolers borrow from other forms of alternative education, including the Waldorf and Montessori philosophies.

Finally, those who patchwork together an approach from a variety of sources and philosophies, including prepackaged curricula, online resources, and learning-through-doing, are often referred to as "eclectic" homeschoolers.[32] Many, if not most, of the homeschoolers whom I interviewed used this term to describe their approach to homeschool instruction. As some of these parents explained to me, everyday experiences can become part of the "curriculum" very easily: a trip to the grocery store can turn into a math lesson on weights and measures, a nutrition lesson, a budgeting lesson, or even a lesson in manners and etiquette. Like unschoolers, then, many eclectic homeschoolers see the boundary between "school" and "life" as fluid.

This observation points to one of the common misconceptions about homeschooling: that it takes place always, or even primarily, in the home. No matter the approach they take to education, nearly all of the homeschooling parents I interviewed described activities that their children took part in outside the home with other children—often, but not always, other homeschoolers. Many belong to homeschool co-ops or organize specialized classes for small groups of children that could be taught by a parent. Those with young children usually attend regular "park days," where homeschoolers gather at a local park or playground for play and social time. Most children take part in what would typically be called extracurricular activities, including sports teams, science or robotic teams, scouting, and 4-H—though homeschoolers tend to talk about these as curricular, rather than extracurricular, pursuits.[33] Families also go on regular outings, at times with other homeschool families, to museums, zoos, and plays and other cultural events, and many of the children are regular fixtures at their local public libraries.

Homeschooling Outcomes

One of the most frequent questions I get when I tell people that I research homeschooling is whether it "works"—in other words, is homeschooling an academically viable practice? While outcomes (academic or otherwise) are not the subject of my research, the question of outcomes is certainly a valid one. Homeschooling advocates are often quick to cite studies that show that homeschoolers have better academic outcomes than their peers, saying, for example, that homeschoolers tend to perform at least one grade level ahead of their peers in public and private schools, that they score higher than students in public schools on various standardized tests, and that they attend and graduate from college at higher-than-average rates.[34]

That said, many scholars argue—and rightfully so—that it is important to take the statistics on academic outcomes for homeschoolers with a grain of salt.[35] Because homeschoolers are a diffuse population, it is hard to collect random samples of homeschoolers, so there is likely some degree of sampling bias influencing these statistics, wherein those who choose to take part in research are not statistically representative of the whole population.[36] Additionally, the practice of homeschooling itself has a high degree of selection bias: those who opt in to the practice of homeschooling are not representative of all parents in a lot of ways.[37] Perhaps most notably, homeschooling parents tend to be highly involved in their children's education, and it is likely that they would have been highly involved even if their children were enrolled in public schools. Because parental involvement is a key predictor of academic success, it is highly likely that these youth would have better-than-average academic success no matter where—or how—they were educated, and most of the existing studies of homeschool outcomes do not contain the necessary data and/or control variables to account for this selection.

This does not mean that homeschooling is more or less the same as any other academic option. What it does mean, however, is that we cannot necessarily rely on measures of academic success, such as test scores, to determine whether homeschooling "works." My research indicates that it could be helpful to approach this question by looking at differences in skills, such as critical thinking, time management, and self-motivation, between homeschoolers and those in traditional schools. Many parents I interviewed argued that homeschool students are better prepared for college courses than their peers in public schools because the methods of learning are more similar; homeschoolers are used to taking charge of their own learning, rather than relying on classroom instruction as the primary site where learning takes place. In other words, it may not be *what* they learn but *how* they learn that makes many homeschoolers successful, not just in college but in the workplace and beyond.

Current Trends: Who Homeschools?

The number of homeschooled students has increased continually over the last several decades.[38] While education analysts estimate that somewhere around ten to fifteen thousand children were homeschooled in the United States in 1970,[39] most current estimates place the number of homeschooled children in the United States at between 1.5 and 2 million, with some estimates over 2 million.[40] According to data from the National Center for Education Statistics (NCES), approximately 1.75 million students, or 3.3% of school-age children in the United States, were homeschooled during the 2015–2016 school year (the most recent year for which data are available).[41] However, these point-in-time estimates only provide us with part of the picture: a 2012 national poll found that 7% of mothers would prefer to homeschool their children than send them to public, private, and charter schools,[42] and scholars estimate that between 5% and 12% of all students will have been homeschooled at some point during their K–12 education.[43]

Demographic research on homeschoolers has shown that homeschooling parents tend to be more highly educated than nonhomeschooling parents, with a greater percentage having received high school degrees, engaged in postsecondary education, and received a college diploma. Most research finds that homeschooling families tend to be middle class; both low-income and high-income families tend to be underrepresented among homeschoolers. Homeschoolers are disproportionately likely to be white, though there is evidence that this disproportionality is shrinking, as the number of minority children being homeschooled has increased in the last decade. Homeschoolers also tend to be in heterosexual, married, single-income families with one stay-at-home parent—usually the mother.[44]

Two noteworthy changes have taken place in recent years regarding who homeschools and why. First, homeschooling in the United States is no longer dominated by Evangelical Christians in the way that it once was. In the 1980s and into the 1990s, much of the growth in homeschooling was due to the practice being taken up by conservative Evangelicals. In 1999, the majority of homeschoolers—about 65%—were primarily motivated by a desire to educate their children in ways that aligned with their religious convictions.[45] This has changed in recent years. According to the NCES, in 2012, 64% of homeschooling parents said that "a desire to provide religious instruction" was one of the important reasons why they homeschooled; this number fell to just over half of homeschooling parents (51%) by 2016. In both 2012 and 2016, only 16% of parents said that providing religious instruction was the *most* important reason they chose to homeschool.[46] By comparison, in 2007 (the first year the NCES asked parents to choose the *most* important reason), 36% of parents chose religious instruction—and this was the most common response.[47] In both 2012 and 2016, however, the most common response homeschooling parents gave to the question of the single *most* important reason for homeschooling was "a concern about environment of other schools," with 25% of parents choosing this response in 2012 and a remarkable 34% doing so in 2016.[48]

Second, scholars note that the last decade has seen a marked growth in homeschooling by nonwhite families.[49] While caution is recommended when using NCES data to estimate homeschooling rates by racial/ethnic group due to the very small sample size of racial-/ethnic-minority homeschoolers, and sometimes-inconsistent reporting of statistically adjusted versus nonadjusted estimates, it is evident that there is a shift. NCES estimates have the percentage of homeschoolers who are white decreasing from 75% in 1999 to 59% in 2016, and the percentage who are Hispanic increasing from 9% in 1999 to 26% in 2016. The percentage of homeschoolers who are from other minority groups has remained relatively more stable, however, with the percentage who are Black at 8–10%, the percentage who are Asian/Pacific Islander at 2–4%, and the percentage of those identified as other at 4–7%.[50] However, other scholars argue that there has been an increase in participation in homeschooling by Black families.[51]

The reason for this growth, particularly in Hispanic homeschoolers, is not clear. The limited research that has been done that focuses on nonwhite homeschoolers has been conducted almost entirely on Black homeschoolers, with almost no research on Hispanic or Asian/Pacific Islander homeschoolers.[52] This research has tended to show that some Black homeschoolers choose to homeschool in part as a means of racial protectionism, either to prevent their children from experiencing racism in schools (including racialized discipline, low expectations, and other racial microaggressions from teachers, administrators, and peers) or in response to a specific incident of racism, if their children had already been enrolled in traditional schools.[53] Some of these parents are also motivated to homeschool by the ability to include culturally relevant materials in their children's education (though, researchers point out, some also homeschool for reasons that mirror those of white parents, particularly for those who are fundamentalist Christians).[54] Homeschooling researcher Cheryl Fields-Smith argues, on the basis of a review of periodicals, blog posts, and other informal documentation, that there is good reason to believe motivations might be similar for many Hispanic parents as well.[55]

Conclusion

Taken together, these trends indicate that homeschooling is both increasing in popularity and growing more diverse. What does this mean for how we understand education in the United States today? In the chapters that follow, I take up this question, drawing upon the data I collected to examine the diverse perspectives homeschoolers have on a number of issues, including childhood, education, government, and family, with particular attention to places where homeschoolers' views tend to converge and diverge.

2

What Is Childhood?

Contrasting Views of Childhood Gender and Sexuality

Claudia and Jamie, two of the parents I interviewed for this project, were both ardent proponents of homeschooling who spoke eloquently, and at length, about why they saw homeschooling as the best educational option for their children. Despite this commonality, however, there was a lot that Claudia and Jamie did not agree on. Among the topics they diverged on were the advantages of homeschooling, particularly when it came to their assessment of issues related to bodily autonomy, gender, and sexuality. Their differing perspectives are representative of two competing understandings of childhood gender and sexuality that I found in my interviews and fieldwork for this project.

I interviewed Claudia, a Black, heterosexual, middle-income, married mother of three children, at a quaint independent coffee shop in her suburban hometown. Claudia, who identified as politically conservative and very religious, told me of how, at a church retreat a number of years prior, she came to be "convicted" that God wanted her to homeschool her children. At some point, our conversation turned to the topic of children and dating. When I asked how she felt about dating, and how she saw romantic relationships happening in the context of homeschooling, Claudia told me,

> My experience, with having boyfriends, it just—it never ended well. It was always broken hearts, and lots of tears; it just never ended well. And I don't think it's necessary to go through that in order to find someone to eventually marry. [. . .] My husband and I agree on that, because he and I started out that way, just friends, and over time it just slowly became more romantic. And once we realized that that's how we got to this point, it's like, oh, this is the direction that we should go [with our children]. Just maintaining friendships. And if it naturally goes someplace else, then we'll

let it naturally go there, but we won't force it. We have run into a little bit of the boyfriend/girlfriend thing [with our oldest son], but we just nipped that in the bud right away, it's like, nope, we're not going to do that.

Claudia told me with a sense of shock that she felt as though some of the teenage girls in their homeschooling group were flirting with her son; one girl in particular would frequently hit him in what Claudia interpreted as a flirtatious manner. She explained that, while dating and romantic relationships were far more intense an issue in public schools, homeschoolers are still interested in dating and relationships. But Claudia felt that homeschooling was a better context for children to learn about and understand romantic relationships, for several reasons: first, homeschoolers have a closer relationship with their parents and are more likely to tell them what is going on in their lives; second, the homeschooling families know each other well enough that they can set boundaries and ground rules about dating; and finally, the parents of homeschoolers have greater control in deciding whether, when, and under what circumstances their children are allowed to date.

This last reason was especially important to Claudia. She told me that part of the reason she and her husband were not going to permit their children to date while they are young is that children—even older teens—are just not ready to handle romantic relationships. She explained,

> There's this book that I read a few years ago, I think it's called *What You Should Be to Marry My Daughter*. It's written by a pastor. And at the end of the book, he says, it's not required that he be complete, now, but just be moving in the direction of all these levels of maturity in all these vast areas. And so I think that that book kind of led me to the fact that you just, when you're sixteen, seventeen [years old], you're just not ready. [. . .] And he bragged early on, "My daughter has never cried her eyes out about a boy. She has never had to be on some type of suicide watch." Because he's a counselor, and he's had all these people come into his office about all this stuff, and he's like, "We've never done that, because we realize that those types of relationships, they're just not ready for them." It's too much for them to handle; feelings are inevitably going to be hurt. And it's just too much for them.

Claudia felt that it was extremely important that she protect her sons and daughter from romantic relationships during their preteen and teenage years, for two reasons: first, because such relationships bring about stress and heartbreak that children are not able to handle; and second, because the end goal of relationships was heterosexual marriage, and she did not see dating as an ideal way to find a spouse. Homeschooling allowed Claudia to have—or at least, to feel that she had—a greater level of control over her children's experience of love, romance, and sexuality.

Claudia's feelings about the importance of maintaining control over her children's experiences stood in stark contrast to those of Jamie, whom I interviewed several weeks later at a picnic table outside of her suburban YMCA. A white, bisexual, middle-income, married mother of one daughter, Jamie identified as politically very liberal and not at all religious. She explained that one of the major reasons why she and her husband decided to homeschool—or more specifically, unschool—their daughter, Emery, who had just turned seven, was to help her develop a sense of personal autonomy. Jamie explained how it was very important that they consciously cede control, and let Emery make decisions for herself:

> We do try to give her as much autonomy as possible. We let her make as many decisions for herself as much as we possibly can. And everything that we don't let her make a decision on, is up for negotiation. We try to leave it up to her as much as possible, because if she can't make her own decisions even when we're here to support her, what's she going to do when we're not there to support her? How is she going to make any decisions for herself? I mean, you see it all the time, you know, kids leave the safety of their home, and the support of their parents, and they go kind of crazy, because they've never had that opportunity before. Or God forbid, they've never been able to make any choices, so they don't even know what they like to do; they don't know what they want to do with their time, because they've never been given the opportunity to figure it out.

One of the clear benefits Jamie saw of raising Emery in the way they were raising her was that it provided Emery with a sense of self, and more specifically, a sense that she deserved to be treated with respect. Jamie gave a compelling example of this in describing a recent visit from Emery's grandfather:

My father-in-law was here visiting last week, and he is of an older generation—and he is not nice to little kids. He teases them, and he gets joy out of making them cry from teasing them, and stuff. [. . .] But she stood up to him. He was teasing her, and she didn't like it. And she told him to stop. And he continued. And I told him to stop. And he continued. And she left the room. And she was afraid I was mad at her. I was like, "I'm not mad at you, you did exactly what you were supposed to do, you asked him to stop, and he didn't, and that's not your fault. That's on him." And she stood her ground, and she was very firm, and said no. And [later] when she had her chat with him, she told him, "I don't deserve to be treated like that. I told you to stop, and no means no."

Jamie was impressed with Emery's firmness. "It's not easy for kids to stand up to adults, especially if it's an older family member," she said. "But she stood her ground. She knows that she deserves more respect than that, because we've told her that she deserves more respect than that."

Jamie wanted Emery to know that she deserved to be treated with respect, even as a child, and even by the adults in her life. But, she went on to tell me, she did not see traditional schooling as providing an environment in which children are treated respectfully. She explained, "It's not really very respectful to tell a kid what they can and can't wear every day, or how they can and can't do their hair, or what have you, or what they can and can't play with. I just don't think that's very respectful of them at all."

For Jamie, it was of utmost importance that Emery develop a sense of autonomy, which included a sense that she could make decisions about her own life and her own body, and that she could say no to others who tried to get her to do things that she did not want to do. Unlike Claudia, who saw homeschooling as a way to exercise control over her children's behavior, keeping them from having the kind of autonomy they would have, but not be able to handle, in public school, Jamie saw homeschooling as a way to provide Emery with the ability to exercise control over her own life, giving her a higher degree of autonomy than she would be able to have in public school.

* * *

Claudia's and Jamie's perspectives align with the two central critiques of gender and sexuality in American public schools that emerged in my fieldwork. In this chapter, I discuss these critiques, and demonstrate that they correspond with two competing ideologies of childhood: one that views children as "in process," as developing toward selfhood, and the other that views children as already selves, capable of exercising agency and autonomy. These two different ideologies of childhood result in differences in homeschooling practices, and highlight the way the "homeschooling experience" may look very different for children depending on their parents' ideological standpoint. I further argue that these two different viewpoints are the subject of a much broader cultural debate about the nature of childhood that is currently ongoing in the United States, a debate that centers on the question of whether "who kids are"—including their gender and sexual identities—is innate, or something that is learned or cultivated. This debate is playing out in local elections and at school board meetings, on parenting blogs and in the opinion pages of newspapers, in classrooms and in churches,[1] and it has important implications for how we understand children's rights, and the responsibilities of individuals, families, schools, and the state to provide for children. Thus, the way in which homeschooling parents talk about childhood matters not only for how we understand homeschooled children but for how we understand childhood more generally.

Childhood Gender and Sexuality

Understandings of childhood are historically and culturally situated; in fact, the very idea that there is a distinct phase of life that falls between infancy and adulthood is, historically speaking, relatively new.[2] The emergence of the idea that childhood is marked by a special, even sacred quality is even newer. As sociologist Viviana Zelizer chronicled, compulsory education only emerged in the United States when the "productive child"—who was expected to contribute to the labor and upkeep of the household, through housework, caring for younger siblings, and/or paid labor—gave way to the "sacred child"—who was believed to be in need of protection from the adult world.[3] As the ideology of the sacred child took hold, schools were seen as the ideal place for children to spend their days, both to protect them from participation in labor and to care for their developing minds. The concept of the sacred child has thus always been intimately linked to ideas about the role of education—and, in particular, public schools—in children's lives. As the role and importance of public schools have been increasingly questioned in recent years, have our ideas about childhood also changed?

And what, exactly, is "sacred" about the sacred child? One key component of this ideology of childhood is the concept of childhood innocence—but children's innocence has always been somewhat contested, and these debates often play out in the context of education. For example, behind debates about abstinence-only versus comprehensive sex education in schools is the question, do children need to be protected from knowledge about sexuality, or does keeping them from such knowledge harm children?[4] Not only do changes in social beliefs about education warrant an examination of changes in understandings of childhood, then, but they also indicate a need to interrogate broader social anxieties about childhood gender and sexuality.

Theorists of childhood gender and sexuality emphasize the importance of the institutional context to how children experience and understand gender and sexuality.[5] Two institutional contexts that are especially important in children's worlds are the family and education. The family is generally the first context in which children learn about gender and sexuality, both through explicit talk about these concepts and through the implicit lessons that come from taking part in gendered family life.[6] Schools, too, are spaces where children both receive implicit and explicit messages about gender and sexuality and also "play" with gender in their interactions with other children.[7] Parents perceive the environment of schools to be highly gendered, and their concerns about peer influence at school tend to be formulated in racialized, classed, gendered, and sexualized terms: that is, parents construct racial, class, and gendered "others" as potentially dangerous influences on their own (assumed-to-be) innocent, impressionable children.[8] Because parental concern about the school environment is a common reason parents cite for opting to homeschool, we would thus expect gender and sexuality to factor into their narratives about this decision.

In this chapter, I look at the ways in which gender and sexuality appear in the narratives of homeschooling parents in order to expand our current theoretical and empirical understandings of gender and sexuality in the context of both education and the family. Looking at a case in which the lines between these institutions are blurred opens a space for novel conceptualizations of gender and sexuality in childhood. I ask, in what ways are parents' concerns about school environment and academic instruction grounded in their conceptions of gender and sexuality? How do homeschooling parents resist—or reproduce—popular notions of gendered childhoods?

Childhood Gender and Sexuality in Parents' Motivations for Homeschooling

There is great variation in the motivations of homeschooling parents, and certainly not all of these motivations center on issues of gender and sexuality. In fact, few of the parents whom I interviewed for this project would be likely to consciously identify "gender and sexuality concerns" as one of the reasons why they homeschool. Yet themes related to gender and sexuality popped up frequently both in these interviews and in the talks at the homeschooling conferences I attended.

The themes that arose throughout my research largely cluster around two central critiques of gender and sexuality in American public schools. The first is that schools are too sexual and are a threat to the sexual innocence of children; thus, pulling children from the school environment and educating them in the home can serve as a way to protect "innocent" children from the influence of their peers, the school curriculum, and a perceived broader liberal agenda in public schools. This idea appeared frequently in the religious homeschooling events I attended, and many (but not all) of the parents who invoked this critique identified as conservative and/or religious. The second critique is not that schools are too sexual, per se, but that they promote a narrow understanding of gender and sexuality: that the heterosexual and/or traditionally gendered space of the school forces children to adhere to a model of gender and sexuality that is, at best, constraining or alienating and, at worst, dangerous. Many of the parents who invoked these ideas were politically liberal and nonreligious, and many (but not all) were unschoolers. In the following sections, I will discuss and give examples of these two critiques, and in doing so, will argue that they stem from two differing ideological constructions of childhood.

Critique #1: School as Overly Sexual

I began my interviews by asking my respondents to describe the process of deciding to homeschool their children and their motivations for doing so, and followed this up by asking them what they currently saw as the main advantages and disadvantages of homeschooling over the public-school model. One of the common critiques of public schools—and at times, private and other alternatives to public schools—that arose in response to these questions was that schools are overly sexualized spaces. Several different reasons were given for this critique, including that school curricula strayed away from what "should" be taught in school, and that children in schools are exposed to inappropriate sexual ideas and behaviors through their peers.

CRITIQUES OF CURRICULA

For Sharon, the former public-school teacher whom we met in the introduction to this book, the instruction in schools around sex and sexuality was a primary motivation for homeschooling her son, Luke, sixteen. Sharon was white, middle-income, and married; she had a college degree, though her husband, who was the primary breadwinner of the family, never attended college. When I asked Sharon how she came to the decision to homeschool, she told me, "We are a Christian family. We wanted that Christian environment. And you can't really do that with the public schools. It's almost like there's everything *but* Christianity. I mean, they can teach all of these other things, but if you want to bring the Bible into it, you can't. And so I realized that, and it was like, okay, I just know that this is something that we need to look at doing, is to homeschool." While she did not explicitly mention sexuality in this comment, from what I had heard at the homeschooling conferences I had attended prior to her interview, I suspected that beliefs about sexual morality figured prominently in this distinction that Sharon made between "Christianity" and "everything else." This suspicion was confirmed when I later asked Sharon to expand on her thoughts about public school, and she brought sexuality more explicitly into the conversation: "In the next town over, there was a big thing last year, they're pushing the kids at the high school to accept alternative lifestyles. But they don't want you to teach about a heterosexual lifestyle. You know, you can't do both. It's like, okay, they're going to take the alternative lifestyle, and they're going to say we accept the gay lifestyle, but then if someone in that school doesn't believe that perspective, they don't accept that person." These comments reveal that for Sharon, public school is an overtly sexualized space, and specifically, one that teaches a version of sexuality that she finds unacceptable. She believes that in public schools, homosexuality—or what she referred to as an "alternative lifestyle"—is taught as a valid and acceptable form of sexuality, a notion that Sharon strongly disagrees with. Because the validity of same-sex sexuality is taught as if it is fact, rather than one of many possible beliefs, Sharon constructs the public school as a space that is threatening to her own worldview.

Several other parents expressed the sentiment that certain things were not appropriate to be discussed in school, but nonetheless were. Claudia, whom we met at the beginning of the chapter, said that "sex education is—I don't think that that's something the public schools should teach." She explained that sexuality was something that parents should teach to their children, and that "signing over that responsibility to the school, I think is just wrong." She told me that even if her children went to a private Christian school, she would not want them learning sex education in school, because "you never know" where the conversation might go, when children are able to ask questions and have an open dialogue about sexuality.

While, for many of these parents, their concerns were due to the conflict between their religious beliefs and certain teachings about sexuality, not all of the parents who felt this way were religious. For example, Vanessa, a white, low-income, married mother of four children, who identified herself as politically moderate and nonreligious, said, "I think that's my overall issue, is that things are pushed, you know, in the schools. They teach about sex, I think it's in fourth grade now. And just from being around my children and knowing them as well as I do, none of my children would be ready to hear about that, at that age." She later went on to say, "I just don't think that the school has any place teaching about sex, in general—that's a parent's job, to teach them about their values and about their sexuality." She gave an example, clearly struggling to find the right words as she tried to articulate how she felt about it, of a news story about controversies surrounding teaching about same-sex families in California public schools:

In California, you know—like I said, I will accept my children, you know, if they're gay, straight, whatever, if they're purple, green—I don't know, but in California, I've read that where they've actually started teaching that it's—I can't even remember what I read now, I read too much. They're pushing, though—let me back up. We have, we were part of a homeschool co-op that we really enjoyed, but it was a little too much for us because it was very intense. But it was a homeschool group where we were all very eclectic, secular, and it had one family that was two moms and two girls, so we're very accepting of each other, and didn't have any issues. But the funny thing is, is that none of my children knew that that family was a homosexual family. It never came up. It was never an issue. I didn't have an issue with the family, but I also didn't—something in me didn't want to push an agenda on [my kids], if you will. So for me to hear that schools are making it discriminatory to *not* include, you know, same-sex couples, or you're not allowed to say this is bring-your-father to school day or whatever, because the family might not have a father—I feel like it's going in the opposite direction, you know?

Vanessa expressed a lot of ambivalence about teaching her children explicitly about same-sex families. On the one hand, she professed not to mind her children knowing a family in which the children had lesbian mothers, but on the other hand, she felt as though talking about their sexuality directly would be "pushing an agenda" on her children by exposing them to something for which she felt they just were not ready. Either way, Vanessa, like several other parents I spoke with, felt that it was important that discussions about sexuality happen within the family, rather than at school, so that parents can decide what to expose their children to, and when.

CONCERNS ABOUT PEER INFLUENCE

For other parents, the official curriculum of schools was less of an issue than the lessons children learned in school from their peers. Jasmine, a Black, married, middle-income, stay-at-home mother of two (soon to be three), explained to me that, before having children, she had never imagined she would homeschool. But when she and her husband began thinking of having children, she was "starting to see the types of things that public schools were teaching, and the types of kids that were coming out of public school, and things I was hearing out of young kids, and things they were exposed to, I was like, oh my! You know, six-year-olds talking about things that six-year-olds shouldn't be talking about." When I asked her for an example of the types of things to which she was concerned about children being exposed, she recounted hearing a child at her church talking about sex: "There's a little boy, he was probably six or seven, and he was talking to someone about—he knew how babies were made. And, he knew, pretty in detail, how babies were made, for a six-year-old. And I was like, oh my goodness! And then I heard his mom talking about it and how she was mortified that he knew all this stuff, and that he had learned it from kids at school. And I was like, oh my gosh, at six! That's kindergarten!" Though Jasmine implied that the knowledge this young boy was recounting was factually correct ("he knew pretty in detail") and focused on the biological process of "how babies are made," she felt that this was not knowledge that a young child should have. In noting that he had acquired this knowledge from his peers in a school setting, Jasmine constructed schools as spaces in which children are not protected from this knowledge—and thus as potentially threatening spaces.

This concern about what information children are exposed to was not limited to very young children. Janice, a white, married, middle-income mother of four, did not homeschool her older three children, now adults and parenting their own children, because at the time, she was not really aware of homeschooling. Janice and her second husband had adopted their now-teenaged son, Mark, as older parents, and she explained her decision to homeschool him in relation to her older children's experiences in public school, saying, "I wish they hadn't been in that environment. And there was just a lot of garbage that I didn't need my children being raised around. Not that I'm interested in protecting Mark to the point where he couldn't function in society. But there's some things a sixth-grade girl doesn't need to learn until she's in high school." When I asked her to clarify, she named both sex education and the language students used in school as examples of things to which middle and high school students should not be exposed. Interestingly, her example implied that it was more important to protect girls from exposure to this knowledge than boys, indicating that the protection of children's innocence is a gendered process.[9]

CHILDREN AS INNOCENT

Parents frequently justified their concerns about what their children would learn in school by invoking a discourse of children as innocent. For example, Veronica, a white, married, low-income mother of five, stated that because they were a Christian family, "I try to keep them... [sighs] sheltered in a way? But not so sheltered that they're weird? [Laughs] You know, just try to keep their innocence as long they can. I think in public school they lose their innocence sooner." For Veronica and Janice, as well as other parents, children's loss of innocence is seen as inevitable; it needs to happen in order for them to transition from childhood to adulthood, and is also necessary to some degree so that they will not be so naïve as to be unable to function in society. However, this loss of innocence is something that they see themselves, as parents, having the power—and even the responsibility—to delay for as long as possible.

This is not to say, of course, that homeschooled children are not exposed to ideas about sexuality. As many scholars have pointed out, the general lack of explicitly sexual content in children's social worlds does not mean that these social worlds are not filled with messages about sexuality—particularly about the normative expectation of heterosexuality.[10] This was quite evident in the four Christian homeschooling conferences that I attended as part of my fieldwork for this project, where one of the frequent themes that arose was that homeschooling allowed parents to spend more time with their children, and thus helped Christian parents to more effectively model for their children the proper relationships between husband and wife, and parents and children. In all of these talks, there was an ever-present expectation of children's future heterosexuality: boys were always framed as future husbands and fathers, and girls as future wives and mothers, all within the context of heterosexual families. Importantly, however, these talks made clear that children are always expected to be heterosexual in the future, but not in the present; as children, they are, or should be, more or less asexual. Speakers emphasized that sex and sexuality were very dangerous for children, and a sexually permissive culture was frequently cited as one of the many "enemies" of the homeschooling movement. The overall message was that any exposure of children to sexual themes—outside of the normativity of marital heterosexuality—is threatening and harmful.

There was one notable moment of rupture in this discourse, however, in the form of a talk at one conference, which focused on protecting children from child sexual abuse. The speaker, Jennifer Hillman, a young mother of two daughters, was at the conference promoting a program she had developed called "Bailey Bee Believes," the aim of which is to educate and empower both parents and children in order to reduce the incidence of child sexual abuse (CSA). Hillman argued that a necessary step toward eradicating CSA is to talk about it openly in our communities, and that giving children access to *certain* knowledge can make them less likely targets of CSA, and more likely to report inappropriate behavior from adults. She advocated for teaching children the proper terms for their anatomy, including genitals, because, she argued, predators rely on children not having the vocabulary to tell others about experiences of abuse. Hillman's presentation countered the dominant discourse about sexual knowledge that I saw at the Christian homeschooling conferences. She complicated the idea that any exposure of children to sexual themes is dangerous, by arguing that *not* educating children about some things actually puts children at higher risk for sexual abuse, and thus for the loss of their innocence. The fact that this presentation felt so surprising and norm-breaking to me is illustrative of how otherwise strong and consistent these messages were across these conferences.

Given the strength of the messaging around children's sexual innocence at these conferences, it is perhaps unsurprising that the parents who saw public schools as damaging to children's innocence were primarily conservative Christians who framed sexuality as a moral issue. However, not all of the parents with such views were religious, and for those, and even some of the religious parents, concerns were not framed around morality. Aspen, a white, middle-income, politically conservative but nonreligious mother of two, cited "protecting their innocence" as one of the main reasons she and her husband decided to homeschool their sons. Aspen explained, "The things that children are exposed to in school before they're emotionally or mentally prepared to deal with them are shocking to me. And scary, and it's just gotten worse over the years, and we just felt like, you're a child for such a short period of time, and once you're exposed to something you can never take it out of your brain and un-learn it, and we just wanted to protect that, and them, as long as possible." For Aspen, children's innocence did not need to be protected for moral reasons, but rather because a failure to do so might damage them emotionally or mentally. Another parent, Ruth, who was a white, middle-income, married mother of three, identified herself as very religious, but nevertheless explained her desire to protect her children from sexual themes in biological, rather than moral or religious, terms. She stated, "I have read that all of this constant exposure to sexual themes can trigger their hormones? And I don't know how accurate that is, but girls are going through puberty younger and younger, and I thought, well, if that's a part of it, then I'll just try to delay it as long as I can."

What both Aspen's and Ruth's comments imply is that, underlying this desire to protect children's innocence is a fear that being exposed to certain ideas and concepts about sexuality has the potential to change children. Other parents implied this as well, often with comments about not wanting their children to "grow up too fast." Margaret, a white, middle-income, bisexual, heterosexually married mother of two, who identified as politically moderate and nonreligious, talked about trying to limit outside influences on her daughter while also being open enough with her that she is not too sheltered: "We have a very open dialogue with her, we don't censor things, she's not as sheltered as I think a lot of homeschool kids are. We try not to—we're trying to prepare her for the real world, but also still, you know, give her time to be a kid, and not feel like she's being forced to grow up too fast. I want her to enjoy being a kid." These parents all understood that their children need to "grow up" eventually, and that their innocence could not be maintained indefinitely, but they all felt it was preferable that their children avoid this change from innocent child to knowing adult for as long as possible.[11]

SEXUAL MORALITY: BEHAVIOR OVER IDENTITY

For some parents, however—particularly the more religious parents—the fear of children being exposed to certain knowledge was also a fear that children would come to adopt, as acceptable, what they saw as "unacceptable" perspectives on sexuality. This was accompanied by a fear that their children would then *behave* in unacceptable ways. Claudia, whom we met at the beginning of the chapter, explained the dangers of putting children in public school in the following way:

> Even if you talk to a child, and prep them, and encourage them, and send them out into a public-school setting, they're going to make mistakes. They're going to. I think the pressure is quite a bit, and it's for such a long period of time. It's a long period of time to make the right choices, you know, to do things, or to not do things that would be wrong, in your parents' eyes. And even for adults—you're in the workplace, you find yourself listening to a joke that you know you shouldn't listen to, and then, not even calling the person out, "Hey, that's completely inappropriate." So it's not specific to age; it's just one of those across-the-board type of things that is just a people thing. And it takes practice, to make those right decisions and stand firm in what you believe. That takes practice.

Claudia felt that the temptation to think and behave in ways that are morally wrong was not exclusive to children, but she believed that children have the added disadvantage of not having enough practice in making "right decisions." Claudia saw homeschooling as a way to prevent her children's thoughts and behaviors from going in the "wrong," or morally unacceptable, direction.

For the most part, these parents frame children's gender and sexuality in terms of behavior, rather than identity. Their goal is not necessarily to shape who their children are, but to shape how they act. They aim to influence their children's gender and sexual expression by focusing on who they *should* be—what some referred to as their "character"—which the parents see as being defined primarily by how people behave. They see it as their duty to protect their children from certain influences, and to guide them toward, or lay a strong foundation for, "correct" gendered and sexual expression.

How to lay this foundation for "correct" behavior by guiding children's character development was the topic of many talks that I attended at the Christian homeschooling conferences. In fact, a frequently repeated message at these conferences was that, while the "school stuff"—like learning to read and write and do math—is important, the *most* important lessons you teach your children through homeschooling are those focused on their character. A talk that reality-television star Michelle Duggar, perhaps the most famous homeschooling mom in the United States, gave at one of these conferences was centered on character development, which she argued is the most important task in raising children.[12] She described how her family has charts of various positive and negative character traits posted around their house, and that her children learn from a very young age to name and define these character traits, as well as to identify their opposite. As part of her talk, she listed what she believes are the top three character traits to develop in children: attentiveness (as opposed to unconcern), obedience (as opposed to willfulness), and self-control (as opposed to self-indulgence). She defined attentiveness as "showing the worth of a person by giving undivided concentration to his words and emotions," and explained that this trait is especially important for homeschooling children if they are going to learn from their parents at home. She defined obedience as "the freedom to be creative under God-given authority." She emphasized that obedience from children did not just mean they do as they are told, but that they do so instantly, cheerfully, thoroughly, and unconditionally. Finally, she defined self-control as "instant obedience to the initial prompting of God's spirit." To illustrate how her children learn these character traits, Michelle showed a video of Josie—child number 19—reciting the definition of "self-control" over and over again, with great enthusiasm (and more than a little bit of hamming it up for the camera). Michelle explained that Josie was learning self-control as she was being potty trained.

Perhaps unsurprisingly, much of the talk about training children and guiding their character development was gender specific. A few speakers gave two separate talks on the same subject (e.g., etiquette, the most important homeschooling lessons, learning styles) that were separated by gender. Interestingly, these talks often contained very similar content, but they were always framed as being different, based on gender. For example, one of the Texas Homeschool Coalition keynote speakers, Todd Wilson, Christian author and founder of Familyman Ministries, gave one talk called "Raising Dangerous Sons in a Safe and Mediocre World," followed later that day by a talk called "Ten Things to Teach Your Daughter before She Graduates." While there were certainly some gender-specific points made in each talk, there was also clear overlap. In fact, the primary message of each of these talks was very similar: that parents must model for their children how to be good husbands/fathers or wives/mothers, and be devoted to God and to their families. Dividing the content into two separate talks, however, had the effect of reinforcing the idea that boys and girls are very different from each other, and that all boys have certain needs, while all girls have other needs.

At the Catholic homeschooling conference I attended, the talk of "virtues"—a concept that seemed to carry the same meaning as "character" did at the fundamentalist Protestant conferences—was also very gendered. The development of virtues was also framed as being of importance primarily so that girls will be able to inhabit the roles of wife and mother, and boys the roles of husband and father, later in life. While the speakers emphasized the importance of virtues for all children, some of the virtues were very gender specific. For example, when speakers described the virtue of modesty, the focus was almost exclusively on the importance of girls being modest in how they dress (one of the speakers, Colleen Hammond, wrote a book on this very subject, titled *Dressing with Dignity*). Physical endurance was noted to be a virtue that is especially important for boys. Much of the focus on the preteen and teen years had to do with developing virtues that would aid children in maintaining sexual abstinence until marriage. For example, in her talk, Hammond named fortitude as an important virtue to develop for children ages eight to twelve, and suggested developing this trait by keeping meatless Fridays as a family (which, since the reforms of the Second Vatican Council in the 1960s, is no longer a mandatory practice for Catholics). Hammond explained the practice by asking how, if parents cannot teach their children to avoid meat on Fridays, parents can expect them to avoid giving in to "the baser feelings" in the coming years, like when they are teenagers and they find themselves alone with someone they really like.

Many of the parents I interviewed echoed the sentiment that parents needed to be able to instill their values around gender and sexuality in their children as a means of guiding their gendered and sexual behaviors. Danielle, a white, high-income, married mother of two, told me that she did not mind teenagers being taught about sexuality in the context of a biology or anatomy class, but, like Sharon, she felt that schools should not promote certain sexual behaviors, including "alternative lifestyles" and "lesbian, gay, and transgender issues," which she thought were "mom and dad's arena." She told me,

> I'm not necessarily opposed to him learning about, you know, gay and lesbian issues, or what is a transgender [sic], you know, I mean that's the world we live in. But that should come from me. And that should be something that I can explain to him, okay, well this is what gay means, this is what lesbian means, this is what rainbow coalition means, this is whatever. And it's up to me to make sure that he understands that they are still people, and you still treat them with respect, and you don't hate on them. But what they're giving them in the schools is that this is normal behavior. That it encompasses all the normal range of human behavior. And you have to accept it, or you're a bigot. And I don't agree with that either. That's something that's a philosophy, it's a political-type discussion, that is probably better served in the home, where you've got mom and dad that can, you know, guide them.

For Danielle, it was important that she be involved in any conversation her children had about same-sex sexuality, so that she could include her perspective that same-sex behavior is unacceptable, and thus that it is not something that her son should engage in.

In short, these parents worried about public school because, as Claudia put it, at school, "other people are able to influence their thoughts, their choices." Claudia and Danielle, like other parents who utilized the childhood-innocence discourse, were not worried that, for example, public school would make their children gay; in fact, none of the parents I interviewed expressed such a fear. Rather, they worried about the school's influence on their thoughts and their behaviors. Claudia summed up the importance of homeschooling in this project, saying, "The values, and the things that we hold dear—they'll be lost for them if I don't take these early years and share with them why we think the way we think, and why it's the righteous way to think—if we didn't establish that first and let them get all their questions out and have open dialogue and discussion about them, then they may not have a firm foundation, a firm beginning." She later added, "There's a lot of opportunity there, to teach what's appropriate. But, without supervision, they're going to make the wrong decisions. They just need guidance, into making the right decisions."

I argue that in emphasizing behavior rather than identity, these parents rely on an understanding of childhood gender and sexuality as malleable, rather than fixed, and as marked by choice (see table 2.1). It is not how their children choose to *identify*, but rather a question of how they choose to *behave*, that defines their character, or "who they are" as a person. Such beliefs are evident in Claudia's statements about how children need to be guided in such a way that they will be more likely to make the right decisions, choosing righteous beliefs and appropriate behaviors, as adults. Or, as another parent, Donald, put it, rather than putting his children in situations where they would face such decisions, "We want to slowly develop them." In other words, although these parents believe there is only one correct way to enact gender and sexuality, they paradoxically adopt a social-constructionist view of gender and sexuality in childhood.

TABLE 2.1. Characteristics of the "School as Overly Sexual" Critique

Critique:	School as overly sexual
Understanding of gender/sexuality:	Defined by behaviors
What defines "who you are":	Character • Evidenced by behaviors • Formed during childhood
Goals of parenting:	• Protect children's innocence • Shape children's character • Lay foundation for right behavior/choices (including gender & sexual expression)
Theory of childhood gender/sexuality:	• Malleable • Social constructionist

Critique #2: School as Constraining Gender and Sexuality

Alongside the critique of public school as overly sexualized and a threat to childhood innocence, a second, very different critique featured prominently in my interviews. In this critique, parents—usually politically liberal and mostly, though not exclusively, nonreligious—were critical of schools for being spaces where children's gender and sexual expression are constrained. As with the previous critique, parents saw this constraint as coming about both from the school curricula and from students' peers. Rather than focus on what children were exposed to from their peers, however, these parents spoke more about the differences in the type and quality of peer culture and peer interactions that exist between public school and homeschooling.

CRITIQUES OF CURRICULA

Several of the parents I interviewed were strongly critical of sex education in schools, but rather than be concerned that children were exposed to more than they could handle, they were concerned that they were not being exposed to enough information. One parent who felt this way was Raya, an Indian-immigrant, middle-income, married mother of two sons, both of whom had previously been in public school. When her older son, David, was in middle school, she signed a permission slip allowing him to participate in the school's sex education program, but was surprised when he came home one day with a flier promoting abstinence. In her mind, abstinence should not be part of a sex education curriculum; thus she explained her reaction to the flier:

> I think, first of all—kids are going to have sex. Alright? But I think the biggest problem is, that they turn it into this awful, terrible, not okay thing that only the bad kids do. I think instead of presenting it as this awful, terrible thing, if you just taught them the facts, okay, here's what it is, here's what can happen, here's what you should do, and if you could abstain? Eh, you won't have to worry about any of those things. But I think that teaching them that you expect them to abstain, is guaranteeing that they will not come and talk to you if they are thinking about it. I mean, if I had a daughter and she was going to do it, I would be like, "Honey, you can do it, in our house. So if something goes wrong, or if you don't want to do it, you're comfortable." Instead of "Oh my god, I don't even want to hear that you're going to do this."

Raya believed that teaching abstinence is unrealistic because teenagers are sexual beings. Beyond limiting their access to information that would help them make decisions about sexual behavior, she also thought that abstinence-based education was unnecessarily moralizing. Raya identified one of the lessons of this type of education as being that people who do not abstain from sexual activity are "bad," which discourages teens who are engaging in, or considering engaging in, sexual activity from seeking out their parents' advice on their relationships. Raya believed that this can lead teens, particularly teen girls, to engage in sexual activity in which their comfort and ability to consent may be compromised. In expressing this belief, Raya sounded much like the Dutch parents in

Amy Schalet's examination of how Dutch and American parents differently understand teenagers and sexuality; unlike the American parents, the Dutch parents thought it was important for their teens to be able to have sex in the home so that they could do so in a comfortable environment.[13] Raya recognized that this stance was rare among American parents, and attributed her own adoption of this view to having lived in several other countries before moving to the United States in her twenties.

Mia, a white, low-income, married mother of two sons, also critiqued abstinence-based sex education. She was among several parents who felt that sex education that is primarily or exclusively morality based, or even just primarily biology focused, misses important educational components because it is divorced from concepts like respect, consent, pleasure, and sexual violence. Mia told me a story about how, when her older son was eleven, she seized on his question about a condom they had seen on the ground earlier in the day to have a very comprehensive conversation about sex. Though her son had been hesitant to talk about it at first, she recalled,

> That night after dinner he said, "Mom, I want to know more about that thing," and we had the *whole* talk. I mean, all of it. Rape, birth control, abortion, adoption, condoms—all of it. And the emotional side, you know, don't push a girl, no means no, and you don't have to do it with everybody. Don't let anybody tell you you're manlier if you do it. And he was like, "Why do people do that?" And I said, "Because it's fun, and because it feels good." You know, it was a little weird at first, but I was trying real hard to make it not weird, and so once I started being like, really just, calm about it, he had all kinds of questions. And it was great.

Like the parents featured earlier in this chapter, Mia said that she was glad that she, rather than a school, was the one to provide sex education to her son. However, unlike these other parents' reasons, Mia's was that she wanted to address a more comprehensive range of issues than her son would be exposed to in a school setting. She commented that she "want[s] him to know everything, real and true and open and honest," and that such a holistic understanding of sex would not be what he would get if he took a sex education class in a public school. She also explained that, after this conversation, she was not worried about him talking about sex with anyone else, because she knew she had covered so much ground with him already.

For Maria, a Latina, low-income, married mother of three daughters, the lack of open discussion about sexuality in schools discourages children—particularly girls—from taking ownership of their sexuality. She explained, "I think it's really, really important for my kids to own their sexuality, especially as girls. That no one else determines their sexuality, and they own that, and they call the shots with that. And they have to be comfortable with that. It's so much part of our identity, how we feel about ourselves, how we see ourselves, how we interact with others." Maria did not think that girls' ownership of their sexuality was something that was promoted by the larger culture in general, but felt that it was *particularly* hard to develop this in the context of schools,[14] because even though sex is at the forefront of teens' interactions with each other, it is in the background—if present at all—in instruction and discussion in schools. In not allowing sexuality to be normalized, Maria argued, schools are spaces in which it is difficult for girls to become comfortable and confident about their sexuality—and thus, following her logic, about their very sense of self.

CONCERNS ABOUT PEER ENVIRONMENT

Parents who expressed this second critique also noted that children's interactions with their peers could be a source of worry about their children's development of a gendered or sexual sense of self. Several parents I interviewed talked about how the peer culture of schools encourages conformity to certain gender and sexual norms. This peer culture was described by these parents as being a hierarchical social system in which a person's ability to have and sustain social relationships is largely determined by their place in this hierarchy, and in which nonconformity can mean being relegated to the bottom of the social ladder.[15] Parents with this concern were sympathetic to children's difficulties in resisting peer pressure, and acknowledged the potentially devastating effects of being socially ostracized in school, but worried that this culture caused children to act in ways that would compromise their "true selves." Mindy, a low-income, white, single mother of one daughter, Emma, stated that "there is a lot of pressure in schools, to do drugs, to drink, and while

I'm sure that she's going to get some of that anyway, and probably will experiment with all of those things, I think it's different than the kind of pressure you feel to conform in school." It was not the behaviors themselves that concerned Mindy; she seemed to expect that her daughter, currently six years old, would eventually "experiment" with drinking, drugs, and—as she brought up later in the interview—sexual activity. What Mindy worried about was that Emma would do these things not out of genuine curiosity but because of feeling pressure to do them. For Mindy, these behaviors are not essentially "bad," but they are made "bad" when they happen in a way that is not guided by her daughter's own desires.

This concern about the pressure to conform appeared frequently when these parents talked about dating. This group of parents did not have qualms about their children dating—and many wanted it to be very clear that they were not discouraging it—but rather, their concerns were rooted in what might be motivating their children to do so. They were critical of what they saw as children and teens dating because of pressure, rather than desire. Aaron, a white, low-income, married father of three who identified strongly as a libertarian, had recently left his work-at-home job that allowed him to share homeschooling labor with his wife (his older children's step-mother and youngest child's mother) to take a job teaching music at a public middle school. Aaron's oldest daughter, Becca, was a year younger than his current students, and while he said she was "as boy crazy" as his students were, he saw differences in how they date. Becca had a particular boy whom she liked, and they saw each other a few times a week and hung out casually, whereas his students were engaged in what he saw as all-consuming—and sexually active—relationships. He said, "It's all about status, and that part does not happen in the homeschool groups. Because they—I mean, they make friendships, but because they're not around each other all the time, they don't have to have, like, social justifications for this hierarchy of who's the coolest." He further explained that he thought part of the appeal of the school relationships is their forbidden quality: students at his school were not even allowed to hold hands in the hallway, and he thought the children sometimes engaged in physical relationships so as to rebel against these rules, whereas "if Becca was holding hands with this boy that likes her, whatever." Aaron was not concerned with Becca and her friend being physical with each other because they would be doing so out of genuine desire, whereas he thought his students "don't know why they're doing it. They just know that it's cool." For Aaron, as with Mindy, it was not the behaviors themselves that were good or bad, but the intention behind them that determined their moral value.

A few parents talked about these pressures as being especially difficult for youth who may have nonheterosexual identities. Shannon, a high-income, married mother of two who identified as having a mixed race/ethnicity, said that she thought homeschooling, "to some extent, allows young people to find their sexuality in a more freeing environment. I think that not having that pressure to conform is good in allowing kids to find themselves, whoever they might be, because maybe they might be pulled to a direction, that you might be gay." Shannon went on to note that this can be hard for children who know they are gay at a young age and feel pressure not to come out, but also for children who may still be unsure, but might feel pressure to declare a sexual identity before they are ready. For Shannon, what is most important is that children have the ability to figure themselves out on their own timeline, whether that means claiming a sexual identity earlier or later than they may be pressured to do in the school environment.

CHILDREN AS AUTONOMOUS

Within this view of childhood, rather than seeing children as innocent, parents see their children as autonomous beings who are capable of exercising agency over their own lives. The practice of allowing children autonomy was a major theme in the sessions that I attended at the Texas Unschoolers conference. This theme was especially evident in a session in which the topic was talking to children about sex and sexuality. The main purpose of the session was to discuss ways of promoting bodily autonomy. Like the session on the "Bailey Bee Believes" program that I attended at one of the Christian conferences, the advice given at this session included teaching children proper names for their anatomy and using these terms without shame, and making it clear to children that they alone have the ability to grant—or deny—someone permission to touch their bodies. While the "Bailey Bee Believes" session leader had advised beginning these practices at age two, the leader of this unschooling session advised beginning them from birth. While it is unrealistic to begin asking for a child's consent to be hugged or picked up from birth, the session leader noted that it was possible to begin laying the groundwork for these practices from infancy, for example, by telling a baby "now I am going to pick you up," as a precursor to someday asking to pick them up. She also advised speaking aloud the anatomical terms for body parts when children are infants, not so much for the child's benefit as for the adult's. She explained that most of us have some degree of discomfort using these terms that stems from inexperience using them, so telling your infant child "now I am going to wipe your labia" or "now I am going to put diaper cream on your anus" gives parents the chance to get comfortable using the words early on.

In contrast to the session at the Christian conference, in which the information was framed as important to preventing child sexual abuse, this danger discourse of sexuality in childhood was largely absent from the unschooling session, where the purpose of engaging in these practices was framed as giving children a sense of ownership over their own bodies. This session also included an acknowledgment that children are capable of understanding, and experiencing, sexual pleasure.[16] One of the takeaway messages of this session was that children are entitled to information about their own bodies, including about sex and sexual pleasure, and that to "shelter" children by denying this information is harmful, not because it places them at risk of abuse but because it denies them full bodily autonomy.

Like Jamie, who was featured at the start of this chapter, several of the unschooling parents I interviewed talked about how they went out of their way not only to teach their children about theoretical concepts like consent and bodily autonomy but also to allow their children, in practice, a great deal of bodily autonomy. Carolyn, a white, middle-income, bisexual, heterosexually married mother of three young sons, spoke at length about the responsibility she felt she had raising sons in what she identified as a rape culture. One of the ways she sought to counteract the culture of men's sense of entitlement to women's bodies was through emphasizing bodily autonomy. She makes it clear to her children not only that they never need to, for example, hug someone if they do not want to but also that they need to respect other people's boundaries as well, including through reading their body language to tell if they do not want to be touched. She described how, when her boys interact with their cousin, Anna, who is an only child and is younger than they are, "sometimes she gets overwhelmed. And I'll be like, I can see from Anna's body that she's had enough. And so we talk a lot about, you need to read people's bodies as well as listen to their words. The words are absolute. If somebody says no, stop, don't, whatever, then that is it. But you also need to look at their bodies," she said, because sometimes a person can be saying "no" through nonverbal communication. Importantly, this was a lesson that Carolyn, like other unschooling parents, did not think children learn in school—that in fact, in training their bodies to conform to the demands and expectations of teachers and other adults, they learn its opposite.

GENDERED AND SEXUAL BEINGS: IDENTITY OVER BEHAVIOR

The parents who engaged in this critique of public schools tended to talk about gendered and sexual expression in terms of their children's identities or personalities (see table 2.2). To these parents, gender and sexuality were already a part of who their children were, and their expression of gender and sexuality was seen as a reflection of something innate. In keeping with this understanding of childhood, these parents tended to focus far less on who their children would be in the future, and more on who they are in the present. This was evident at the unschooling conference as well, where childhood was framed as a stage of life like any other. There was no talk of training children to ensure certain adult behavior, and only some focus on preparing them for adulthood—notably, in the theme of anxiety about unschoolers being prepared to attend college, which came up on more than one occasion. Overall, there was far less of a focus on shaping who children will be as adults and more of a focus on allowing them to be who they already are. This was explicit in one talk that Lisa, one of the leaders of the conference, gave about mindfulness and parenting in the present moment. Lisa noted that if you ask parents what they want for their children, almost all of them will answer "for them to be happy." But, she argued, what they really mean when they say this is that they want their children to be happy in the future. Lisa explained that she had come to see unschooling as an intentional way of letting go of this future orientation, and instead focusing on the goal of having happy children—and a happy self—in the present moment.

Like the parents who saw their children as innocent, these parents also feared that school might change their children—not by changing their innate identity but by causing their "true" or "natural" selves to be suppressed or distorted to fit within the constraints of the public-school environment. For example, Julia, a white, middle-income, married mother of three, told me the following story:

> There was one time I was sitting on my couch, and my son was five. He wanted these fairy wings, and a fairy wand at Target one time, so I bought them. They were a dollar. And I watched him, running around the living room, wearing his fairy wings, with his fairy wand, dancing, just totally free, not even self-conscious at all, and I was just like, f—— everybody else. I would not expose him to any kind of ridicule for being who he is, whoever he is. I know there are people who look down their nose at [homeschoolers] who [they think] are pulling their kids out of society. I dare them to look at their little boy dancing around in fairy wings, and think about sending him to school. I want my kids, every day, to know that it's okay to be who they are.

Julia saw her children as being able to be "free" to be their authentic selves in the context of homeschooling, whereas in public school, she argued, they would be ridiculed if they expressed themselves so freely. Such ridicule had the potential either to suppress her children's expressions of their true selves or to damage their self-identity. Or, as Jamie, whom we met at the start of this chapter, put it when she talked about how much her daughter, Emery, would chafe at the structure and rules of school, "People have asked me, 'Don't you think she'll adjust?' And I'm like, I do. And I don't want her to."

While the more conservative and religious parents tended to see gender and sexual expression as malleable and defined by behaviors, the more liberal and less religious parents tended to see gender as fixed or innate, and as a part of a person's core identity. While these parents did think children could "adjust" themselves to fit into the rigid gender and sexual norms of public schools, this was definitely not preferable, as they saw such adjustment as compromising their true or natural identity. Rather than seeing it as their job as parents to shelter and guide their children, these parents saw their responsibility as being to ensure that their children grow up in environments in which they are supported and nurtured in being and becoming their true selves.

As Natalie, a white, middle-income, married mother of three, said when I asked her whether she believed that parents should have the right to homeschool their children, "I don't feel like that's my right. I feel like it's my responsibility, in fact, to allow my child to be who they want to be. And not to stand in the way of that, but to actually help with that. Even if it's not someone that I envision they would be, because they are a human, and they have the right to self-determination." For parents like Natalie, childhood is not contrasted sharply with adulthood, as it is for those who maintain childhood as a space of innocence; instead, children are viewed as having in common with adults their personhood, and with that, the right to make decisions about their lives. The parents who engage in this second critique of public schools tend to have a more flexible understanding of gender expression. They do not necessarily believe that there is a "right" or morally preferable way of "doing" gender. However, these parents feel this way because they believe that the "right" way for each person to express their gendered and sexual self resides within that person's core identity. Though they acknowledge that there are many ways of being a gendered person, paradoxically, they have a more essentialist ideology of gender and sexuality than do the conservative, religious parents.

TABLE 2.2: Characteristics of the "School as Constraining" Critique

Critique:	School as constraining
Understanding of gender/sexuality:	Part of identity
What defines "who you are":	Core sense of self • Innate • Includes personality, temperament, other aspects of identity
Goals of parenting:	• Allow children freedom to express themselves—exercise agency • Protect from situations in which core self would be damaged/suppressed
Theory of childhood gender/sexuality:	• Innate • Essentialist

Conclusion: Are Children "Born This Way"?

The parents whose voices are featured in this chapter share a sense that there are aspects of the public-schooling model that are fundamentally incompatible with what they believe childhood should look like. However, as demonstrated, the substance of their critiques is very different: for some of these parents, schools are overly sexual spaces, while for others, they are constraining or limiting to children's education and identity development.

I argue that the reason some parents see schools as too sexual while others see schools as sexually limiting stems from the fact that these parents hold different ideologies of childhood gender and sexuality. On the one side, some parents want to limit their children's knowledge and behaviors in order to create a strong and upright "character." They want to limit these because they understand children as fundamentally innocent, as different from adults, and as having a malleable gender and sexuality that can be easily influenced in the "wrong" direction. On the other side, some parents want to expand children's options for knowledge and behavior so as to protect their core sense of self. They want to expand these because they see children as fully human and, like adults, capable of exercising agency, and as having an innate gender and sexual identity that can be damaged by the constraints of public education.

In other words, there is not agreement among homeschooling parents about what childhood is, and there are important implications for the children of these parents of these differing beliefs about childhood. In her recent book *Growing Up Queer: Kids and the Remaking of LGBTQ Identity*, sociologist Mary Robertson uses feminist scholar Sara Ahmed's concept of a "queer orientation" to capture the way in which sexual and gender identities—"the possibilities of straightness and queerness"— are shaped by our social worlds, through our interactions with others and through what we imagine to be possible.[17] Ahmed argues in *Queer Phenomenology* that when we are children, our families play an important role in orienting us toward—and away from—certain possibilities. "Spatial orientations (relations of proximity and distance)," she argues, "are shaped by other social orientations, such as gender and class, that affect 'what' comes into view, but also are not simply given, as they are effects of the repetition of actions over time."[18] In Ahmed's analysis, the repetition of compulsory heterosexuality[19] within the family acts as a "straightening device," one that literally produces straight orientations.

But might different family experiences orient children differently toward ideas about gender and sexuality? I argue that the case of homeschoolers, as detailed in this chapter, indicates that this is certainly the case. In this chapter, I have demonstrated that parents' different understandings of childhood lead them to orient themselves differently in relation to their children, and orient their children differently vis-à-vis their own expressions of identity and desire, with different sets of repeated actions taken to shape—or not—their children's behavior. The parents who participated in my study are thus likely raising children with very different orientations toward gender and sexuality, such that not only their present experiences but the realm of possible gendered and sexual futures for these children will be more or less constrained, depending on the view of childhood their parents take. And while the particular case of homeschoolers offers an unusually clear window into this phenomenon, because parents who homeschool are so accustomed to having to account for the unusual decisions that they make about their children's education, all children are oriented by the institutions with which they interact, and thus are oriented by the ideologies of childhood that shape these institutions.

3

Educating the Unique Child

Veronica was the first parent I interviewed for this project. She was a low-income, white, married mother of five children, four of whom were grown and out of the house at the time we met. Neither Veronica nor her husband had completed college degrees, and her husband, who had formerly been in the military, was now on disability after a serious car accident. Veronica was a fast talker with a bubbly personality who told me as we began our conversation how much she *loved* talking to people about homeschooling. Veronica was not typical of the parents I interviewed for this book. Her five children each had a different history with homeschooling, and each spent different amounts of time, at different ages, being homeschooled. At times, her children went to public school because of the needs of the family—such as their financial need for Veronica to work—but at other times, their schooling decisions were guided by each child's individual needs, such as her middle son's need, due to his ADHD, to have the flexibility that homeschooling gave to learn on his own timeline, or her younger daughter's need to learn alongside other peers to accommodate her competitive temperament. In this way, her story exemplifies a common theme that I heard throughout my interviews, which is the theme of this chapter: the parents I interviewed almost universally shared an understanding of children as unique, and of homeschooling as a way in which they could focus on their children's unique needs.

Though Veronica considered herself very religious, and religion played an important role in her family's homeschooling life, her initial reasons for homeschooling—which she first began almost twenty years prior to our interview—had nothing to do with religion. Rather, she told me, when her oldest children (now twenty-five and twenty-six years old) were in first grade, "I was having some problems with the school. The teacher was reading a book that gave my son nightmares—and when I asked the teacher about it, she's like, 'Oh okay, I'll take care of it!' Well, what she did was she put him outside in the hall when she read the book to the rest of the class." Veronica went to the school to speak to the principal about the situation, but she felt as though he brushed her off. "I was just in a place where I was disgruntled with the public school system," she continued. "And then I met a woman who homeschooled. I had never heard of it. I didn't even know it was an option. [And I thought] 'All right,' [snaps fingers] 'let's pull them out right now'; because the situation I was in, I was unhappy."

Veronica admitted that she jumped into homeschooling "without much of a thought process—which wasn't a good thing." Lacking a solid plan, she found homeschooling to be harder than she had initially expected, and, after what she called an "unsuccessful" year, put her children back into public school. Homeschooling remained in the back of her mind, however, and a couple of years later, she met another mother who homeschooled and realized that she really wanted to try it again. At the same time, she began to feel convicted that her children's education was her and her husband's responsibility, as given to them by God. At first her husband was not thrilled with the idea, but eventually he came around, and they decided to start homeschooling again. This time, Veronica explained, she was much more deliberate in her approach, and relied on her new friend for advice on how to "do it right."

Veronica's homeschooling story, however, only became more complex (and hard to follow) from there. Veronica continued to homeschool even when, two years later, she was forced to return to the paid labor force when the family came under financial strain. So as to continue homeschooling, she worked nights and weekends for about a year, while homeschooling during the day. But, because she was getting so little sleep, she found that it was becoming "unproductive," and so she re-enrolled her children in public school. For a while, her children seemed fine with being in public school, but when the younger of her two daughters started middle school, she asked to be homeschooled again. Though at first she would not say why she wanted to be homeschooled, her daughter eventually admitted that she was being picked on a lot at school. Despite Veronica's efforts to improve the situation, her daughter was "just miserable," so Veronica agreed to homeschool her again. Her middle son, then in high school, decided that he also wanted to homeschool with his sister. Veronica explained that she thought her son preferred homeschooling because he had ADHD, and it was easier for him to learn when he did not have to spend long periods of time sitting still. At that point, then, Veronica was homeschooling two of her children (and caring for her youngest son, just a baby at the time), while two others remained in public school.

This arrangement did not last very long, however. While her middle son thrived in the homeschooling environment, her daughter struggled with it. Veronica explained that she did not think homeschooling worked well for children who had hyper-competitive personalities: "My daughter was like that. The one that wanted to be homeschooled ended up going back into public school and she did better [there] grade-wise, work-wise, because she didn't want that person to get a higher grade than her! Whereas at home, it was just herself, so it wasn't motivating for her. So I think if you have a child that needs that extra competitive drive or whatever motivation, then [public school] can be good for them." Unlike his other siblings, Veronica's youngest son, who was ten years old at the time of our interview, had been homeschooled his entire life. And while Veronica did not seem opposed to the idea of him attending public school if he wanted to, she also did not seem to think that was a likely scenario.

Furthermore, Veronica felt there were distinct advantages to homeschooling, especially when she reflected on the ways she thought public education had changed—for the worse—since her older children were young:

> I wonder, in ways, if it—because of the way they're teaching towards the test now, if it, if kids are . . . what's the word. . . . Their creativity and natural desire to learn is kinda stunted? So, that's kinda, it's more [. . .] institutionalized, I guess? Factory type, is what it makes me think of. How they're all treated the same instead of—which I can't imagine how to make it more to where they're more, it's more individualized, for, you know, 'hey he is great in this [area], let him'—I don't know how to fix it, but that's what I see.

Veronica had a lot of experience with public schools—more than most of my respondents—so she had a lot to offer in terms of her views on how public schooling and homeschooling differed. One of the things

Veronica appreciated about homeschooling was the way that it allowed for a more individualized, tailored experience, in which a child could take an area that "he is great in" and pursue it further than he could in a public-school classroom.

* * *

As discussed in the previous chapter, sociologist Viviana Zelizer has chronicled how, during the first half of the twentieth century, the understanding of children as sacred took hold as the dominant ideology of childhood in the United States.[1] Rather than using the language of children as sacred, the homeschooling parents I interviewed used the language of children as unique to describe their own children and why they choose to homeschool. In his 2001 book on homeschooling, Mitchell Stevens argued that homeschooling is one of several educational approaches that focuses on children's individualism—something that he noted was a growing focus, in the late 1990s, of different educational "reform agendas."[2] In the decades since, as school choice and neoliberal ways of thinking have taken a firm hold on American education, this focus on children's individualism has become a centerpiece of American education discourse. In this chapter, I argue that, as part of this shift, the ideal of the *unique child* has taken hold as one of the dominant ideologies of childhood in the contemporary United States, and that this ideology has made homeschooling all the more attractive an approach for a growing number of parents, even those who might not have considered homeschooling in earlier decades. I also ask what this understanding of all children as unique means for the ideal of the sacred child. Are all children similarly sacred, or are some more sacred than others? Is their individuality—their particular set of unique traits—their defining characteristic? Is their individuality what *makes* them sacred? Additionally, I ask what the implications are of this focus on children as unique. I argue that one important implication is that it leads parents to prioritize their own children's unique needs over the needs of other children, and of society as a whole.

Homeschooling as a Solution to Children's Unique Needs

The parents I interviewed identified the ability to tailor a child's education to their own unique temperaments, aptitudes, interests, and other personal needs as a distinct advantage of homeschooling over any other educational option. I discuss each of these in the sections below.

Temperaments

One of the common ways in which parents discussed their children's unique needs was in terms of personalities or temperaments. This was something that transcended differences of political leaning, religion, and homeschooling approach. Take, for example, the following two excerpts, in which two parents, who each initially put their oldest child into preschool, explain why they ended up pulling them out and homeschooling after less than a year:

> *Cynthia*: Especially knowing Jason, he's the sweetest, most tender-hearted kid, and they just—he really is a bully magnet. He doesn't mean to be, he does nothing to deserve it, but [he] just totally [is]. And so we just wanted to protect him, and build him up, and help build his confidence. Because he was really unique.

> *Maria*: What was difficult [for my daughter] was the scheduled day, and the forced socialization. She loved her friends, but her nature is very much an introvert, and her nature is methodical, and if she starts something she wants to immerse herself in it and finish it. So she would spend the whole ride home crying, just to relax, just to have that emotional release now that she was in a safe place. So that really clued me in to, that's not where she wants to be. That's not an environment that best suits her.

Thematically, these quotations are so similar as to be practically interchangeable. Yet the first comes from Cynthia, a white, middle-income, married mother of two who identifies as politically conservative and very religious, and the second from Maria, a Latina, low-income, married mother of three who identifies as politically very liberal and only somewhat religious.

Maria was described in the previous chapter, wherein I discussed her strong views of childhood gender and sexuality. Maria spoke at length about how she wanted her daughters to feel ownership of their bodies and their sexuality, and how she worked to instill that in them from a young age. In contrast, Cynthia and her husband, Donald, felt quite differently from Maria about this issue. Like many of the other religious parents I discussed in the previous chapter, they felt it was their duty to protect their children's innocence as long as possible, and thus took solace in the fact that their preteen daughter still enjoyed playing with dolls, did not feel the need to act too "grown up," and was not yet interested in dating. Despite these stark differences, though, on this, Cynthia and Maria agreed: homeschooling was a better fit for their children's individual, unique temperaments than other forms of schooling. This type of agreement "across the aisle" of political difference is something that we have certainly come *not* to expect in today's divisive political climate, and thus indicates that these parents are drawing on a discourse that resonates across these differences.

Their emphasis on their children's unique needs is especially noteworthy because both mothers had put their children in nontraditional educational environments for preschool, already believing that they would not succeed in a traditional classroom environment. Jason, who is on the autism spectrum, was in a preschool classroom that intentionally integrated autistic and neurotypical children, with a very low student-to-teacher ratio and teachers who were trained and experienced in teaching young children with autism. Maria—who told me that she had long been attracted to nontraditional education methods and had researched many different options before her daughter started preschool—had enrolled her daughter in a Montessori program specifically because of the child-led focus of the Montessori philosophy. And yet, despite having sought out programs that they felt would be particularly responsive to their children's needs—far more so than the average preschool environment—both Cynthia and Maria found the schools they had chosen to be ill suited to their children's temperaments.

Interestingly, both Cynthia and Maria had other children whom they described as having very different temperaments compared to their eldest children, but each was still able to articulate reasons why she thought homeschooling was ideally suited for each child. For example, Maria told me,

> My youngest and my oldest, they are more academic, they are very independent learners, they both enjoy reading and being solitary, so I can just let them be. My middle kiddo is very sensory, very kinesthetic, learns by doing and moving and is a big action kid, and is the kid that is always bored. Where the other two can occupy themselves. There's a term in unschooling called "strewing," and you just fill your environment with opportunities and materials, and for oldest and youngest that's sufficient. Middle kid, she can look around her and there's tons of stuff, and there's nothing to do, in her mind. She needs to be engaged. So that took a while, [. . .] until I could really see their groove and how they responded to things and what they needed, for us to say, "This works for this one."

When her children were young, Maria invested a lot of time and energy into figuring out what "worked" for each of her children—something that she noted "is always changing, too," which is part of the reason why "I never, ever invested hundreds of dollars in curriculums, because it was unrealistic" to expect to find a single curriculum that would work for all three girls. Taking a more eclectic approach, "picking and choosing, doing a combination of things, going to book fairs, picking stuff up, trying it, seeing what worked and what didn't," she said, allowed her to truly tailor the homeschooling experience to each individual child.

Also of note is that homeschooling looked very different for these two families: while Cynthia's children used structured curricula and had a regular schedule of work to complete, Maria's children were unschoolers who had a considerable amount of say in what they wanted to learn, and when. Nevertheless, for both of these mothers, homeschooling is understood as being able to meet the unique needs of almost all children, regardless of how much the children may differ from each other in their individual needs.

This was not something all of the parents I interviewed agreed on. Like Veronica, some parents felt that some children were better off in a public-school environment. Shannon, a mother of two who was introduced in the previous chapter, assessed her individual children's temperaments, and thus educational needs, very differently—to the point that she did not think homeschooling was the solution for both children. At the time of our interview, Shannon was homeschooling her older child, Ethan—I will talk about Ethan's story in more depth in the next section—but she had another child, a three-year-old daughter, with a very different temperament. When I asked Shannon about her plans for her daughter's education, she told me, "She will probably go to school. She's very social, she thinks she's prom queen already, at almost four. And I don't know how to deal with that! So she, we will probably put in school. I don't think she'll enjoy sitting at home for hours reading books, as much as my son does." Just as her son took well to the homeschooling environment, Shannon predicted that her daughter would have a difficult time *not* being in school, because she was such a highly social child who was not content spending time alone. When I asked if she would be open to homeschooling her daughter if public or private school did not seem to be working, she hesitated: "Um, I'm open to it? But I am not—I'm not an adamant homeschooler. It's not, you know, 'Kids should never go into the school system!' Because there are those [parents] out there. But I am open to it."

Melinda, like Shannon, had an older son and a younger daughter who she felt had very different temperaments. A white, middle-income, single mother, Melinda was unschooling her son, Calvin, age eleven, while her daughter, Kayleigh, was in second grade at a private school. Melinda had begun unschooling Calvin the previous semester, and she was very pleased with that decision. Calvin had some behavioral issues that meant he had to be medicated to make it through the school day, and whereas school had been a major source of frustration for him—and as a result, for Melinda—he was thriving in the unschooling environment. According to Melinda, he had grown more confident and "was able to stop taking the medications," which in turn helped him "to accept himself for who he is, you know, and start to nurture and feel better about himself." But Melinda really liked Kayleigh's current teacher, whom she had had the previous year for first grade and who "looped" with the class for the second-grade year. In fact, Melinda told me that this teacher was the main reason she kept Kayleigh in school for the second grade instead of unschooling her as well. Melinda was leaning toward homeschooling Kayleigh starting the next year, but she expressed some concern about whether the unschooling approach that was working so well for Calvin would work as well for Kayleigh. "Calvin's very outgoing and unstructured. Kayleigh's timid and relies on structure," Melinda explained. "At home, she would be more likely to say, can I have this workbook? You know? And do fifty pages in one day. And I'd be fine with that. It's just, whatever she wants to do. But Calvin would never, ever, ask for a workbook. Ever." That said, Melinda expressed that she felt that unschooling would work for almost any child, as long as the parent was open to tailoring the approach to the child's individual temperament.

Aptitudes

Parents frequently named the ability to customize the educational experience according to their children's academic strengths—and, for some, also their weaknesses—as a major advantage of homeschooling. This includes the ability for children to move at their own pace, even—and especially—when that meant they were doing work at varying grade levels in different subjects. In this way, as one respondent put it, homeschooling functions similarly to having a private tutor. For example, when I asked Aspen, a white, middle-income, married mother of two sons (ages six and nine) what she saw as the primary advantages of homeschooling, she began by saying, "For example my younger son, if I were to put him into first grade in a public school next year, he would be completely bored out of his mind, because he's reading at a third grade level, and they can't—that's just too far of a gap for a teacher to help keep them stimulated. So that's a huge advantage of being home, because I can cater to whatever level he's at, very easily." For Aspen's older son, on the other hand, the benefit of homeschooling was the opposite—that they could move as slowly as he needed to with reading. When they first began homeschooling, her older son would have been in second grade, and, she said, "He hated reading. Didn't want to read for a minute, I mean just absolutely hated it." The extreme degree of his aversion led Aspen to speculate that he might have dyslexia—something she noted runs in her family—or some similar learning difficulty that was causing him to be very frustrated with reading. Rather than shell out the money to have him tested (which can be hundreds of dollars when done privately, rather than through the public school system), Aspen decided to just "act as if" he had a learning disability, and started over with reading instruction using a method that was recommended for children with dyslexia. This meant using lesson plans that were far below his grade level. Aspen explained that this could not have been done in public school without holding her son back a grade or more, which would not have been ideal because it would not have allowed him to advance in other subjects, like math, in which he was doing just fine. She seemed very proud to report to me that, after two years of relearning phonics, her older son now reads happily for an hour or more at a time.

Other parents agreed with Aspen in their assessment that homeschooling was advantageous in that it allowed children to move at a different pace in different subjects, working ahead of their public-school peers in subjects that they were good at, and working at grade level or even below in the subjects with which they struggled. As Anita, a Latina, middle-income, married mother of four, explained, "I like that I can have them on different levels, if their reading is not—let's say Ryan, who's in fourth grade, let's say his reading comprehension may not be fourth grade level, well, I can do the third grade curriculum." This ability to tailor the pace of each subject to each child's aptitudes led Anita to say that homeschooling was more like "a one-room schoolhouse" than the current public-school model, where "you're this age, so you're in this grade, so you should be doing this stuff. Because I don't think everybody is like that, everybody doesn't work that way."

Jacqui, a white, middle-income, married mother of three, agreed with the idea that teaching large groups of same-age students as if they had the same aptitudes was less than ideal. Jacqui had been very active in her local homeschooling community for years, and in addition to running free information sessions for people who were considering homeschooling, she also moderated a large homeschooling listserv. She explained to me that when they are first starting out, a lot of parents want the safety blanket of a full, boxed curriculum, but she tried to steer them away from that approach:

> I know people who say, "Well, I want the curriculum because I'll have all my bases covered." But it doesn't—you know, you don't know how your kid learns. Like my daughter, when she was learning math, it took me a while to realize that if she *saw* the problem, she would have trouble

with it, but if she said it out loud, she could get it. Or if they wrote it on a whiteboard, sometimes they could understand something that they couldn't understand in another way. It's like, they wouldn't be able to do that in school.

Homeschooling, Jacqui explained, allowed parents to figure out a child's individual learning style, which then provided an even greater ability to tailor that child's education to their unique set of strengths and weaknesses.

The feeling that schools were not able to adjust to the unique needs of their child was expressed perhaps most clearly in the narratives of parents of children with disabilities or other special needs, such as autism, ADHD, or behavioral or developmental disorders, and in the narratives of parents whose children were considered gifted. These narratives, which I discuss in depth below, make especially clear the ways in which parents see schools as unable to accommodate their unique children, and thus view homeschooling as a better—or, in some cases, the *only*—option.

DISABILITY AND SPECIAL NEEDS

Cynthia and Donald, whom we met earlier in the chapter, did not initially plan on homeschooling their children, Jason and Sara. Cynthia always intended to be a full-time, stay-at-home mother, but, she said, "I had no aspirations of homeschooling." Jason was diagnosed at eighteen months with a Pervasive Developmental Disorder, which, in his case, was a precursor to an eventual autism diagnosis. They were living in another state at that time, where, because of his diagnosis, Jason qualified for early-intervention services, to which Cynthia credited Jason's positive development in his early years.

When Donald's job caused the family to relocate to Texas, they were excited because it afforded them the opportunity to move to a school district that was known nationally for having an excellent special education program. Jason started in a special integrated preschool that was designed specifically for children with autism. They explained to me that they loved the teachers in the program, but almost immediately ran up against some problems with the school policies. Cynthia explained, "One of the other children with autism kind of bullied him. Unintentionally, I'm sure, I mean, he was four [years old]! But he scratched Jason down the front of his face, like he had claw marks. And another time he was bit in the cheek, kind of a chunk—and the teachers, neither time, could tell us what happened exactly. Because of the other child's privacy." While they were sympathetic to the school's need to protect the other child's privacy, Cynthia and Donald felt that not knowing which child was responsible made it impossible for them to address the issue with Jason by, for example, coaching him to stay away from that particular child. Although the school said that it was addressing the issue, Cynthia and Donald felt as though they were being asked to blindly trust in the school, as they were kept in the dark about what "addressing the issue" actually meant. And so, while they loved Jason's teachers, they were frustrated by the feeling that the teachers were very limited in what they could do to intervene.

At the same time, Cynthia was researching what services Jason would be eligible for when he moved from the preschool to the elementary school, and learned that the level of intervention was generally proportional to the severity of the case. Since Jason was among what his parents described as the more "high-functioning" autistic students in his class, he would not be eligible for many of the services to which they had expected he would have access, given the reputation of the school district for being excellent for children with autism. This information was weighing heavily on them when the second physical injury occurred only a few months into the school year, and Cynthia and Donald made the decision to pull him out. Though they still liked his teachers, they felt as though the school policies—including the size of the classroom and the student-teacher ratio—were keeping them from being able to really address Jason's specific needs. Donald explained, "I thought well, then, if we can't do anything about it, then we can't take the risk of having him in there, getting further injury, if that takes place. If you guys are not able to watch over him and make sure the interactions are safe, then we have no choice but to say, you know what, we need to pull him out." At that time, they were not sure whether they would continue to homeschool long-term, or just do it for a year or two, or whether they would homeschool their daughter, Sara, who was more developmentally typical. However, after a couple of years of homeschooling, during which Cynthia developed both confidence and a support network of other homeschooling mothers, they decided to stick with it long-term.

Mia, a white, low-income, married mother of two, was another parent who felt that homeschooling allowed her to prioritize the unique needs of a child with disabilities. Mia's older son, Joey, had multiple diagnoses, including developmental and behavioral disorders and mental health issues.[3] Mia did not attempt to sugarcoat her son's behavioral issues during our conversation, and described Joey to me as "a difficult person." As an elementary school student, Joey was prone to frequent verbal and physical outbursts and almost daily panic attacks. Because of this, the only way Mia, working alongside Joey's teachers and doctors, could figure out for him to be "functional" (i.e., nondisruptive) in the classroom environment was for him to be, in Mia's words, "heavily medicated." Legally, of course, Joey was entitled to accommodations for his disabilities—for example, Joey was allowed to finish at home any work he did not complete in class—but these accommodations sometimes felt more like a burden than a benefit. Mia explained, "He was at school all day doing nothing, a zombie on medicine, and then coming home and having four or five hours of work to do that he didn't do all day, plus homework." This was the case through first, second, and into third grade, and Mia described the whole experience as "miserable."

In the middle of third grade, Mia started to question the direction in which her son's doctor wanted to go with his medication as they tried to manage his multiple diagnoses by increasing his doses and trying new combinations of medicine. Mia clearly felt that managing her son's conditions—including making decisions about his medications—was her responsibility, and she spent a lot of time researching the various medications in order to inform her decisions about her son's care. She told me that "it was just getting to the point where the side effects of the drugs were not even worth what they were helping." Especially in cases of multiple, overlapping diagnoses, the management of childhood disabilities through psychotropic medications is more of an art than a science. Where one medication might improve some symptoms, it may exacerbate others, and most medications have a range of possible side effects. As sociologist Linda Blum, who studied mothers of children with invisible disabilities, explains, "Medications are simply not a quick fix, but instead, their limited benefits require extensive maternal management."[4]

Mia was a former public-school teacher who had taught high school until her second son was born, which was around the same time that Joey started elementary school. As such, she was not ideologically opposed to public schools, and in fact felt as though, as a teacher, she understood how "the system" worked, and did her best to advocate for her son. She did not blame the teachers themselves for their inability to help her son:

> I was a teacher and I know that side of it. I know how hard it is for them. They don't—they're so busy, they don't have a lot of resources. I mean, could they have [done more], if I was their top priority, if I was the parent that was most threatening? Maybe. But they had others that were scarier and more threatening than me, and that demanded more attention. I mean, even though I was advocating for my son, and I knew what he needed and I was working for him, I felt so bad for [his teachers] because I knew they didn't really have a lot of options.

Though Mia felt that it was her responsibility to advocate for Joey, she demonstrated some ambivalence about this role by invoking the stereotype of the "threatening" parent. On the one hand, Mia wanted to maximize her son's educational opportunities, but on the other, especially as a former teacher, she felt guilty pushing too hard, knowing that there was only so much his overworked and underresourced teachers could do to cater to the unique needs of each child. Mia told me that Joey would cry daily after school, talking about how much he hated it, and getting all of his work done in the evening was putting a strain on the whole family. Recognizing these constraints, Mia reached the point where she felt that public school was no longer an option for Joey. She brought up the idea of homeschooling to her son, who, she said, loved the idea. They withdrew him at the end of the school year, and have homeschooled ever since.

Not all of the people whom I interviewed who were motivated to homeschool by a child's special needs had such severe difficulties as did Mia and Joey. But some still got to the point where they felt that homeschooling was the only way to adequately meet their child's needs.

As a single mother, Allison, who was white and middle-income, had never imagined that homeschooling would even be a possibility for her. She had two daughters, two years apart in age, who were both Black and had been adopted internationally. Her older daughter, Therese, was seven years old when she was adopted, and her younger daughter, Rose, adopted one year later, was six. Both came to the United States with limited English-language exposure. Allison initially enrolled Therese in kindergarten because she felt that, even though she was seven years old, it would have been unfair to expect her to keep up with her peers in first grade without a basic language foundation. When she discussed this decision with school administrators, Allison was led to believe that it would be easy to move Therese into the appropriate grade level with children her own age after a year or two.

Allison found this process to be much more difficult than she expected, however, and things were even more difficult with Rose, who had even less exposure to English prior to her adoption. By that point, the family had moved into what Allison described as a "very rigid" school district in order to live with Allison's mother, who helped care for the girls. Because it was one of the largest school districts in Texas, Allison felt, it followed rules and policies very strictly, leaving little leeway for families with unique circumstances such as theirs. The school had open-classroom kindergarten classes—something Allison referred to as an outdated relic of earlier educational philosophies—with the exception of one class, which had a closed classroom.[5] Allison requested that Rose, whom she suspected might have learning disabilities, be placed in the closed classroom, as she figured that it would be difficult for her to pick up a new language in the loud and highly distracting environment of the open classrooms. Despite this request, however, Rose was placed in an open classroom, and astonishingly, she did not receive any specialized English-language-learner instruction despite the fact that her teacher was certified to teach English language learners.

Toward the end of the school year, the teacher told Allison that, because Rose's language skills were not where they needed to be, she was recommending that she not be promoted to first grade. Consistent with the neoliberal expectation that mothers be familiar with a range of expert advice about childhood, but reject this advice if it is not what they believe is best for their child,[6] Allison did her own research and talked to administrators in the school district. This confirmed her suspicion that it was, in fact, against state policy for a student to be held back simply because of concerns about language acquisition. Still, the struggle that Allison went through to get Rose placed into first grade left "a bad taste in my mouth about the whole thing, and it was very stressful." As it became clear that Rose did, in fact, have learning disabilities, Allison said that she became increasingly stressed out with all of the time and energy she needed to spend interfacing with the school. She explained,

> Even though I'm entrusting my child's education to the school, I feel like I have to do so much advocacy with the school to get her what she's going to need. [. . .] So I see the writing on the wall, this is how it's going to be with this school district, with both of my kids. And it's very stressful on me, as a single parent, to have to keep going up to the school to advocate for my child, when I feel like they're not really listening to me. Basically, it made me very sick to my stomach and stressed out dealing with the school, knowing that my child has special educational needs.

The time and energy Allison spent advocating for her children was taking a toll on her, both physically and mentally. It was especially difficult for her as a single mother, without a spouse or partner to support her in this endeavor, because going to the school to meet with teachers and administrators often required taking time off work. Allison's frustration with the situation led her to ask her mother whether she thought homeschooling would be possible. Allison knew that she would need her mother's help, because, as she explained, one of the functions of public school is to provide child care for working parents, which is especially important to single parents who, as the family's sole breadwinner, rely on work in the paid labor force to support their families. Allison's mother agreed to think about it, and eventually agreed to help out by watching the girls during Allison's work hours. Allison told me,

> That was how I ended up making the decision. I felt so stressed out and frustrated with trying to get my children's educational needs met in the school district because they're so cookie-cutter rigid about everything. I didn't feel like—I told them every time I would meet with them, I said, "I understand that you are looking out for the educational needs of all of

the children, but I am looking out for my child, and my child is most important to me." I have to look out for my child and what I feel like is best for her, and I felt like that was getting lost in what was actually happening.

Allison's narrative of her path to homeschooling echoed that of many other parents with whom I spoke: she had children with what she perceived as "unique" needs, she attempted to work with the school system to make sure these needs were addressed, and she became increasingly frustrated with an inflexible system that, in focusing on the educational needs of the many, was unable to meet the needs of the individual. Simply put, Allison, like other parents, felt the school system was designed for "cookie-cutter" children, and her children did not fit the mold. Thus, despite the difficulty of taking on homeschooling as a single parent, Allison explained that she made the decision because "I felt like I could do that more than the system would."

While all mothers face pressure to manage their children's educational experiences, research has shown that mothers of children with disabilities face increased, and at times competing, pressures in how to act to maintain their status as a "good mother." This is the case because some of the very things these mothers feel they must do to advocate for their children are also stigmatized, such as "administer[ing] psychoactive medications to their kids and seek[ing] added services from overburdened schools and healthcare systems."[7] In Linda Blum's study of mothers of children with invisible disabilities, mothers saw it as their responsibility "to expertly negotiate the many maze-like obstacles of the educational and medical systems governing invisible disability" and "to be relentless in efforts to mitigate her child's issues and the stigmatized difference surrounding them."[8] The mothers in my study who had children with disabilities, including Cynthia, Mia, and Allison, expressed similar pressures and frustrations as they attempted to advocate for their own children's unique needs within their schools without coming across as *too* needy or threatening. As Allison explained, the frustration of feeling constantly at odds with the school was at least in part due to the tension caused by the school officials being responsible for *all* children at the school, while mothers are responsible only for their own children. And while schools are generally judged on the basis of the aggregate performance of all children in attendance, mothers are judged on the basis of their perceived success or failure in choosing what is best for their own children. The mothers in Blum's study overwhelmingly reported feelings of blame for failing to live up to an impossible standard of expertly managing their children's disabilities.[9] I contend that the mothers in my own study who had children with disabilities opted to homeschool as a way of attempting to live up to this same impossible standard.

GIFTEDNESS

The idea that some children have particularly unique needs was, of course, not limited to parents of children with disabilities. A few of the parents whom I interviewed had similar struggles with their school systems, but on the opposite end of the spectrum from those with children with disabilities. These parents had children who tested as "gifted" or "profoundly gifted"—children with IQs far higher than the average, who were capable of doing work far more advanced than that assigned to their same-aged peers. Robin, a white, middle-income, married, lesbian mother of two, was one such parent. Her son, Hugo, who was ten years old at the time of our interview, was reading before he was two and doing grade-school-level math before he was in preschool. She explained that she "knew right away" that public school was not going to be a good option for her son, because she recognized how hard it was for a teacher to give special attention to a child who falls so far above the mean. They tried one private program, but it was geared toward gifted but not "profoundly" gifted students—or as Robin put it, "They want the obedient gifted kids, not the difficult gifted kids," implying that Hugo was among the "difficult" children (something she substantiated with a story of how the teachers "lost" then-four-year-old Hugo at recess one day). She looked into other programs, both at charter schools and at private schools, but found each school unwilling to do "grade skipping," or placing children above the grade level for their age—something she felt Hugo would definitely need to avoid being bored. "He's insane when he's bored," Robin explained, laughing. "You don't want this kid bored in a classroom, for like ten seconds." Robin said it felt as if "doors [were] slammed in our face right and left." As she put it, "I had always said, I really like the idea of homeschooling for other people. I could never be a homeschool parent. I could never be patient enough to homeschool, and so I would never want to do it." Nevertheless, that is exactly what she ended up feeling she had to do. "It became clear that that was literally our only choice," she said. In Robin's narrative, though sending Hugo to public school was technically an option, she did not see it as actually being one, because she did not think his unique educational needs would be met and predicted that he would be impossible to educate as a result. Thus, from Robin's perspective, she did not choose homeschooling—homeschooling was forced upon her.

I asked Robin what they were currently doing—and planning on doing—for their daughter Addie, age six, and Robin expressed some ambivalence. Addie was also academically advanced, but not to the same degree as Hugo, and she was much better at sitting still and listening, so "she would definitely work in a classroom." However, even though Robin felt as though Addie *could* do regular school, she also did not think it would necessarily be the best fit, and thought that there would be advantages to homeschooling. Ultimately, Robin and her wife decided to ask Addie what she wanted, and Addie said that she preferred to be homeschooled. But, Robin pointed out, "If she had said I would really rather go to school, we would have found something. We wouldn't have sent her to public school down the street, though. It would've been a charter school of some sort." There were several reasons for this, she explained: they had seen the experiences of some of their friends with children in the local public schools and were not happy with how the children were treated, they were concerned about rumors they had heard of a "drug ring" at one of the local elementary schools, and they did not want their daughter to be subject to high-stakes standardized testing.[10]

Shannon, who was mentioned at the beginning of this chapter, was, like Robin, the mother of a gifted son and a more typically developing daughter. When her son, Ethan, was in first grade in what Shannon described, using air quotes, as a suburban "good school," he acted out a lot—he disrupted the class frequently, and would not finish his worksheets. Because of this behavior, Shannon found herself "having to volunteer" in Ethan's classroom to help keep him under control. (Note Shannon's paradoxical phrasing here—if you "have to" do something, this implies that it is not voluntary, and thus, "volunteering" would not be an accurate description of the activity.) It seems that she had internalized the idea not only that, as a mother, she was required to manage her son's ability to be in the classroom but also that the teachers and school administrators expected this of her. Midway through the year, the teacher, whom Shannon reported she had gotten along with very well, recommended that Ethan be tested for ADHD. As was the policy in their school district, this triggered a series of tests—as Shannon put it, "a full gamut of testing, not just for one specific item." They did not get the results back until the end of the school year, at which time Shannon and her husband were shocked to find out that Ethan did not have ADHD, but rather, he had a genius-level IQ and very high speeds of processing information, which, they were told, led him to act out in school out of boredom.

Shannon described Ethan as having "asynchronous development," meaning that he was very advanced academically, but lagged behind his peers in social development. This qualified him for intervention from the school, so Shannon worked with the school over the summer to develop an IEP—an Individualized Education Program, which schools use to delineate the services or accommodations for which children with special needs qualify.[11] But in the end, it was determined that the only accommodation her son qualified for was thirty minutes per week of speech therapy. As Ethan's mother, Shannon felt that she knew better than the school what type and amount of services would be effective in meeting Ethan's needs (and that thirty minutes per week of speech therapy was not it), so she started looking into other options. While Shannon and her husband considered private school at first, they struggled to find one that seemed like the right fit. Shannon started considering homeschooling at the recommendation of the school psychologist at the public school. In so doing, Shannon weighed one piece of "expert" advice (that of the school psychologist) over another, conflicting piece of advice (that of the group that determined her son's IEP) to make the choice she felt was best for her child—something scholars argue is required of mothers, as "managers" of their children's lives, in the neoliberal era.[12]

Shannon homeschooled for a short time, but when the family moved out of Texas for work, the educational options available to them changed, and they eventually put Ethan in a private school for academically gifted children. However, Shannon came to realize that there were a whole host of ways in which private schools, too, could be inflexible and bureaucratic, and that, most importantly, "Even in a private school, designed for gifted children who have difficulties, he still wasn't getting the guidance in how to handle social issues, and social situations."[13] Thus, they started homeschooling again after Ethan finished a few years at this school, and continued to do so when they moved back to Texas.

Interests

Kelly was a white lesbian and the mother of one child, Alexis, who was twelve years old. Kelly adopted Alexis at age seven from the foster care system, and Alexis came to Kelly—then a single parent—after having lived in an abusive home for the first three years of her life and then in multiple foster homes for the next four years. Alexis had been labeled "mentally retarded" by the foster care system, and when Kelly adopted her, she was told Alexis would never be able to read. However, Kelly—who had education degrees and worked at a Montessori school—did not trust this diagnosis and sought out additional expert advice. Kelly was glad she had trusted her instincts on this, as Alexis eventually was diagnosed with Asperger Syndrome (and, at the time of our interview, was an avid reader).

After trying—unsuccessfully—multiple different types of schools over two years (Montessori, which was not a good fit because Alexis had not yet developed the self-regulation skills that the Montessori approach required; public school, where one of Alexis's aides found out the family was not Christian and started using Christian magazines for Alexis's reading lessons; and a private school, which was unsustainably expensive on Kelly's teacher's salary), Kelly began homeschooling Alexis when she was nine. Homeschooling as a single parent required some tricky maneuvering, schedule-wise, but overall, Kelly was really pleased with it.

Kelly felt that homeschooling was ideally suited for Alexis as someone with Asperger's, because when Alexis was interested in something, she pursued it with a passionate focus. Kelly explained, "She spent about, I don't know, a year, really, really into horses. She could tell you more about horses than I could. [. . .] Because once she's focused on something, she will consume all aspects of it. So when she shows an interest, I try to push that for as long as she's interested." Homeschooling worked well for Alexis because it gave them the flexibility to focus on one thing at a time. As Alexis's interest in a certain topic intensified, Kelly would look for ways to incorporate that interest into books, projects, field trips, and other subjects (for example, she tied Alexis's interest in horses into a history lesson by talking about George Washington's horse). When Alexis's interest in that topic waned, Kelly could pivot away from that, toward whatever the next interest was. "But," she explained, "I don't think the public school is set up for that at all." Nevertheless, after a couple of years, Alexis expressed an interest in trying public school again, so at the time of our interview, Alexis was just starting her first week at a public middle school. Kelly was unsure of how it would go, but was willing to give it a try, especially because the special education class that Alexis would be a part of focused a lot on social and emotional skills.

Catherine, who was mixed race/ethnicity (white, Hispanic, and Native American) and a married, middle-income mother of one teenage daughter, agreed with the idea that public school just does not allow children to pursue their unique interests the way homeschooling does. She said,

> Yeah, they [public schools] have to curtail it; if they really want to learn more about this particular animal it's like, no, we'll have to do that later, or read about it on your own time, and they're going to lose interest in it, and they won't go back. But if you focus on it when they want to learn it, and they'll just go after it, for everything they possible can about it, and then they'll say, "Did you know?!" And it's like, "No, I didn't!" That's why little kids who are really into dinosaurs, they know everything about dinosaurs, because their parents have let them just check out every book in the library, you know? Just let them do it! If you stop them, they just won't have that same energy to go back to it.

For both Kelly and Catherine, then, the flexibility and individualized attention that homeschooling allowed gave their daughters the ability to pursue their unique interests, at times even in all-consuming ways.

Jacqui, whom we met earlier in the chapter, also really loved how homeschooling allowed each of her now-teenage children to pursue their own interests. She described her approach to homeschooling as eclectic, saying, "We have a very basic core that I think that they all need to know. And then beyond that, they basically pursue their interests—and they're all very different." This led to different approaches to each child's education. Regarding her oldest, Silas, who was eighteen, she explained, "My oldest son is a STEM guy. Like, he's applying to places like MIT. So he's wanting to do high-end STEM stuff. So for him, [our approach] was to exhaust all the math and the physics classes at the community college so he'd get that all on his transcript and maybe place out of something so he doesn't have to repeat all that when he goes to college. And so his focus really was about the math and the science." Her daughter, Talia, who was sixteen, had different interests. "She's much more of a wanderer," Jacqui told me. "She loves to travel, she likes foreign languages, right now she's taking—well, she just spent, in the summer, she spent two months in Peru, and is also taking Russian, and is applying to go to Russia next summer with the [US] State Department." As for Maddox, the youngest, who was fourteen, Jacqui said, "My youngest is not academic at all, totally different from the other two, and wants to play music and he's just a much more laid-back, noncompetitive kid. And so they're all very different." Jacqui felt that homeschooling was the best way to be able to let each of her three children pursue their own interests. But, she noted, not all homeschooling approaches lent themselves to pursuing individual interests—for example, she argued that using a boxed curriculum would constrain children's interests in ways similar to the way they were constrained in public school.

Some of the parents I spoke with anticipated that the issue Jacqui raised, of the potential for a more rigid curriculum to constrain children's interests, might become important to them as their children got older, but felt that, when children were young, it was important to keep them focused on "the basics." Aspen, whom we met earlier in this chapter, and whose sons were six and nine, said that, for the moment, she kept things on a daily schedule and made sure they covered several main subject areas each day. But, she explained, "I can see that completely loosening up as the basics are mastered. I can see how, once you can read and write and do basic math solidly, then your interest needs to guide, you know—because again, you're not gonna remember it, you're not gonna delve deeply into anything if you don't have an interest in it." Similarly, Virginia, a white, married, high-income mother of four children (ages eight, seven, almost four, and almost two), who had been homeschooling for two years, speculated, "Later on we may switch when the kids really develop interests, maybe more literature based, or science based, whatever their interests are as they develop. We'll see where they go, and we'll choose curriculum from there. But right now, we're just doing the basics."

Other parents, however, felt that it was important to let children's interests guide their learning even from an early age. This was particularly clear in my interviews with parents who were unschooling their young elementary-aged children. Julia, a white, married, middle-income mother of three, explained her attraction to unschooling by saying that "unschooling is basically like organic, true learning. And it's centered around the child's interests. It's not necessarily letting the child decide what he's going to do all day every day. But it's finding out what interests them, what drives them, what makes them want to keep exploring a topic, and putting stuff in front of them." Melinda, whom we met earlier in this chapter, also loved the way that unschooling allowed her son, Calvin, to pursue his interests. They had recently joined a homeschool co-op, and Melinda was surprised that the two classes Calvin chose to do at the co-op were Latin and archery. "When he was in public school, he despised everything that had to do with learning," she explained. But since they began unschooling, "What's arisen for him is this real desire to learn things. And so he sought out things like Khan Academy, you know, virtual learning tools. He asked to take Latin, which I'm like, 'What?!' So it was his choice."

Both Julia and Melinda felt that the learning that was taking place for their children through unschooling was a superior type of learning to that which children do in public school—that it was more "real" or "organic" because it arose from a child's genuine desire or interest. For Melinda, this meant that unschooling could be a useful approach for all kinds of children, including those who struggle in public-school settings but also those who do well in such settings. "One of the things that's interesting about unschooling is that it has the potential to benefit every single child because it is uniquely, inherently unique for that child," she said. "So like, the child who is struggling at really making it could benefit, but also the child who does really well."

Unschoolers were not the only parents who talked about the benefits of children being able to pursue their own interests through homeschooling. Some focused on the ability to instill the idea of learning as a lifelong endeavor, while others focused on the academic benefits derived, and still others focused on the personal benefits. Claudia, a conservative, religious homeschooler whom we met in the previous chapter, was about as far from unschooling—in both her methods and her philosophy—as one could get. But she, too, saw the ability of homeschoolers to pursue intellectual interests as a definite benefit, and something that would follow them into adulthood. She told me, "I want them to have freedom. Not—certainly not freedom in the sense that they could buy anything that they want, that is certainly not what I'm speaking of. I mean freedom to study. Like, wherever their interests take them. We discuss lifelong learning. It's like, you want to just be a lifelong learner, not necessarily to be rewarded with a degree or anything like that, but I teach them to study the world, in order to know God better." Echoing other parents whom I interviewed, Claudia felt that the dominant approach to education in our society frames learning as something that only takes place in the school environment. She identified two major drawbacks to this understanding of learning: first, it leads to an expectation that learning should always be rewarded, rather than it having inherent value, and second, it makes it seem as if learning is something that stops when one graduates, rather than being an ongoing, lifelong endeavor.

Several parents identified what they saw as clear academic benefits to allowing children to pursue their own interests. In other words, for these parents, not only is learning more *fun* when one is interested in the topic, but one actually learns *more*, or more deeply, when one is interested. Tracy, a mixed-race (white, Asian American, and native Hawaiian), married, high-income mother of two, explained that she was having a hard time getting her in-laws on board with the idea of homeschooling. Their daughter—Tracy's sister-in-law—had gone to Harvard as an undergraduate and was currently finishing up her doctorate, also at Harvard, and they worried that homeschooling might foreclose similar academic options for their grandsons. She recounted a story in which her sister-in-law came to her defense when her in-laws raised this objection, noting that her best friend at Harvard had been homeschooled. "She goes, 'They have a whole department that understands homeschoolers, in fact a lot of the students that come here have been homeschooled, and they like it, because they haven't had the cookie-cutter education, trying to be in the top ten. They've been able to take their interests to the next level, when normally, you wouldn't have that opportunity, necessarily.'"

But not all of the advantages to pursuing individual interests that parents discussed were of an academic nature. Some parents also felt that this practice had deeply personal benefits as well, including that it fostered a stronger sense of self. Natalie, a white, middle-income, married mother of three young children, explained this by comparing her children's experience with unschooling to her own experience in the public school system. "I was really good at school. And so I thought school was good for me. But it turns out that it was really—it damaged a lot of my sensors, you know, like not knowing who I am or what I'm interested in. For the longest time. And that's—that's too bad." Natalie felt that, by not being allowed to pursue her own interests as a child, she was not able to even figure out *what* those interests were, and she felt that this "damaged" her. For Natalie, then, pursuing one's own interests from a young age is a means of developing a sense of self. Maria, whom we met in the previous chapter, expressed this same concept when she said that she sees focusing on what her children are interested in, rather than on them developing a certain set of skills or knowledge, as a way of respecting her children as individual people: "My focus, on what they learn, is not preparing for a test or graduating from grade to grade, it's, well, what are they interested in? Who are they right now? How can I nurture and feed that person right now, and support them right now?"

Personal Needs

The final type of unique needs of children that motivated some parents to homeschool was more personal—particularly health issues that interfered with a child's ability to be successful in school. Among several reasons why Maura, who was first introduced at the beginning of the book, decided to leave work to homeschool her daughter, Merri, was her frequent illnesses, "which seemed to be exacerbated by being around a whole bunch of other children. There were respiratory issues; she was missing a lot of school because of those. And it turned out she was allergic to just about every kind of antibiotic that works for respiratory issues, so there were some hard times around her health there."

Maura noticed that "every summer she would be home, and she would get totally healthy. So that weighed into part of it."

Although Maura had not even heard of homeschooling when her son (from a previous relationship, who was already out of high school when Merri was born) was young, she had actually begun considering homeschooling as soon as Merri was born. Maura wanted to raise a confident daughter who saw herself through her own eyes, rather than constantly worrying about how others saw her, and she did not think this would be easily achieved if Merri was in public school. Because Maura worked full-time and derived both pleasure and a sense of identity from her job, however, she initially put Merri into public school. She finally made the move to homeschooling because of Merri's health problems.

Unlike Maura, Erica—a white, middle-income, married mother of one daughter—did not consider homeschooling as an option from the get-go. Erica had a degree in special education and quite firmly believed in the public school system. When her daughter Allie was eighteen months old, she was diagnosed with severe food allergies, and Erica's husband proposed the idea of homeschooling, as it seemed like a way to protect Allie's health. Erica explained, "I would say by the time she was about three, that we had decided it was going to be the route that we went. Both because educationally, we felt like I was perfectly capable, and we also learned more about food allergies, and how they're handled in schools, and [felt] that [homeschooling] would also be the safest option." Erica perceived the home to be a safer environment, especially while Allie was young enough that she needed more adult assistance in handling her allergies, such as knowing how to avoid certain foods and how to administer emergency treatment. Allie was only kindergarten age at the time of the interview, and Erica did not see homeschooling as a lifelong commitment. Rather, she saw it as something that they would take year by year, making a conscious choice every year as to what was the best option for Allie's education.

Erica explained that her greater ability to control what was—and more importantly, was not—in the environment at home was a definite advantage of homeschooling. This was a job she appeared to take quite seriously: when I set up our interview over e-mail, she noted that they were a nut-free home, and asked that I not bring in any foods with nuts and that I wash my hands before coming, especially if I had consumed anything containing nuts that day. When I arrived, there was also a sign on the family's front door declaring it a nut-free space. It was obvious that Erica saw it as her responsibility to manage Allie's nut allergy, indicating that she understood the management of children's health to be, as sociologist Jennifer Reich puts it, "maternal terrain."[14] In fact, Erica's process of making the decision to homeschool very closely mirrored the process that the mothers in Reich's study of vaccine refusal went through in deciding not to vaccinate their children—one that Reich describes as exemplifying the demands of neoliberal motherhood. Erica (and her husband, whose idea it was for her to homeschool) saw it as the mother's responsibility to make decisions regarding her child's health *and* her education, and before she made any decisions, she researched the various forms of expert advice on the topic, filtering the available advice to make the decision that she felt was best for her child. She also sought to "control risk through management of social exposure,"[15] taking many steps to ensure that her daughter's world was not physically contaminated in ways that could have (admittedly serious) health consequences. Like the mothers in Reich's study, Erica saw herself as an expert on her own child, and thus the person in the best position to make these decisions, which she described through the language of individual maternal choice.

Conclusion: Changing Conceptualizations of Childhood in the United States

In her book *Tumbleweed Society*, sociologist Allison Pugh argues that "childrearing is deeply cultural, a collection of beliefs and practices we might interpret for meaning as we might a poem or a painting; we can read it to understand not only how people conceive of their obligations to children but also what kind of world they are raising their children to face."[16] Whether they used boxed curricula, were more eclectic in their approach, or were radical unschoolers, the parents I interviewed overwhelmingly saw the ability to tailor a child's education to their unique needs, interests, aptitudes, and temperaments as a major advantage of homeschooling. What does this focus on children's uniqueness mean for how these parents understand who children are and what they need?

To answer this question, I return to *Pricing the Priceless Child*, Viviana Zelizer's now classic and widely cited book on changing cultural conceptions of childhood. In this book, Zelizer traces the development of the concept of childhood in the twentieth century as children went from having monetary worth to the family, in terms of their capacity to labor, to being understood as priceless. The priceless child, Zelizer notes, is precious to the point that to talk about children in terms of their economic value is to break a major social taboo. She argues that, while "profound changes in the economic, occupational, and family structures" played a role in this shift away from understanding children in terms of their economic worth, this shift "was also part of a cultural process of 'sacralization' of children's lives."[17] However, in the book's conclusion—first published over thirty years ago—Zelizer wonders whether the increase of women in the paid labor force is indicative of the demise of the sacred child, who "is losing the undivided attention of its primary caretaker."[18]

I argue that, contrary to Zelizer's prediction, the continued dominance of the ideology of intensive mothering[19] in the age of neoliberal motherhood[20] indicates that the "sacred child" has not lost its grip on American mothers. However, I also argue that the narratives of the homeschooling parents featured in this chapter point to what may be the next step in the ideological progression Zelizer first identified: from the productive child to the priceless child, and now to the unique child, wherein children are still priceless, but each for their very own reasons. Children who are priceless demand investment from their parents, and one of the primary ways in which parents do this investing is through providing their child with an education.[21] But if these priceless children are also *unique*, what they demand is individualized, personalized educational investment. In other words, this is not a one-size-fits-all investment strategy—mothers are expected to invest in the education that will be best for *their* child. When this is something the government promises yet fails to provide—the subject of the next two chapters—it is left up to mothers to find an alternative, with homeschooling becoming an increasingly popular and normalized option for these mothers.

Just as Zelizer argued that the shift from the productive to the priceless child cannot be understood simply by looking at changes to the economy, the workplace, and the family, I argue here that the shift to understanding children as unique, while influenced by changes in the economy, workplace, and family, must also be understood as a cultural process. In other words, I am not proposing a one-way, causal argument linking economic restructuring and neoliberal educational "reforms" to the rise of homeschooling. Rather, I am arguing that what we are seeing is something of a feedback loop in which these structural and policy changes, and their corresponding ideologies of market competition and individual choice and responsibility, both feed into and are fed by the ideal of the unique child. The belief that children require an education that is tailored to them as individuals makes the ideology of school choice attractive to parents. As the next chapter will further demonstrate, parents use the rhetoric of school choice to explain their decisions to others, and the more this happens, the more "commonsense" this logic appears when it is reflected back to parents in policy debates about education.

To be clear, the progression from the priceless child to the unique child does not directly parallel the progression from the productive to the priceless child. In the latter situation, the ideal of the priceless child supplanted that of the productive child, making it a society-wide taboo to discuss children in terms of their economic worth (though it is worth noting that children—particularly poor and nonwhite children—are still not priceless in the eyes of current welfare policies, which penalize the poor for having children).[22] The unique child does not replace the priceless child, but rather, broadens its scope.

The parents whose narratives are featured in this chapter make it clear that the ideology of the unique child is central to the decisions they make about their children's education. While a few parents considered, or even planned on, putting their children (back) in public schools at some point, overwhelmingly, the parents I interviewed felt that public schools—and even most private schools—just could not provide the degree of personalized education that their children needed in order to flourish. This is somewhat ironic given that the current dominant model of education in the United States is the school-choice model, in which schools are supposed to vary in their strengths, focus, and/or pedagogy in order to cater to children's varying needs. While homeschooling parents largely adopted the language of school choice in how they discussed their decision to homeschool, as the analysis in the next chapter will show, their narratives contained both implicit and explicit criticisms of the US education system—including, for some, an overwhelming sense that choice was all but absent in their decision to homeschool.

4

Views of Education

What Do Children Need out of an Education, and Who Should Provide It?

We first met Raya, an immigrant, Indian American, middle-income, married mother of two sons, in chapter 2, where she had some very critical things to say about how sex education is taught in the United States, particularly the focus on abstinence, which she saw as both unrealistic and unnecessarily moralizing. Raya's critiques of public education did not stop there, however. In fact, the precipitating event that led her to homeschool had nothing to do with curricula and everything to do with how her older son, David, was treated by his peers in school.

In many ways, Raya's story exemplifies the themes of this chapter. First, she identified certain things that she felt children in general, and her children, specifically, needed out of their education: both physical and emotional safety, an education that was free from the influence of certain moral and political agendas, and a high-quality education that met their unique needs. Second, when she perceived the school to not be meeting those needs, she felt that it was her responsibility, as her children's parent, to find a solution to this problem. Because she and her husband knew the needs of their children better than the teachers and administrators, they felt they were best poised to make this decision.

Raya's son David, who would have been in the eighth grade at the time of our interview, has autism, and had been homeschooled on and off over the years, depending upon whether or not Raya and her husband felt his needs were able to be met by their school district at various points in time. Like Shannon's and Robin's sons, whom we met in the previous chapter, David was academically advanced, and had been a self-directed learner from a young age. Learning about all sorts of "advanced" topics was something of a hobby for David; Raya said, for example, that he was currently "really into" quantum physics and string theory, in the same way another parent might say their child is "really into" video games or baseball.

When David was in the seventh grade and enrolled in public school, he started having issues with other boys, such as "a lot of teasing him in the hallways, there was a lot of putting their feet up on the back of his chair, kicking him, and inking the back of his shirt." He especially had trouble in the hallways between classes. Raya explained, "What he told us, is all the kids know where the video cameras are not. So they know that the teachers stand at certain spots in the hallway, and they know exactly where the blind spots are. And if you need to walk through one of those blind spots to go to your class, you're in trouble. So they'd grab his backpack, they'd unzip it and throw things down." The bullying began to affect David's mental health, Raya said, making the decision to go back to homeschooling an easy one. She explained, "It was very easy to pull him out. As soon as we saw that he was starting to say, you know, 'I want to kill myself, I wish I was dead'—that's not worth it for us." She later said, "Quite frankly, when we pulled the kid out, that was not a choice[. . . .] We just knew he couldn't go anymore."

Raya's younger son, Jude, was about to start third grade when Raya and her husband took David out of public school, so they gave him the option of homeschooling, but told him that they felt as though he would do better in school. Raya described Jude as "very bright" but neurotypical, and reported that he did not have the same social issues in school that his brother had. However, in the fourth grade, after a couple of bad experiences with teachers with whom he did not get along well, Jude started backsliding academically, not wanting to do his written work, and having an extreme emotional reaction to the suggestion of working on things at home. Raya, who has a background in education, and her husband, a psychologist, were not particularly worried about this; they felt that this was a temporary phase that Jude was going through, which he would eventually come out of. But Jude's teacher, who was worried that Jude would not be able to perform well on upcoming standardized tests, started talking about needing to have him tested for ADHD and medicating him. Raya was adamantly opposed to this idea, as David had had bad experiences with extreme side effects of medication. At the time that I interviewed her, Raya had just pulled Jude out of public school a couple of weeks prior.

During my interview with Raya, her ambivalence about the public schools her sons attended was evident. She critiqued their overly moralistic approach to sex education, and she was vehement in her assertion that school had become an unsafe place for David and that she did not want to risk his mental health, and especially his life, by keeping him in school. She also pushed back against the way the school, and Jude's teacher in particular, seemed quick to jump to medication as a solution to a whole host of classroom-related "difficulties"—this being especially frustrating because, unlike David, Jude did not have any diagnosed mental health issues or learning disabilities when his teacher started talking about him needing medication. Nevertheless, Raya still was not someone who had written off the public school system entirely. While she did not see David ever going back to public school, she seemed pretty sure that Jude would, potentially as soon as the next academic year, though she hoped that she could get him into a neighboring school district, where the quality of education was among the highest in the state.

* * *

Raya, like many other parents I spoke with, used the language of choice to describe her move from public schooling to homeschooling. This is not a coincidence. In this chapter, I argue that parents have internalized the logic of the school-choice movement, a movement that has come to be the dominant model for thinking about education in the United States. Because this model has reached such a level of cultural acceptance that it has come to be understood as "commonsense,"[1] when parents perceive an incompatibility between what they think their children need out of their education and what schools are providing, they search for other options. And, for many of the parents I interviewed, it was in considering these options that they came to see homeschooling as the best—or even the *only*—option for their children. Ironically, while they talked about this decision using the rhetoric of school choice, many said that they "chose" to homeschool because they felt they had "no other choice."

School Choice and Neoliberal Education Reform

Homeschoolers are stereotypically understood as existing at the political and ideological extremes. While some of the parents I interviewed certainly fit this stereotype—we met some of them in chapter 2—this certainly was not true of all the parents I met while doing this research. In reality, I found that plenty of parents do not sit comfortably at these extremes. These are parents who are not opposed to public education per se, though they certainly have their critiques of it. Rather, they opt to homeschool their children because they find that the public (and at times, private) schools they interact with do not live up to their expectations for their children's education. When this happens, they shop around for alternatives. Though the data I collected for this project cannot prove this statistically, I have a hunch that, due to the increasing normalization of homeschooling in the United States, parents who may not have previously considered homeschooling end up considering it under these circumstances, and as a result, this group may be a rapidly growing segment of the homeschooling population.

The parents I interviewed are having these experiences in the context of changes to public education that began in the 1980s and have since intensified, resulting in the increased standardization and even privatization of public schools.[2] In the process, education in the United States has moved away from a model of the common school—the ideal that all children should be provided with a similar educational experience, and thus that all schools should, ideally, be similar to each other—toward a model of school choice. The main theory behind the school-choice model is that the quality of education for all students will increase if schools are forced to compete with each other in order to offer a continually better "product" to children and their families.[3]

This trend is part of the larger neoliberal transformation of the American—and the global—economy. Lisa Duggan defines neoliberalism as a "vision of national and world order" marked specifically by "competition, inequality, market 'discipline,' public austerity, and 'law and order.'"[4] Neoliberalism is not solely a set of economic policies; rather, it includes corresponding political and cultural shifts that are masked by the supposedly "neutral" language of economic policy. Duggan argues that the cultural and economic elements of neoliberalism intersect at what she identifies as neoliberalism's "key terms": "privatization" and "personal responsibility." These key terms are critical for understanding the impact of neoliberalism on both education and the family, because, as Duggan notes, "This rhetoric promotes the *privatization* of the costs of social reproduction, along with the care of human dependency needs, through *personal responsibility* exercised in the family and in civil society—thus shifting costs from state agencies to individuals and households."[5] These "individuals and households," however, are not gender neutral: under what has come to be known as "neoliberal motherhood," women largely shoulder the burden of this increased privatization of care work within the family,[6] as well as the burden of making informed but personalized decisions about how to raise their children.[7]

Scholars of education have noted numerous ways in which neoliberalism has affected public education, as education has shifted from being considered a public good to being considered a market commodity, and schools themselves are increasingly run on the principles of corporations.[8] Perhaps most obvious is the increased emphasis put on "accountability" of teachers and schools, which is executed through increased standardized testing. This accountability is applied to teachers through initiatives to link teacher pay to test outcomes, and to schools, which are ranked and compared to each other, through test scores used to indicate which schools are offering a better—or lesser—product.[9] This commoditization of education is accompanied by an increase in the "technicization of knowledge,"[10] with the new dominance of the language of "best practices" and "teacher effectiveness" transforming knowledge acquisition into something that is understood to be measurable and observable in supposedly objective ways. Under this model, teaching practices, teachers themselves, and even entire schools can be categorized as successes or failures, a process that serves to further entrench educational hierarchies and disparities, as schools serving low-income and racial-minority students are at much higher risk of being labeled "failing."[11]

Some scholars have argued that the very goal of education has shifted under neoliberalism, from being a public good that benefits society to being a service that is responsive to the needs of the economy.[12] These two goals correspond to what Kevin B. Smith refers to as competing ideologies of education: the commonwealth ideology and the market ideology.[13] The increasing dominance of the market ideology of education has led to the reshaping of the role of school administrators, such as principals and vice principals, from educators to a managerial class. This is evidenced by the creation of new degree programs within schools of education, specifically for training school administrators as experts in management, rather than educational philosophies and techniques.[14] Because public schools aim to produce workers well suited for the "New Economy," which emphasizes personal responsibility in creating and shaping one's own career path, the goal of the school becomes the creation of "responsibilized" citizens, who are highly individualized and capable of being entrepreneurial in all areas of their lives.[15] With public funding for education dwindling, students—and their parents—are increasingly told that it is up to them to take responsibility for their own education.

Paradoxically, one of the effects of this increased competition—in which schools attempt to make themselves stand out as being particularly "successful" through high test scores—is that schools have become increasingly standardized,[16] leaving little room for teacher creativity or responsiveness to the needs of their particular students. This has resulted in a fundamental change in the relationship between teachers and students; Raewyn Connell argues that due to the "intensified testing regime" and "formidable pressure to teach to the test," teachers who want to serve the interests of their students are rendered unable to do so because "the current institutional system creates contradictions between short-term results and long-term effects."[17] This conflict, along with the undermining of teachers' unions and increased job insecurity for teachers, has led to the weakening of teacher power, including both individual and collective efficacy.[18]

At the same time as schools have become more standardized, pressure on mothers to provide individualized attention to their children's needs has also intensified. The dominance of school-choice rhetoric places responsibility squarely on the shoulders of mothers—not the school itself—to ensure that their children's educational needs are met. And so, while the public-school model in the United States has always relied on the unpaid, often invisible, labor of mothers for its everyday functioning,[19] in the context of the increased privatization of education, mothers face a new imperative: to look out for their children's interests by constantly "choosing" the best educational option. Referencing the frequent refrain she hears from mothers talking about their children's schooling that "I just have to do what's best for my own child," Amy Shuffleton argues that rather than expressing selfishness or irrational anxiety, "Our national unwillingness to support children and families means that these mothers are accurately identifying a problem: if they do not tenaciously defend their own children's interests, those interests will go unaddressed."[20] And so, when the neoliberalization of education is combined with huge funding cuts to public education more broadly, both the risks and the responsibilities associated with children's education are being increasingly transferred to families—in particular, to mothers.

I argue that the increased standardization of schools, and its accompanying decrease in individual and collective efficacy of teachers to advocate for students, when combined with the increased pressure for mothers to manage the individual needs of their children, effectively pits motherhood and public schools against each other. Mothers are forced to take an oppositional stance toward public schools to ensure that their children's needs are met, and when these needs are not met, the responsibility falls on the mother, not the school, to find an alternative solution. Thus, in some cases, homeschooling becomes the "better" option when public—and sometimes also private—schools are not perceived to be meeting children's needs.

What are the needs of children that mothers feel schools are not meeting? What are the concerns that mothers have about schools when they are choosing where and how to educate their children? One concern, of course, is the feeling—as discussed in the previous chapter—that schools are unable to meet the *unique* educational needs of each child. But the parents I interviewed raised other concerns as well. In the sections that follow, I will discuss two sets of concerns that these parents had with schools: bullying and children's safety, and quality of education. For the parents whom I interviewed, when they felt that their children's education was being compromised in one or more of these areas, they sought out alternatives—and came to feel that homeschooling was the best possible way to give their children the education they need.

Bullying and Student Safety

When Shannon, whom we met in chapter 3, and her husband first made the decision to homeschool their son Ethan, they did so because of Ethan's "asynchronous" development—he was academically gifted and had a very high IQ, but socially, he lagged behind his peers. Around the time they began homeschooling, however, they moved from Texas to Massachusetts for work. Initially, they were excited to be moving to a state where the public schools had such an excellent reputation, but upon doing some research, Shannon was dismayed to realize that gifted education was "nonexistent in Massachusetts public schools." As a result, they continued to homeschool for another year, hiring a private, live-in tutor to accommodate their work schedules. Shannon told me that that year was "a fantastic year." However, when they found a private school nearby that seemed to be exactly what Ethan needed—a school for gifted children who had difficulty fitting in socially in other schools—they were excited at the possibility that the school could meet both Ethan's educational *and* his social needs.

This expectation, however, was not met in reality. Ethan attended this school for three years, and over that period of time, he experienced teasing and bullying from other students in the program. Ethan, Shannon explained, "has a follower-type personality, where if somebody's picking on him, again, he's not picking that up appropriately? And he wants to be like them. And he wants them to like him. And he would start modeling their behavior." The bullying was not physical, she explained, but "was setting him up. He had one [kid] in particular who would set him up to do things, in front of the teachers, so that he would take the fall. He would ask him to do something foolish in front of the other kids and he would do it, thinking it's funny, and instead be humiliated." Shannon tried to talk about the issue with the school administrators, but felt that the school was unwilling to do anything about it, because they feared alienating parents who were "high donors" at the school. "We had problems with bullying for all three years we were there, with the same kids," she said. "And that wasn't going to change."

Over time, the bullying grew increasingly worse, to the point that, Shannon reported, Ethan was crying every night. She told me that "because he was lonely at school, he knew he wasn't fitting in, and he was trying desperately, I could see him sinking. I had a real concern that I was losing him emotionally, because of his fear of going to school and his fear of handling himself with other people, and wanting to be cool, and wanting to fit in." Shannon said it worried her, given "all of the stories you hear" about young people getting depressed and even suicidal from bullying. They made the decision to go back to homeschooling, so as to not risk things getting to that point with Ethan. At the time of our interview, they had been homeschooling again for two years.

Although some have been critical about the rise in discourse about school bullying, arguing that schools have gone to an extreme of calling any interstudent conflict bullying, what Shannon described here, and what Raya described in the opening vignette of this chapter, both fit within the understanding of bullying as a social experience, as theorized by Todd Migliaccio and Juliana Raskauskas. They argue that bullying includes three predominant characteristics: it is repeated over time, it is performed with an intent to harm, and it is characterized by an imbalance of power.[21] In Raya's example, the neuro-typical boys at David's school were exercising power over David, whose Asperger's put him at a distinct disadvantage in the social hierarchy of the school. In Shannon's case, the children who tormented Ethan also occupied a higher place in the school's social hierarchy—they were part of the "cool" crowd, of which Ethan was desperate to be a part. This exercise of power was especially evident in that "the intention of bullying is to dominate in a public venue, exhibiting power in the group."[22] In other words, most bullying occurs in the presence of other people. For both David and Ethan, that these events typically happened in full view of other students, and sometimes even in front of teachers, reinforced this power differential, and led to the feelings of humiliation that both mothers identified as being central to their sons' extreme emotional distress.

While it is tempting to interpret David's and Ethan's cases as outliers due to their being so highly advanced academically, several parents I interviewed also discussed actual or hypothetical experiences of bullying and teasing in telling me what they disliked about public schools. Veronica, whom we met in the previous chapter, talked about how her youngest daughter "started getting treated like crap" by her peers when she became pregnant in high school. Jenny, a mixed-race (white and Hispanic), middle-income, married mother of two children, told me specifically that her fear of bullying was a major factor motivating her decision to homeschool. She said, "Around the time that Caleb was going to start going to kindergarten, there was like, in the news about all these kids being bullied, and like, committing suicide. And Caleb's very sensitive, and I was like, 'Oh, he's going to be bullied.' And so I didn't want to put him in."

For Allison, the single mother of two adoptive daughters whom we met in the previous chapter, bullying was not on her mind when she decided to homeschool, though in retrospect, she did note that her older daughter was teased by her peers in kindergarten for still watching TV shows that were considered "babyish," and she now felt that homeschooling allowed her daughters to feel comfortable having interests that their same-aged peers might tease them about. That said, Allison noted that, as her daughters approached middle school age, the prevalence of bullying had become a reason she continued to homeschool: "It didn't factor in in my decision when I started and everything, but since then it definitely, you know, it does factor in. I'm a social worker at the hospital, I see kids who are bullied a lot, especially, you know, who come to the hospital, who are depressed or self-injuring and things that like, because of bullying. And my sister's also a middle school teacher, so [bullying] is something that I'm very familiar with, with the schools." Allison later brought up the argument she had heard that children need to encounter bullies, because they will need to learn how to deal with difficult people in their life—an argument that, as a social work professional and as a parent, she found ridiculous. "I understand some people say you have to be around negative people and everything, but like, I just don't prefer for my kids to be bullied in order to learn how to deal with bullies." Furthermore, she said that "I see the schools not really able to handle the bullying situation," which made her all the more intent on continuing to homeschool her daughters.

Finally, some of the parents I interviewed theorized that the increase in attention to school bullying, and an increased frustration among parents that schools seemed ill equipped to deal with it, was bringing about an increase in homeschooling. As Jenny noted, "I know a lot of people do homeschool because their kids were getting bullied. I see that a lot on [Internet] forums." Jacqui, whom we met in the previous chapter, and who moderated a large online listserv for homeschoolers, also gave this assessment. She noted that in the past couple of years, she had seen a sharp increase in parents talking about bullying as a motivation for homeschooling, saying, "I've seen a lot of people join the group because their kid is bullied, or something. Like we had one last week that was, 'My junior, fifteen-year-old, was getting sexually harassed, and nobody would deal with the issue, it's the only thing we could do was take her out.' Or, 'My son is in middle school and he's getting bullied so badly'—you know, you've heard the stories."

The parents I interviewed who brought up issues related to bullying did not tend to discuss it in specifically gendered or sexualized terms. That said, many of the experiences they described were clearly gendered experiences. It is not a coincidence that it tended to be parents of boys who described the most actual or anticipated experiences of bullying. Scholars have theorized bullying as a social practice linked to social status, and social status as tied to embodying appropriate, hegemonic masculinities and femininities.[23] The link between hegemonic masculinity and heterosexuality means that, in particular, boys who fail to embody a certain degree of heterosexual competency through interest in girls, or who are perceived as nonheterosexual due to their association with feminine traits such as sensitivity, are often subject to bullying and teasing from their male peers, even in the elementary school years.[24] Because boys often perceive academic success or an interest therein as feminine, being especially studious or enjoying learning can make it difficult for high-achieving boys "to project a coherent and stable hegemonic masculinity."[25] The bullying that David and Ethan experienced, and that Jenny feared Caleb would experience, is likely linked to their lack of embodiment of hegemonic masculinity.

For the girls mentioned, including Veronica's daughter who was pregnant, and the unnamed girl on Jacqui's listserv who was sexually harassed in school, bullying is also gendered and sexualized. Girls who embody stigmatized forms of femininity, as Veronica's daughter did when she was pregnant and thus clearly marked as sexually active, are also subject to bullying in schools,[26] and scholars have argued that boys engage in sexual harassment of their female classmates as a way of demonstrating their (heterosexual) masculinity to each other.[27] It is no wonder, then, that some scholars have called for a rethinking of our discourse on school bullying to more clearly name it as a form of gender policing.[28]

Quality of Education

Several of the parents whom I interviewed decided to homeschool because they had issues with the quality of their children's education. They shared stories of drawn-out, often very frustrating experiences of trying to work with their school to address their children's needs before ultimately deciding to homeschool. One such parent was Tracy, a high-income, mixed-race (white, Asian American, and Native Hawaiian), married mother of two middle school–aged sons. Tracy was educated in private schools, and recalled noticing at the time that the quality of the education she received was better than that of her public-school friends. As an example, she said that she began writing research papers in the sixth grade, whereas her public-school friends did not do this until high school, if at all. With these memories in mind, she and her husband elected to enroll their first child, Hunter, in private school. He remained there until the second grade, but when their younger son became school-aged, they realized that they could not afford to pay private school tuition for two children—their family income was lower at the time, and varied widely from year to year because Tracy's husband worked a job that paid primarily on commission. They lived in a town that, Tracy said, "everyone knows is a very good school district," so despite her initial hesitation about public schools, she decided that their local public school would be an acceptable option.

Tracy described Hunter as a bright, academically inclined child. When Hunter was in the fifth grade, however, school became difficult and he began to struggle to finish the massive amount of homework he was being assigned—up to three hours a night, mostly in math. Tracy felt that this was a lot of work for children at this age, especially because the amount of work did not seem to be paying off in terms of increased learning. She soon found out that other parents also had problems with Hunter's particular math teacher; they complained that she was an ineffective teacher who caused her students to struggle with what should have been basic concepts. Tracy requested a meeting with the vice principal and all of Hunter's teachers to try to resolve the problem, but the meeting was completely unhelpful, and she felt as though the teachers simply blamed Hunter for not completing more of his homework during free time at school. Tracy explained,

> Basically, I was *that* parent, who complained. We finish up, I take it to the next level, I talk to the principal, about what one of the teachers said, and she finally said that she believed that the teacher said that my son was a procrastinator. And I said, "So what you're telling me is, I'm imagining it,

even though all these other parents are coming in and complaining about the same thing?" So I found out very quickly, she was not going to help. I talked to the vice superintendent, who's in charge of academics, and he agrees with me that something is wrong, but over time made it very clear to me that he's not in charge. How are you not in charge? So all of a sudden I'm feeling like I have no say in anything, I have no control over my child's education, I have no control over the direction that he's going. I had him yanked out of the math class. I said, "I'm telling you now, I want him out. I want him in a different math teacher, if he has to switch his schedule around, we'll switch his schedule around—I don't want him in that class anymore."

The frustration Tracy felt was apparent as she told this story: the pitch of her voice went up, the speed of her speech quickened, and her hand gestures became more and more animated.

Although she seemed pleased that she had been able to get Hunter into a different math class—where, she reported, he began to thrive—Tracy's frustrations soon began to grow again when the vice superintendent called her to say that, based on Hunter's scores, he thought he had been placed in the wrong math class to begin with, and that he should have been in the highest level of math class for his grade. "I said, 'What does that mean? I got a thing in the mail that said he's in compacted math,' which was the middle tier—and he goes, 'Well, you didn't protest it?' And I said, 'Why would I, if they said that his test scores came that he was supposed to be in this class, why would I protest that?'" Tracy had trusted that the school would place her son in the appropriate class, but now felt that her trust had been misplaced. The vice superintendent only reaffirmed this feeling by making it clear, by asking why she did not protest Hunter's placement, that it was ultimately Tracy's responsibility—not the school's—to make sure her son was placed in the correct classes.

A drawn-out and increasingly hostile battle ensued involving the school administrators, the school's math coordinator, the district's "gifted and talented" coordinator, and the summer math teacher, whose class Hunter would now have to pass in order to be placed in the higher tier the following year. Tracy came to feel more and more powerless, as if all of the school's policies and procedures—many of which were initially concealed from her as a parent—were more important to the administrators than her child's education. Tracy told me that she felt as though she was "placed on the back burner," ignored, and even mistreated by the school's administration. As the new school year approached, she said, "I became very overwhelmed. I started Googling everything I could about homeschooling. I looked at my husband, and I said, 'I can't do this anymore.' We can't afford private school, [which] would be anywhere from six to ten thousand dollars per student. I didn't have a choice. I literally felt that way." Two weeks before school was supposed to start again, Tracy wrote to her sons' schools to inform them that she was withdrawing them in order to homeschool.

The rhetoric and logic of school choice appears consistently throughout Tracy's narrative. She took a while at the beginning of our interview to explain why her sons were in public school to begin with, when she obviously would have preferred to have them in private school. Public school only seemed like a viable choice to her because her family lived in a "good school district"—in other words, because the local public schools offered a good enough "product" to compete with that offered by private schools. Even though the decision to send her sons to public school was made out of perceived financial necessity, she still framed it as an informed decision. And, it was perhaps because of the research she had done about the school district that Tracy trusted the authority of those at the school at first, for example, by not questioning Hunter's placement in the middle-tier math class. However, this trust diminished over time, which led Tracy to become more directly involved with the school. As she described to me, the summer before she ultimately pulled her children out of public school, it seemed as though the drama-filled process of trying to get her son placed in the right math class consumed the majority of her time and energy. The process was exhausting and affected her both physically and mentally—she described feeling overwhelmed and experiencing heart palpitations as a result of all the stress.

I argue that Tracy experienced such an intense degree of stress because she felt that, as her children's mother, she was ultimately responsible for ensuring her children's educational success, and that she was failing at this task when she "suddenly" felt that she had "no control over her children's education." Neoliberalism has changed not only education but motherhood as well. As I will discuss more in chapter 6, motherhood under neoliberalism has also taken on a market logic, such that motherhood is experienced as a managerial role.[29] Tracy found herself unable to manage her children's education in the public-school environment, and thus felt she had no other choice but to find a different option.

Tracy's own class privilege, as a privately educated, high-income mother, likely contributed to her confidence in engaging with the school and advocating for her children,[30] but it may have also intensified her feelings of anxiety. As sociologist Jennifer Reich explains, the "active management of childhood" that characterizes intensive mothering affects mothers at all socioeconomic levels, but "is marked most intensely by those in the middle and upper class who have the material and cultural resources to invest most heavily in their children's development and . . . are most fearful of their children's downward mobility."[31] It is likely that Tracy was motivated to homeschool out of concern for not just the current efficacy of her children's education but also the implications for their future economic success.

Nevertheless, there is also evidence that Tracy experienced some ambivalence about her managerial role. She invoked the stereotype of being "*that* parent"—the pushy mother who cannot just let the school do its job, is always complaining, and feels the need to interfere, using the school's time and resources in ways that distract from the purpose of education. And yet, despite seeing "that parent" as annoying, she still felt as though she had no choice but to embody the stereotype in order to ensure that her children's educational needs were met.

Interestingly, Tracy's husband barely appeared in her narrative of how she decided to homeschool. Tracy, alone, interfaced with the school and ultimately made the decision to remove the children from public school when she could not handle it any longer. Her husband really only appeared in the narrative as the one who made money for the family (but not enough for the family to afford Tracy's preferred schooling option). For Tracy, the work of managing children's education was *mothering* work, not *parenting* work. It was also very embodied work, which, as mentioned above, took a physical toll on her body and on her mental health. Despite the fact that Tracy felt as though her only choice was to homeschool, she framed the decision as something that was beneficial not only to her children but also to herself, because it allowed her to avoid sacrificing her own mental and physical health. Although a lot of her time and energy went into homeschooling her sons, this was not a great departure from the enormous amount of time and energy she had been putting into their education while they were in public school, overseeing hours of homework and interfacing with teachers and administrators as issues arose.

While some parents, like Tracy, had concerns about the quality of the education their children were receiving when they were already enrolled in public school, some avoided public school altogether because the public schools they had access to were considered low-quality schools. For example, Jenny, whom we met toward the beginning of the chapter, explained that when her children were getting close to school age, the area in which they lived was zoned to a very low-rated public school. She, and especially her husband (who was white and, she explained, grew up in New England and was therefore "kind of a snob about education"), did not want to send their children to a low-performing school. She considered private school, but most of the private schools in their area were religious, and as she was nonreligious, she was adamantly opposed to sending her children to a religious school. These factors, in addition to the fact that the family moved frequently for her husband's work, combined to make Jenny "just feel it would be easier to do it on my own."

As did Tracy, Jenny narrated her decision to homeschool as being one in which she weighed various choices for schooling but ultimately "chose" homeschooling because she perceived it to be the choice that would offer the highest quality of education, and would put the least burden on her and her children. Jenny was not ideologically opposed to public school in any way—in fact, she planned to send the children to public school eventually, definitely for high school, and potentially for middle school as well. But the market logic of school choice meant that Jenny and her husband were able to "know" what kind of education their children would get at their neighborhood elementary school because of its low rating, which was likely a result of subpar performance of the students on standardized testing. Similarly, Margaret, a white, middle-income, married mother of two children, Ashley, age seven, and Cole, eighteen months, also referenced the rating of the public school in her area. Margaret decided to homeschool Ashley when the family moved and found themselves in a new school district. Margaret explained,

"Well, she did public school for kindergarten and first grade. The school district was great, we actually had a very, very good experience with her teachers. I mean, she excelled. She thrived. It was not a bad experience. But, life kind of happened, and we moved here and [this is] not a great area—the school is rated really poorly, not just test scores but in general."

Standardized testing, and its use to grade the performance of specific teachers, schools, and school districts, is one of the hallmarks of neoliberal education reform. This practice contributes to parents' ability to gather data about their public-school options in order to make decisions about their children's schooling. And yet, when I asked parents to tell me what they saw as some of the positive and negative attributes of public schools today, almost across the board, the culture of frequent standardized testing was raised as one of the negatives. Margaret, who earlier in the interview had noted that the low test scores of the schools in her current district were part of the reason she did not want to send Ashley to those schools, later spoke about the culture of standardized testing being something that she did not like about public school: "I hate testing. I feel like it wasn't as bad when I was in school, but now I feel like there's so much pressure, and there's so much centered around the test, and I just feel for the kids that aren't good test takers. I feel like in some cases maybe they're a good judge of how kids are learning, but at the same time, I've looked at some of them, and I'm just like . . . you know? I hate the idea of teaching to a test." This comment on standardized testing touches on three common critiques that other parents I interviewed also articulated. First, Margaret notes that testing puts a lot of pressure on children. This was something that Alma, who had volunteered in her sons' classrooms prior to deciding to homeschool them, also discussed. "I saw how anxious the kids were," Alma said. "I saw how much pressure there was on the kids, and kids having to throw up before they took their test, because, you know, I moderated a lot of those tests. And I just felt bad for them. Kids that I knew, because I had seen it, knew the material. They just got stressed out over this test. It was so high stakes."

Second, Margaret articulates a distaste for the idea of "teaching to the test." Other parents expressed similar feelings. For example, Jenny felt that teaching to the test is something that takes away from the opportunity for "real" learning. At twenty-eight years old, Jenny was among the youngest of the mothers I interviewed, so her own middle- and high-school years, in the late 1990s and early 2000s, corresponded with the increase in the use of standardized testing in public schools. When I asked Jenny what she thought were some of the good or bad things about public schools, she first said that she did not think there was anything bad about them. But then she quickly amended her answer, saying, "I kind of hate the focus on standardized testing. I remember when I was in school, they would take, like, a whole six weeks off [from teaching], just to really drill us on how to pass that test, so the school would get a good grade." Since Jenny's own children had not yet been in public schools, she drew on her own experience of standardized testing, in which a sizable chunk of time was devoted to teaching them "how to pass that test," rather than teaching them important concepts, to leverage her only real critique of public schools. Another parent, Ruth, drew on the experiences of friends she had who were teachers, discussing their frustration with having to teach to the test: "They're not learning anything real, if all they're learning is how to answer a multiple choice. And then the teachers talk about how much time they have to spend, working toward that, and even coming up with alternate tests for special needs kids and all these things." Ruth felt that teachers were forced to make standardized testing "be their whole world" and that this was bad for both the students *and* the teachers.

Finally, Margaret's comment implied that standardized tests are not a good measure of academic performance. Similarly, Robin used a health-related metaphor to describe what she saw as the "absolute nonsense" of using one particular type of testing as a stand-in for a more holistic idea of performance. She said, "They think a number on a standardized test is going to give you an indication of how it's actually, how things are actually working. And that's like wanting to be able to describe somebody by taking their blood pressure, and then saying, 'Oh I know you, you're the one who's 123 over 78.' It doesn't make any sense."

Taken together, these excerpts make for a multifaceted critique of the widespread use of standardized testing in public schools. I believe that the fact that parents articulated many different reasons for why they disliked standardized testing indicates that "standardized testing" functioned as something of a stand-in for a larger critique of public schools—that it eliminates any focus on the needs of the unique child.

This is illustrated particularly well in the narrative of Jamie, an adamant unschooler whose story featured prominently in chapter 2:

> As I got older, things started changing, with the standardized testing. And then I moved to Texas, which is very different than where I grew up, [in terms of] standardized testing. [And] I was like, I don't want [Emery] to go through that. That's ridiculous. I don't want my kid to be taught to a test. I don't like that idea at all. So [at first] I thought, it's either going to be homeschooling or private schooling. And then I started learning more about private schooling, and just the differences between the different types of traditional education, and I came to the conclusion that private school really isn't any better than public school, it's just different. Maybe they don't have the testing and stuff, but the culture is still the same, the expectations are still the same, the grooming is still the same. And I realized I didn't want any of that for my kid either. So much of it is classroom management, and getting kids to conform to expectations, because—well, I don't know what else they're going to do with a class full of thirty students, I don't think they have any other option, but I don't like it. It's the same, you know, whether it's a private school with eight kids in a class or a public school with twenty kids in a class or whatever, it's still, "You're going to do what we're going to tell you to do, when we do it, how we tell you to do it. And you have to learn what we want you to learn when we want you to learn it. And if that doesn't work for you, that's your problem." But I didn't like that, I didn't want to do that to my kid, I didn't feel like that was good. If I had any other options, that wasn't what I wanted to do.

Like Jenny, Jamie referred to her own public-school experience, in the years when schools began increasing the amount of standardized testing students did, in narrating her thought process about her decision to unschool her daughter. Unlike Jenny's, however, Jamie's critique of standardized testing was tied to a broader critique of the approach and the goals of most traditional schooling.

Jamie's initial dislike of the culture of standardized testing led her to look for alternatives in the form of private schools. In this sense, she seemed to embrace the ethos of school choice, where she did not feel tied to the neighborhood public school as the only, or the most logical, place for Emery to get an education. She also seemed to embrace the neoliberal expectation that, as Emery's mother, she was in charge of researching what other options were available, and making the choice, based on that research, as to which option was best for her individual child. But the more she researched the available options, the more she began to feel that the different choices she was presented with were all basically offering the same product, just wrapped in different packaging, or as she put it, "The culture is still the same, the expectations are still the same, the grooming is still the same." This led Jamie to the conclusion that she would avoid any traditional school, provided "I had any other option." And she did: she had the option to homeschool.

DIY Education and Deskilling of the Teaching Profession

Why did Jamie—like the other parents I interviewed for this project—think that homeschooling was a viable option for her daughter's education? What makes these parents think that homeschooling will afford their children not just a comparable but a *superior* educational experience to what they would get in schools? What makes these parents feel that they are even qualified to be their children's primary educators? I argue that the trend of the deskilling of the teaching profession is fundamental to understanding the confidence these parents had that they could provide their children with an education that was as good as, or better than, what they would get in public schools. When combined with the principles of neoliberalism, this trend leads these parents—particularly mothers—to see themselves as being not only equally as capable of serving as their children's primary educators but even as ideally situated educators.

When I interviewed Anita, a Latina, middle-income, married mother of four, I ended the interview the way I always did: by asking her if there was anything that we had not touched on that she wanted me to know about her homeschooling experience. It was at this point that her somewhat conflicted feelings about the public school system really came out. She told me that she tries to stay out of political debates about the school system, but that she felt as though she had some insights as to problems with how schools are run—problems that "many people just don't see"—

because her in-laws had worked in "the school system" for many years. And her perspective was that "it's just kind of disheartening." She went on to say, "I wish that the teacher role was just a more professional role. Like, I wish they—you know, back in the day, that was a profession. That was a highly respected profession. And now it's not so much. You know? It's like, the requirements are easier, so more people gravitate toward that, and they don't pay much, so you become undervalued, as a person. It just seems backwards. Especially going through it myself, like, I only have to teach three [children], I can't imagine having to teach thirty, or more. I don't know. It's just disheartening."

In saying this, Anita touched on a crucial point of context for the larger set of critiques of education raised by the parents I interviewed. There is debate within the sociology of professions over what characteristics separate a profession from an occupation or job, but the characteristics that have been most generally agreed on over time include expert knowledge, autonomy (both of individual professionals over their own work and of professional organizations over their members), normative community standards, and social status and other rewards, including income and job security.[32] During the 1970s and 1980s, however, scholars began to observe a breakdown of some of these characteristics, particularly claims to expert knowledge and autonomy over everyday work, and thus began theorizing the "deprofessionalization," or "deskilling," of professions.[33] Two of the forces scholars identified as challenging the status of professions were increased bureaucratization and the rise of market-based concerns and pressures—in other words, the hallmarks of neoliberalism.[34]

In part because teachers have not enjoyed the high pay typically received by members of other professions such as doctors and lawyers, whether teaching could be considered a "profession" in the sociological sense has always been a point of debate. Nevertheless, scholars of education have noted the trend toward deskilling within the teaching profession, and argue that it makes sense to understand this trend alongside the parallel processes occurring in other fields.[35] Of particular importance is the "debilitating effect on the teaching profession" of "the merging interests of an enhanced centralizing tendency of the state and private commercial interests."[36] In other words, just as the state has increased the central regulation of education, it has also increasingly opened education up to the influence of the private sector, and this trend has only intensified as neoliberal education reform measures have taken hold not only in the United States but across the world.

One of the changes that has taken place under this shift is that schools are increasingly run more like businesses,[37] and teachers find themselves being increasingly managed from above, and less able to rely on their own professional autonomy to determine the day-to-day needs of their classrooms or, more broadly, what children need to learn.[38] Teachers face increasing accountability to those outside of the profession due to the widespread use of standardized testing that has accompanied neoliberal education reforms such as No Child Left Behind and the Common Core State Standards, and curricula have become increasingly standardized, or what some have described as "teacher-proof," in order to prepare students for these high-stakes tests.[39] The concept of such "teacher-proof" curricula that can be delivered with less training has coincided with the advent of fast-tracked, less rigorous, and financially profitable alternate credentialing routes, such as Teach for America.[40]

These changes have had effects on teachers beyond the changes to their professional status and work processes. In a case study carried out in a British primary school, teachers reported feeling increased pressure as a result of the "new managerialism" in education, and this pressure leaves them feeling that teaching is "draining their energy, sapping their enthusiasm and placing increasing demands on their working and personal time," and for some, this negatively affected their mental and even physical health.[41] Teachers also report feeling less effective overall, due to an inability to flexibly respond to students' needs and to an increased amount of time spent on bureaucratic tasks, time that takes them away from more student-centered tasks.[42] If teachers themselves feel that recent education "reforms" render them ineffective and unable to give students personalized education that is tailored to their individual needs, it is little wonder, then, that parents also feel that way.

Teachers feel that their ability to rely on their instincts and their situated knowledge of their students is what makes them a good teacher.[43] Interestingly, the mothers that I interviewed spoke similarly about what makes them ideally situated educators for their own children. As teachers' agency to teach responsively decreases, mothers—as the people who arguably know their children best—see themselves as the people best suited to take over this work. For example, Erica, who homeschooled her daughter in part because of her severe food allergies, was at first skeptical when her husband proposed that they homeschool. But, she said, the more they talked about it, she came to realize that a child's mother may, in fact, be the best teacher a child could have, saying that "educationally, we felt like I was perfectly capable—and perhaps, as her mom, even *more* capable—to be her primary teacher." Erica explained that, because mothers know their children better than anyone else, this gives them an advantage that a schoolteacher would not have. Danielle, whom we first met in chapter 2, made a similar argument about mothers having the best capacity to educate their children, but rather than focusing on mothers' superior knowledge of their children, she argued that nobody has a stronger interest in a child's development than their mother. She explained that she was hesitant to homeschool at first, because she associated homeschooling with "those ultra-religious people who live on a farm and have nineteen kids," and she did not see herself as being "radical" enough to homeschool. "But the more I thought about it," she said, "the more I thought, well, who had a better vested interest in my son's well-being and his education, than me?"

In the context of the deskilling of the teaching profession, in which teacher credentialing is seen as less valuable—what good is a degree in education if you can't use it to teach your students effectively?—and expert knowledge is devalued, the issue of whether or not parents have the training needed to teach becomes less important. As Kamilah, a Black, high-income, married mother of three children put it in describing her frustrations with her oldest daughter April's teachers, whom she felt did not want her involved in April's education, "[They say,] 'We know better than you, because we have an EdD or a PhD, or this and that, in child studies or early childhood education.' But you don't have an EdD in educating April, though. *I* have that."

Conclusion: Homeschooling and School "Choice"

To conclude, I would like to return to Raya, whose narrative opened this chapter. Toward the end of our interview, Raya reflected on the immense amount of emotional and intellectual work that surrounded her decisions—made separately from each other, at different points in time—to homeschool her two sons, David and Jude. Raya recalled a conversation that she had with a counselor at David's school when they first decided to pull him:

> You know, one of the terms that David's counselor used, when we first pulled him out and didn't know exactly what his issues were and all that—one of the things she told us is, she said, "What you guys are doing is called 'active parenting.' You're not just sitting back and letting him follow the system and do[ing] what the system tells you needs to be done." Because that's what the school kept telling us, "Let the system work, let the system work." And she says, "When you're an active parent, you're involved, you make the choices, you decide what's best for your child."

Raya paused, and I could hear the emotion in her voice when she continued:

> And it's exhausting. Because you're constantly having to consider your choices. And I've found that a lot of the homeschoolers that we meet are active parents. They have a very strong opinion, on what their child should be exposed to. And, you know, some of them, the ones that we associate with, want their child to be exposed to everything. But, it's just, you know . . . I don't feel like I had a choice, with David. With David there was no choice, it was either homeschool or he would not make it. I didn't think he would make it past fifteen, sixteen. So with him, it was not a choice. With Jude, it is a choice. And I think it's a good one.

The stories featured in this chapter have in common a sense that schools are inflexible, and a perception of teachers and administrators as often unwilling or, more sympathetically, unable to accommodate the needs of particular children. In other words, the stories we heard in this chapter echo back to those in the previous chapter, when we encountered the rhetoric of the "unique child." As in the previous chapter, we see here that parents sensed an incompatibility between the public-school model, on the one hand, and the unique child, on the other. That said, many of these parents expressed a belief that public schools work for *some* children—exemplified in how some homeschool some of their children and not others, or go back and forth between homeschooling and public school—whereas for other children, public school simply fails them altogether. And, when the school fails, these parents believe that it is the responsibility of the parents—and the mother, in particular—to provide a viable alternative. These narratives show the ways in which some mothers feel pushed into homeschooling, talking about it as a "choice" that they were forced to make when faced with a lack of alternatives. But is a choice really a choice, when there are no real alternatives? While homeschooling parents utilize the discourse of school choice to describe their decision to homeschool, I argue that this frequently perceived *lack* of choice reveals that the ideology of school choice is exactly that—an ideology.

5

Giving Up on Government

In late July 2014, I drove from Austin to The Woodlands, Texas, an affluent suburb of Houston, to attend the annual convention of the Texas Home School Coalition (THSC). I arrived the evening before the conference officially began in order to attend the "beginner sessions," which were geared toward people who are just about to start homeschooling, or who are attending the conference for the first time. The first session, called "Ready, Set . . . Now What Do I Do?" featured Tim Lambert, president of THSC, and his wife, Lyndsay, a well-dressed white couple who appeared to be in their early sixties. Tim, in a suit and tie, was tall and had silver-gray hair. Lyndsay, dressed in a long skirt and colorful blouse, had curly blonde-gray hair and the kind of impeccably made-up face that I had come to expect from many Texan women in the years I had been living there. The conference room, which was set up to accommodate around four hundred people, was nearly full, and as the presentation began, volunteers walked up and down the aisles helping latecomers find an empty seat.

The hour-long presentation was divided in half, with Lyndsay presenting first, covering the "mom stuff," and Tim following, with the "dad stuff." Lyndsay discussed what a mother needs to do before she begins homeschooling, including prayerfully considering the decision, "getting your house in order," reading a lot, and choosing a teaching approach. She spoke about the practical things to consider in making the decision to homeschool, like what subjects you can handle teaching, your confidence level, the amount of money you have, the number of children you have and the spread of their ages, and the learning styles of each of the children. She noted that many of the major publishers of homeschooling curricula were in the exhibit hall downstairs, and encouraged parents to spend some time looking at their options before deciding what to buy.

She then turned things over to Tim, who noted that, though mothers usually do the day-to-day work of homeschooling, dads also play an important role. Tim asserted that it is the dad's responsibility to handle all of the "legal stuff," like withdrawing the children from public school, if needed, and handling authorities, such as truancy officers and Child Protective Services (CPS), who may question the legality of homeschooling. He spent a fair amount of time discussing how dangerous CPS can be for homeschooling families, sharing some "horror stories" of children being taken away from their parents by overly zealous CPS workers. He talked about these stories as representing a broader "assault on parental rights" currently occurring in the state of Texas, with recent legislation that had come close to passing through the Texas legislature that would have, among other things, given grandparents the right to intervene in cases where they felt their grandchildren were being harmed by how they were being raised. He called such legislation a violation of the "fundamental constitutional rights of parents," notably "the rights parents have to raise their own kids," stating ominously that "every time the [state] legislature meets, we are at risk." He recommended that all prospective homeschooling parents view the THSC documentary *Taking a Stand in Texas: The Battle for Homeschool Freedom* (which, he added, was available for purchase on DVD in the exhibit hall for twenty dollars).

The next morning, I sat in a similar, though slightly smaller conference room waiting for the 9:00 a.m. session, "Raising Dangerous Sons in a Safe and Mediocre World," to begin. Before the presentation itself started, however, the lights dimmed and a short video produced by THSC—perhaps an excerpt from the documentary Tim had promoted the previous night, I wondered?—was projected onto the screen at the front of the room. The theme of the video was the same theme that Tim Lambert had raised in his presentation: parental rights. The takeaway message of the video was the importance of parents standing firm in their right to teach their children according to their own worldview. In the video, THSC staff members talked about how public schools are anti-Christian, because they teach things that conflict with the Christian worldview. One staff member even said that the state mandating that children attend public schools is the fastest way to erase Christianity from American culture. Over the next two days of the conference, I would see two other such THSC-produced videos, which also focused on parental rights and the threat the state poses to these rights, played before various sessions.

* * *

This vignette illustrates well the theme of this chapter. Among most of the parents I interviewed, there was a shared sense that they had given up on the idea that the government would provide the type of education that children need—even when their assessment of what that would look like differed. Given their belief in a smaller role for the federal government, it likely does not come as a surprise that many of the more politically conservative parents I spoke with tended to express feelings about the role of federal government in public education that ranged from skepticism to downright distrust. Indeed, these parents also, at times, echoed Tim Lambert's general distrust of state and local government, expressing concern about the potential for the government to intrude on their private family life. Perhaps what is more surprising is that many of the moderate and even liberal- to progressive-leaning parents also expressed distrust in the government's ability to provide public education—though, overall, these parents tended to express far more ambivalence about public schools than did their conservative counterparts. Although they did not see public schooling as the right choice for *their* children, many believed, in theory, in the *idea* of public schooling, and the collective responsibility of society to ensure that all children had access to an education. These parents tended to feel that a major overhaul of the public school system was needed, and they had largely given up on the idea that politicians were willing, or able, to make that happen.

Americans' Perceptions of Government

Until the mid-1960s, Americans displayed generally high trust in government, but thereafter, public trust in government began to decline significantly in the United States—and indeed, in almost all Western democracies.[1] The American National Election Studies' "Trust in Government Index" shows that in 2016, trust in government was lower than it had ever been in the time period (1958–2016) for which data are available[2] (though it is important to note that this measure does not differentiate between lack of trust, i.e., skepticism, and active distrust, i.e., cynicism).[3]

There is a large body of literature from both sociology and political science that examines the origins and consequences of Americans' distrust in government—a literature that I will not attempt to summarize in full here. However, there are a few important points raised by this literature that speak specifically to questions of homeschoolers' perceptions of government that I wish to touch upon briefly: the relationship between government complexity and distrust of the federal government, the particular place of public education as a state institution, and the important role of ideology in "activating" Americans' feelings of distrust.

The US government is complex in nature, with its multiple branches, its many partnerships between public and private institutions, and its division of federal, state, and local governance. This "institutional fragmentation" makes the state "less visible" to Americans than it is to citizens of other nations,[4] and also means that Americans can simultaneously hold different perceptions of different levels, or branches, of government. Most notably, "Many Americans . . . see the federal government as a dangerous if distant force, but view local government as a force for good."[5] Adam Sheingate argues that there is an important link between Americans' distrust of government and the complex nature of the American state: "Skepticism toward government is more than a simplistic anti-statism or rugged individualism, aspects of American political culture that are easily overstated. Rather, the history of the American state suggests that the disposition of rank-and-file Americans toward government is itself a product of their institutions. One reason many Americans might possess a skeptical if not hostile view of the federal government is because, for so many, the federal government is a rather distant force in their lives."[6] This analysis suggests, importantly, that when the federal government makes itself visible through involvement in matters generally considered the province of state and local government, members of the American public may see this as a particularly egregious form of government overreach.

Education, which is typically the province of state and local government, is one of the more visible state institutions in the United States. It is one of the government sectors that employs the largest number of Americans, so it is far more likely that the average American will personally know someone employed by a public school district than someone employed by, for example, a federal government agency. Thus, while education is one of the primary ways through which ordinary Americans "see" the state, many Americans actually fail to "see" teachers and school administrators as public-sector employees, and by extension, as arms of the state.[7] Therefore, when the federal government becomes visibly involved in matters related to public education—such as through federal education reform efforts—Americans may perceive this as government encroachment into their lives, even though, technically speaking, public education is by its very existence already a site of contact between the government and the governed.

Another reason to expect that Americans may feel particularly distrustful of the government's role in education is that education is the site of some of our most heated public debates. This includes debates about taxes and the material contributions of citizens to the public good, as well as debates about ideology in the form of what children are taught in schools. Thomas J. Rudolph and Jillian Evans argue, "Citizens' political trust is activated not only when individuals are asked to sacrifice material interests, but also when they are asked to sacrifice ideological principles."[8] Although Rudolph and Evans's analysis looks specifically at the role of political trust in predicting support for government spending, we can imagine that political trust also influences other forms of support for state institutions, such as a willingness to participate in the activities of those institutions. It makes sense, then, that in discussing their support (or lack thereof) of public schools, issues of political trust would arise in parents' narratives, particularly when they understand sending their children to public schools to be a form of participation in an institution that forces them to sacrifice ideological principles. In short, "Political trust has meaningful consequences for American democracy."[9]

These observations about Americans' perceptions of government are important for making sense of the ways in which the homeschoolers whom I interviewed, and the speakers at the conferences I attended, spoke about their lack of faith in government to provide the type of education children need. In the sections that follow, I discuss several specific critiques of the state that arose in my research: critiques of the political agendas of schools, critiques of the inefficacy of the state (particularly as it relates to funding education), and critiques of federal education reform overall.

Schools as Extensions of the State: Perceptions of the Political Agendas of Schools

Several of the parents I interviewed expressed a distaste for the presence of what they perceived as political agendas in schools. As we saw in chapter 2, some of the more conservative Christian parents felt that a liberal (especially pro-gay) agenda was clearly evident in public schools, while many of the more liberal parents felt that their local school districts pushed a conservative agenda. Incredibly, some of the parents who expressed these opposing diagnoses of the direction of political bias even lived in the same school districts as each other. While it is certainly possible that some schools within the same district, or even administrators or teachers within the same school, might have opposing biases that show up in the schools in different ways, it is just as likely that parents might interpret the same event as demonstrating different types of bias.

This was made especially clear to me one October day when I conducted back-to-back interviews in the same town. I was on a four-day trip to one of Texas's major cities, and in order to maximize my time in the area, I had set up multiple interviews each day. On this particular day, I had managed, somewhat miraculously, to set up two interviews in the same suburban town—one, in the afternoon, with Danielle, and another, that evening, with Keith and Kamilah—a fact that I was excited about because the town was about a forty-five-minute drive from where I was staying. Both interviews were with parents whose children had attended public schools in that town for a couple of years, and I was quite surprised when in both interviews, I was told a story of the same incident, in which the children brought home permission slips to watch a live, televised speech on education by President Obama. Both sets of parents were upset by the incident, but for very different reasons.

Danielle, who identified as politically conservative and somewhat religious,[10] had a son, Connor, who started his schooling in a private school in California before the family moved to Texas. (Danielle also had an older daughter, who had just started college when the family moved, and still lived in California.) Danielle did a lot of research about area school districts before the move, and she and her husband bought a house in the school district that they felt was the best in the area. Because of how highly regarded the school district was, she said, "When we moved here, he started third grade here, and went to third and fourth grade at the elementary school right around the corner. And I had absolutely no issues with the quality of the education, but there were little things that really bothered me." One of these, she said, was that Connor frequently came home from school with permission slips to participate in events that Danielle did not think belonged in a public school:

> I remember when he was in—I think it was third grade, was when President Obama was first elected. And they had a permission slip that came home, that the parents had to sign this permission slip in order to allow the children to sit down and listen to a speech that he gave, that was publicized. And so like, the whole school, every elementary school [in the district] televised this speech. And because of the controversy, of you know, the election results and him getting elected in the first place,[11] and what he was apparently going to say and things, they had these permission slips coming home. And that's just one example. There's always permission slips coming home for things that are controversial, you know, can your child participate in sex education, can your child participate in, we're going to have this—there was one that came home in fifth grade that was a permission slip for, they were having an assembly, and they were going to be talking about, like, Islam, versus Judaism, versus Christianity. And it was to kind of—I don't even remember what was going on at the time, but it was to quell some, you know, misunderstandings that were going around. And so things like that in a public school system—I just, I don't think they belong there. Those are the kinds of issues that I think should belong in the home. The parents should be teaching their kids that.

Danielle went on to explain that there were certain topics that she felt were outside of the purview of what public schools were intended to teach. "In my opinion, the school's job is to teach my child to read, to write, to do math, science, that kind of thing. I don't think that they should be teaching my child morals, in terms of sex ed, or religious morals. I don't think they should be teaching them about world events that are not in the context of a history class, things like that." Danielle felt that these examples of things the school would send home permission slips for, including the school showing a speech by the president of the United States, were evidence of a political agenda on the part of the schools in the district, one aimed to expose children to liberal ideals that might conflict with the ideals of their parents.

Just a few hours later, I heard the same event described somewhat differently as I interviewed Keith, who identified as liberal, and Kamilah, who identified as moderate and not very religious.[12] Interestingly, Keith and Kamilah had also moved to Texas from California in the same year as Danielle and her family, and had heard people speak very highly of the schools in their town. They approached the accolades with a bit more skepticism than Danielle had, however, as their three children—April, Daniel, and Alexis—would be among a very small number of Black students in this predominantly white school district.

During the interview, Keith brought up his frustration with the way people at the schools seemed to apply certain policies selectively, and expressed his view that this selectivity revealed their political bias:

> I've had conversations with the school board, I mean, some of the conversations I have are absurd. Like, April's first year at [her school], they sent a note home, that I had to give permission to have her hear President Obama's speech to students. So they send the letter home, and I sign it, but I did call my school board members and I said, you know, I don't understand why this got home. They're like, well, you gotta understand, it could be viewed as political and all that. But in the same folder that came home with the permission slip for that, there was also this nice flier announcing Flag Day. And I don't know why, I thought Flag Day was in June or something, but they do like, American Flag Day or something in September. But they had a school board member speak [that day], on campus, to the kids, and the mayor. So I'm on the phone with my school board member, and I said, "So, here's what my problem is. Your rule is to send home—" and she was like, "Well, it's an elected official, we have to get [parents'] approval." I said, "How come you didn't give me the same right of refusal for the mayor and the school board member?" And she got quiet. I said, "You're an elected official. The mayor—and I don't give a fudge on school board, okay. But the mayor was there. So how come you didn't ask for my permission for that? Because you're telling me the policy applies to elected officials speaking to children. You didn't ask me whether I wanted my child to hear from the mayor."

Keith described their school district as "bright red—there is nothing blue about this school district at all." Keith felt that the district sent home the permission slips for President Obama's speech because President Obama was a Democrat, and they assumed that parents would want the opportunity to opt their children out of viewing the speech. When the person speaking was a Republican, however—as the mayor was—they did not foresee this being an issue. In short, while Danielle interpreted the fact that the school was showing the speech at all as evidence of a liberal agenda, Keith felt that the mechanism that allowed parents to opt their children out of seeing the speech (but not other speeches) was evidence of a conservative political agenda.

The Conservative Critique: The Government's Anti-Christian Agenda

Danielle's perspective was expressed far more frequently in my interviews, despite the fact that I interviewed equal numbers of liberal and conservative parents. In particular, the more conservative and strongly religious parents seemed to lack trust in the government's capacity to oversee education because they saw the government as having an anti-religious or anti-Christian agenda that they did not want imposed on their children. Sonya, a very conservative, very religious, middle-income, mixed-race (white, Native American, and Black), married mother of nine children, was one of these parents. As she put it, "The main problem that I see with public school is institutionalizing children. The attitude the state seems to have, the country, our president [Obama] seems to have, is that they're *their* children. And they're not their children. You know?" Sonya disagreed with the idea that children "belong" to the state, or to society more broadly. She felt that children belong to their parents, and she did not want the government—through public schools—getting their hands on "her" children because "public school is teaching them the opposite of a lot of things that I want them to know," including views on homosexuality, abortion, and evolution that differed from her own.[13]

Sonya was not the only parent who felt this way. Cynthia, who was also very conservative and very religious (and whom we first met in chapter 2), told me that she felt that public schools were moving away from the presence of Christianity and Christian ideas in schools. When I asked her if she could give me an example of this, she started by talking about how she was taught about the creation of the world in science, compared to how she thinks it is taught today. "When I was in elementary school, I had a teacher who was not a Christian," she said. "But she had no problem, when we were talking about science and the big bang and evolution and stuff, she said, 'Christians believe God made the earth.'" Cynthia continued: "She didn't poo-poo it. She didn't make it sound like it wasn't—it's a theory. It's like, we believe it's truth and fact, but some scientists believe that evolution is truth and fact, or that the big bang is truth and fact, but it's all theory. No one has witnessed it and can verify it. So she taught them all as theories, and theories were really theories, and hypotheses were really hypotheses, and that's how it was taught. Today, all of it is taught as fact, even though nothing's changed." Cynthia also felt that even acknowledging God in schools was no longer permitted:

> I think there was a general acknowledgment of God [back then]. Even like, saying the Pledge [of Allegiance], and trying to change the words, and take God out of the pledge. It's kind of frustrating to me, because these things, our country was based on.[14] You know, this is the foundation of our country. And so many, I think so many people in our country love that. And those that don't, don't understand it, or aren't taught it properly. Like, this is what it means, and if you don't like it, you don't have—no one's forced to live here and stay here. And so I guess it kind of bothers me that our own government isn't protecting that, you know?

As Cynthia was speaking, it was clear that this was something she felt very strongly about. She clearly expressed her belief that the United States is a country that was founded on Christian principles, and that it remains a largely Christian nation—that "so many people in our country love that." Furthermore, she took the stance that people who did not believe in these Christian ideals were free to move elsewhere, but that they should not be attempting to have these ideas removed from American public life, including from schools.

That said, when she began discussing issues of gender and sexuality, she began to hesitate quite a bit. She seemed to sense that there might be some conflict between her own beliefs and the American ideals of civil rights:

And then in terms of defining the family, I think the family is being redefined. Because of all the talk about homosexuality and transgender and all that stuff. And I just feel like that's also false. And I'm not saying don't be kind to people, don't love people. Maybe they should have civil rights. I mean it depends, if our country is going to be based on God and His principles, then it will. . . . You know you could have . . . I guess there's different opinions. But I feel like, you know . . . I have an issue with . . . I mean I unders—I don't know the answer. I just have an issue with redefining family.

I asked Cynthia if this was something that she and her husband, Donald, who was also taking part in the interview, had discussed with their children, and Donald immediately jumped in and answered, "Yes." When I asked how they approached the issue, they told me a long story about a friend they had from church, who had been in a lesbian relationship and had had a daughter with her ex-partner, but who "has since become a Christian, and she's totally acknowledged, basically affirmed what the Bible says about all that." Their friendship with this woman had given them the opportunity to have multiple conversations with their children, Jason and Sara, about their beliefs about homosexuality.

Cynthia acknowledged having less confidence talking about her beliefs about homosexuality than about other things, like evolution, because it was a topic that she had not had to discuss much until recently. She mused, "There's always been homosexuality, I mean, you can go way back to Sodom and Gomorrah, maybe even earlier, it's been around. It's not new. But as far as being socially acceptable in America? It's very new. So it's new to me and Donald, it's new to you, it's new to everybody. Ask me in fifty years, I might have more wisdom about it." She went on to explain that she thinks it is very clear that homosexuality is a sin, but that it is not the job of Christians to judge each other for their sins, but rather, "God will judge, and there will be judgment." She also did not feel that this particular sin was worse than others. "Like, I sin too! I mean I covet, or I lie, or whatever. I have my sins. And sin is sin is sin. And I believe all sin nailed Jesus to the cross. And so, whether it's homosexuality or mine, I don't really give one more weight than another." But on the other hand, she said that she definitely did not think it was appropriate for schools to teach that homosexuality is acceptable, and that same-sex parents are just as good and normal as heterosexual parents, because to her, that simply is not true. "I know it's in public school," she said. "It's even in the Common Core curriculum, I've read excerpts from it. They're teaching it as, 'This is a family.' As fact. And it's right and it's true and it's good and it should be embraced. And so that, I have an issue with. I don't necessarily think they should teach anything about [that]."

She went on to echo Danielle's assertion that there were certain things that schools were *meant* to teach, but that other things fell outside of their mandate: "Again, it goes back to, what's my responsibility. I want them to teach math and reading and writing and basic history and basic science and maybe, these days, technology. You know, things like that. I don't want them teaching my child morals, unless it's my, you know, what I want them to learn. And so they can't—I don't want them to compromise that." That Cynthia saw public schools as infringing on parents' ability to teach morality to their children became even clearer later in the interview, when I asked her what materials—books, magazines, blogs, etc.—she would recommend to someone who was interested in learning more about homeschooling. She told me about a book she was currently reading, called *The Thomas Jefferson Education*. She said that one thing she had taken away from it so far, even though it was not the book's central point, was that "public schools are sort of—it's a very socialist idea." She went on: "It ends up being like, the government gets more and more control over your children, and the government educates your child, and decides what they learn, and decides what they can't learn in school, and they decide how much school they have to have. And if you really look at it, you can really see, like looking back, it used to not be like that. Public school used to be a real assistance to the parents and the family in raising their children. But now they've really crossed the line, and they're overstepping." One of the reasons this has happened, she went on to explain, is that so many families now have two working parents, with nobody staying home with the children. "Nobody's at home, so there's less parental involvement, I think, with kids, and less parents are taking responsibility for their kids." Because of this, schools are taking on things that were previously seen as parental responsibilities, which, according to Cynthia, "shouldn't be their job."

Cynthia and Sonya both expressed a belief that public schools were overstepping when they taught, as fact, things that they felt were really beliefs—and in particular, beliefs that were in conflict with their own. Both attributed this overreach to the government: Sonya, in invoking the president, and Cynthia, in noting that this "redefining of family" was happening through the Common Core (which I will discuss more later in this chapter). In this way, they framed public education as a means by which the government can intrude into private family lives by undermining their ability—which they emphasized as being their *right* (ironically, one protected by the very government they seem to distrust)—to parent their children according to their own belief systems.

The idea that the government has an anti-Christian bias was something that I heard expressed repeatedly at the fundamentalist Christian homeschooling conferences I attended while doing this research. The first year I attended the annual conference of the Texas Home School Coalition, the keynote speaker was Ken Ham, founder of the Creation Museum and expert in so-called creation science.[15] Having registered in advance for the conference, I had received an e-mail a few weeks prior explaining that, as a controversial figure, Ham was expected to draw protesters to the conference site and advising me (and the other conference attendees) that nonengagement is usually the best strategy to deal with such protesters. Among the several talks that Ham gave over the course of the three-day conference was one entitled "Learning How to Defend the Christian Faith in Today's World." In this talk, Ham focused on the question of human origins, contrasting the Christian worldview, in which the Bible is understood as a literal account of human creation, with the secular scientific worldview, which bases its understanding of human origins in scientific observation—and is the viewpoint privileged in US public schools.[16] Ham argued that the biblical account is to be trusted because it has been provided by "someone who was there, who never tells a lie"—namely, God. To those who argue in favor of the big bang, he advised retorting with, "You can't know that—you weren't there."

Ham's talk had very little to do with homeschooling—were it not for him mentioning the subject in passing once or twice, there was no clear indication that this talk was meant to be presented specifically to an audience of homeschooling families. It was clear, however, that the assumed audience of the presentation was a Christian audience, and particularly one made up of fundamentalist Christians who subscribe to the "young earth creationist" perspective (the belief that the earth was created just over six thousand years ago, in seven days, as told literally in the opening chapters of the book of Genesis). Ham did not acknowledge that within Christianity more broadly there are a range of beliefs about creation and evolution, or that most mainline Protestant denominations in the United States do not profess the young earth creationist perspective.[17] In drawing on the evolution-versus-creation debate for all of his examples of how to defend the "Christian worldview," Ham's presentation equated "Christianity" with a worldview that rejects evolution, implying that homeschoolers, as Christians, would subscribe to these beliefs. While it is impossible to know what percentage of conference attendees actually subscribe to this perspective, the attendees at this talk seemed to affirm this assumption. As Ham discussed why evolution should not be taught in American public schools, he declared that the reason "we've lost biblical authority in this nation" is that Christians have failed to defend the Bible—to which the audience responded by erupting into thunderous applause.

This idea that a Christian worldview was at odds with the dominant, secular worldview—which was promoted in public schools—was not limited to the fundamentalist Protestant conferences; it also appeared at the Catholic homeschooling conference I attended. Joseph Pearce, who has authored several books on literature and Catholicism, opened the conference with a talk about "the battle for true education." In this talk, Pearce argued that secular culture is a threat to Christianity, and more fundamentally, a threat to truth. Pearce stated that "those who do not believe in truth cannot breathe life into education, they can only kill it," and pointed to public schools and universities as examples of this, saying that they promote a "culture of death" rather than a culture of life. He went on to say that secular education dumbs everything down to the lowest common denominator of Godless mediocrity, and that "everything it touches, it kills." His takeaway message was that in choosing between (religious) homeschooling and secular schooling, parents are actually making the choice between their children being "trapped in the darkness of the culture of death," or being candles in the darkness, helping to lead others out.

The Liberal Critique: The Government's Anti-Education Agenda

While the conservative religious parents had the strongest critique of the agenda of public schools, they were not the only parents who worried that schools were sites of the exercise of state power. Specifically, some of the liberal parents whom I interviewed—most of whom were nonreligious—argued that the state uses schools not to educate children but to produce compliant citizens and good workers. As Kelly, who identified as very liberal and nonreligious, put it, "I feel like [what we have in public schools] is education for mediocrity. As long as you fit down this middle-of-the-road average. And conceptually, big picture, I see that, what does America need? A vast majority of workers in this middle path, right?" Kelly found this frustrating, because at the same time, she felt that children were being told they should strive for excellence, and to go to college so that they could achieve their dreams. "There's sort of a dichotomy there of like, well, we're telling them this is important, but yet we're training them to be mediocre. So, what are we actually, you know, training them to do? Igniting a passion for learning is different than training, and I feel like what they're getting in the public school system is training." And she did not think that this was likely to change. "Unless our society undergoes some sort of massive restructuring," she said, "education for mediocrity is the goal. I mean, and it always will be, because the goal is a workforce."

Kelly, whom we first met in chapter 3, had her undergraduate and graduate degrees in education, and had worked for several years in Montessori schools, which she felt did a much better job of "igniting a passion for learning" rather than simply training children to be "workers in this middle path." But other parents who did not have advanced degrees in education echoed Kelly's statements. Eva was, like Kelly, very liberal, though she also identified as somewhat religious. Eva was telling me how she had mixed reactions from her family when she decided to pull her daughter out of public school—the most negative reaction coming from her brother, who told Eva that if her daughter was not in school, she wouldn't get "socialization."

> And I'm like, do you know what kind of socialization's going on in the classroom? Like, they have to raise their hand to socialize in the class-

room, and then when they're eating lunch, like they can't even—you can't talk! And there's like, they have stuff on the wall like, oh, if you're quiet for a week you get a pizza party. Like, seriously? Wow. Like, it's encouraged, to shut the hell up. Don't speak your mind, because nobody's allowed to do that. So that's not cool. They're training children how to think. How to act, how to think, how to perceive people—that's not cool. You know? That's not cool with me.

In short, Eva felt that one of the functions of school was to produce compliance, and she saw the school doing this through rewarding children for *not* speaking their mind.

Some of the parents I interviewed talked about school as being an effective way of "warehousing" children, or as being a form of free daycare that allowed parents to work. When I asked Holly, who was very liberal and nonreligious, if she saw any advantages to public schools, she replied, "Well definitely, and this is going to sound rude, but the warehousing of the children is an advantage. Because then the parents can work, or do whatever." Maura, who was liberal and nonreligious, also used the language of warehousing, saying, "I'm very much in favor of there being free education available to everyone. But I feel like it's become more of a warehousing situation. I feel like kids are being—the emphasis is more on 'we're going to provide supervision and keep these kids off the street' than it is on education at this point." Similarly, Natalie, who was liberal and nonreligious, said, "I mean, we do need something to happen, just because the adults are locked up getting money, and so the kids have to be locked up somewhere else." Similarly, Keith, whom we met earlier in this chapter, explained that "we started to feel like maybe school, traditionally, is more geared towards daycare. You know, it's a 7:45 to 2:45, Monday through Friday, and then after-school programs, so that the parents can go to work. And be in the workforce." He also echoed the sentiment that Kelly had expressed about the government's goal of producing a certain type of workforce, though he questioned whether this goal made sense in the current economy: "The kids learn to become assembly line workers. And that worked in 1950, but schools are not teaching the children to be leaders. And they're not teaching the children to be critical thinkers, or be different. That's not celebrated, being different, whatever way you're different."

These parents were questioning whether schools actually had the capacity to *educate* children—or at least to educate them in ways that parents saw as being worthwhile. The more liberal parents, and especially unschoolers, tended to be most likely to question whether "schools" and "learning" are compatible. My interviewees drew upon a host of metaphors to convey to me that they viewed schools as something other than places for learning. Various parents compared public school to "warehousing" or "institutionalizing" children; to "sending them off to the coal mines" or a "factory"; to a "cattle chute" or a "conveyor belt" or "puppy mill"; to a "babysitter" or "daycare," "a place to keep kids safe so that their parents can go to work"; to "locking my child in a cage"; and to "a prison" or "prison-lite." Several parents made the comparison between schools and William Golding's famous novel, *Lord of the Flies*, in which the struggle to assert power leads a group of children who have been marooned on an island to descend into murderous chaos.[18] These metaphors describe schools as places where children are managed, shuffled around arbitrarily, perhaps watched and kept safe, but also imprisoned, not as places where learning happens.

The common theme across these metaphors is school as a dehumanizing space. As Dana, a politically moderate, nonreligious unschooler, said, "I would never want my child to have to experience, you know, the simple things, like having to wait to use the bathroom until the instructor says it's okay. Not being able to eat. Not being able to talk. [. . .] Freedom is a huge thing for me. I'm talking about bodily freedom, emotional freedom, all of these things that—I mean I think it sounds really harsh, to associate school and prison, but it's way closer than people even consider. I mean, there's no choice."

Support for Schools as Ideological Sacrifice

In chapter 2, I argued that I saw in the parents I interviewed for this project two competing ideologies of childhood. For some parents, particularly those who were more conservative and religious, childhood is understood as a time of innocence, and children are treated as people-in-process. The role of parents, in this ideology, is to protect their children's innocence while instilling good character in their children.

For religious parents, this is particularly important because instilling good character will help ensure that their children will behave in morally upright, Christian ways as an adult. For other parents, often those who were more liberal and less religious, childhood is understood as just another stage of life, and children as already people. The role of parents, in this ideology, is to provide an environment in which their children's core selves can flourish.

These ideologies, though incompatible with each other, still help explain why parents on both sides of the political aisle express distrust in government when it comes to schools. Earlier, I noted that an individual's political trust is "activated"—or is important to determining their stance on a policy issue—when they perceive that policy issue as requiring them to sacrifice, either materially or ideologically.[19] What the parents featured in the sections above make clear is that they view schools as incompatible with their own ideologies, whether that be because they see schools as promoting an anti-Christian worldview or because they see schools as "warehouses" or "prisons" that are hardly ideal environments for children's flourishing. For both sets of parents, then, enrolling their children in public schools would entail a sacrifice of ideological principles—and, furthermore, would be akin to asking them to sacrifice their own children. Mia, who identified as very liberal and nonreligious, summed up this feeling, which was expressed quite clearly by many of the parents I spoke with during my research, regardless of their political beliefs. A former teacher, Mia had grown disillusioned with public education, and she felt that the growing diversity among homeschoolers was evidence that she was not alone. "More people just don't want to give up their kids to the government. I see the school now as a big government machine and like, I don't want to give my kids to them."

The Inefficacy of the State

In addition to critiquing the perceived ideological biases of schools, several of the parents I interviewed—across political and ideological lines—expressed their lack of confidence in the state by critiquing it as ineffective. Some raised the issue of government funding of schools—either that schools were underfunded, or that funding went to the wrong things—while others felt that there was not the political will, either from politicians or from the grassroots, to make the changes that they thought were needed to the public education system.

As we saw above from Kelly and Mia, some of the most searing critiques of how the government runs public education came from current and former teachers. Another of these teachers was Mindy, whom we first met in chapter 2. Mindy, who was very liberal and nonreligious, had been a special education teacher for several years before deciding to homeschool her daughter, Emma. In fact, Mindy used to teach in the very same highly regarded school district that Danielle, Keith, and Kamilah lived in—the school district that sent home permission slips for students to watch President Obama give a speech to America's schoolchildren. When I asked Mindy if she could imagine ways in which schools could be changed to make them better in regard to some of the issues she had raised earlier in the interview, she cut me off before I could even finish asking:

> Dude, I have thought about that *so much*. Especially when I taught, we would talk about it, what we could do. Number one, I mean, the funding for schools is a joke. You know, God knows we can't support our schools when we've got a billion wars to fight! And, so I think it starts [there]— but that's just it, the problem is so much bigger. We don't care about poverty, we don't care about poor people, we don't care about—so you have these schools that are awful, schools that aren't funded. I mean, even [my former district], which is supposed to be one of the best districts in Texas, we were horribly underfunded. And I'm not sure that money is the only answer, but I'm quite sure it would help.

Mindy went on to say that, while she felt that "compulsory, mass education" could probably not ever replicate some of the benefits of homeschooling, there were schooling models that were far better than what we currently have. One example she gave was of "these amazing schools, where they're project based, and they're small, and they have a lot of freedom." But, she said, "you would never get a government to support that," in part because it would require so much more of a financial investment than our current model.

Angie, a liberal, nonreligious mother of two who will be featured more fully in the following chapter, also felt that the underfunding of public schools was a huge problem—one that she predicted would lead to increasing numbers of homeschoolers in the coming years. "I think that the schools are only going to become more crowded and less popular," she said, noting that public school teachers she knows are "very up in arms" about funding, because "the population grows but the funding doesn't grow, all they can do is cram [in] more and more kids." Angie knows a lot of parents of children with disabilities who are in public schools, and that has informed how she feels about the funding issue: "I see the services that schools are required to provide for special needs kids, and then I'm very happy for that individual kid, but then when you start thinking about the number of kids, say, with autism that are going into those schools and needing one-on-one aides, and think about the limited resources, and what is that doing to your everyday kid down the street? They'll end up in a class, with thirty-five, forty kids eventually, I suspect. Because so many resources are going to so few children, and there are not more resources coming in." Angie felt that the solution to this issue was to increase funding to schools so that class sizes could be much smaller: "What needs to be done is improving the ratios of student to teachers. I mean, the more one-on-one, the more supervision, the more the teacher knows the student." But Angie was not optimistic about this happening. "That's not the direction it's going," she said. "And I don't see any kind of political shift to put a whole lot more money into the system, so I don't see that changing."

Interestingly, Raya felt that the lack of funding hurt children with special needs, in addition to more "mainstream" children, as Angie had put it. Raya, who has appeared in previous chapters, was liberal and somewhat religious (but not Christian). Her older son, David, whom she had decided to homeschool because he was badly bullied, was what she called "twice-exceptional," meaning that he had special needs that were primarily socio-emotional, but was also "profoundly gifted." Raya expressed to me that public schools just are not equipped to handle such children, since the typical special-education classroom model was based on the assumption that children would be academically delayed, not academically advanced. Raya said that she felt it was theoretically possible for schools to better serve such students, "if the teachers were trained in it," but that it would probably only work "in a very wealthy public school," because there would need to be a separate classroom. But more realistically, she said, "I really don't see a public school being able to do it. I don't think the money's there."

Some parents I interviewed commented that, even when money is provided to schools, it often is not spent on the "right" things. For example, Jamie, who was very liberal and nonreligious, said that she thinks that "there possibly are" ways to improve our public schools, "But as long as people don't value teachers, and teachers' education, it's not going to happen. We don't have the money to make it happen. I think as long as people are nickel and diming teachers, and the whole school system and everything, that it's not going to change, because they're so flipping underpaid." She bemoaned the way that schools in Texas invested so much in sports, rather than in teachers, saying, "Like, these really fancy football stadiums we have for high schools here in Texas—like, really? That's what you put your money on, and you've got sixteen hundred kids per graduating class in some of these high schools?" For Jamie, the fact that schools would put in huge football stadiums but underpay their teachers was evidence that spending priorities were severely out of whack.

While many of the parents who expressed these critiques were liberal, not all were. Danielle, whom we met earlier in the chapter, felt similarly to Jamie. She expressed frustration with the fact that there were constantly votes during local elections to raise more money for schools, but then the money was poorly allocated:

> I think there's too many administrators making far too high of salaries, and that money is not getting down to the kids. And every time it seems that one of these public initiatives comes up, to raise more money for the schools, it's really few and far between that we actually see that money going to hiring teachers and, you know, doing that kind of thing. They may build all these wonderful schools, like when they built, a couple years ago, they built [a new] high school up here, and it's very technologically advanced and stuff, it cost a boat-load of money—but the kids aren't getting that much better educated.

Similarly, Julia, who was politically moderate and nonreligious, said, "The money is not being spent properly. It's not right. Stop paying for these tests, this benchmark testing that makes no difference in their lives, it doesn't help them learn anything." This was a viewpoint, then, that crossed political lines: Danielle, who identified herself as conservative, Jamie, who was very liberal, and Julia, a moderate, may have had different political views, but they were in agreement that schools were prioritizing the wrong things when deciding what to fund.

Importantly, many of the parents who felt that change needed to happen did not have confidence in the state's ability to make these changes. As Melinda, who was politically moderate and somewhat religious, explained, "I do believe that there's a massive problem with the system. And I don't think that it's—it's not going to change from the top down. It would have to be something revolutionary, from the bottom up. However, I don't think that's ever going to happen." Melinda was not alone in her assessment of the government as being unable or unwilling to make the kinds of changes that would be needed to reform or completely revolutionize how the country approaches public education. She also was not alone in her skepticism that grassroots, community-led changes could be achieved—at least not in her time parenting school-aged children. Summarizing a view I heard repeatedly throughout my interviews, Aspen, who was very conservative and nonreligious, said, "I think a lot of parents want to have faith in the school changing, and they believe that if they keep the kids in, and just fight for changes, that it'll happen, but I don't think that's going to happen fast enough to help *your* kid." In part, this lack of faith in grassroots change was tied directly to the ineffective ways in which parents saw the state managing education. As Wendy, who was conservative and very religious, put it, "The politicians make that argument"—that parents should try to change the school, not pull their kid out. "But you can't. There's so much red tape, you can't really. It's so sad."

Federal Government Overreach: Critiques of Federal Education Reforms

One of the topics that arose in several interviews that laid bare some parents' lack of faith in the federal government was education reform, including No Child Left Behind and the Common Core State Standards.[20] Some parents expressed the fear that the Common Core was being used as something of a Trojan horse, through which the federal government was forcing a liberal agenda into schools—as mentioned earlier in the example that Cynthia gave of Common Core–aligned activities that, she claimed, were normalizing same-sex parents. Danielle gave some other examples of a perceived liberal spin in the Common Core:

> A couple weeks ago I saw an example where some parent had, like, photographed the page of the book. And it was probably a social studies book, or a civics book or something, it sounded like it was written, like a fourth-, maybe fifth-grade level? But the text read—it had to have been written by a liberal progressive, it had to, because it was talking about Barack Obama, and how, when he was elected a lot of white people didn't want him elected because he was Black. And so, you know, it was up to the Black people in the country to elect him so that we could move forward as a nation. And, I mean, just the wording of things. And there was another example that had to do with the Second Amendment, right to bear arms. And in this—I think it was a history book, not a civics book, they were summarizing the Bill of Rights. They were taking each one of the amendments, and they were summarizing it. And the way they reworded, very subtly reworded the amendment, it said, in times of war, the rights of, you know, the citizens have a right to take up arms to fight for their country. And I thought, are you kidding me?

Danielle seemed visibly agitated, almost disgusted, as she recounted these examples. What she said upset her about the situation was that she saw it as a case of federal government overreach into what should be a local issue. "I think what's going on is that, you know, the federal Department of Education, they're trying to consolidate and they're trying to make uniform, a standard education for all Americans. Rather than allowing local school districts to do it, and parents to decide what their students—they're trying to say this is the education that kids will get in this country." She went on to say that, because of this, "every Common Core example that I have seen, that comes across my Facebook feed or that I see in some of the homeschooling magazines and things, they scare the crap out of me." Danielle was shocked that people in local, state, and even federal agencies and departments would let this happen. She was frustrated that the government was, in her view, arguing that Common Core was just about having common standards, but "that's not what this whole Common Core thing is panning out to be." Instead, she felt it was about ensuring that students across the country were indoctrinated into a specific way of thinking.

That the federal government would use education reforms to indoctrinate children was something that came up at several sessions at the homeschooling conferences I attended, as well. Dr. Duke Pesta, the academic director of Freedom Project Education, an organization that bills itself as being "at the forefront in the fight to educate families without ideological spin or government control," spoke at two of the Christian homeschool conferences I attended.[21] Pesta, who, ironically, is also a professor of English at the University of Wisconsin–Oshkosh—a public institution—claimed that American public schools have been hijacked by those whose primary agenda is to teach "liberal" sexuality to children as young as five years old. This, he explained, was being done in part through the introduction of the Common Core, which in one talk he referred to as "educational terrorism." He argued that Common Core is less an educational project and more of "a sociological rebranding of what children are." In other words, he claimed, Common Core is primarily an ideological project, the main goal of which is to convince children that they belong to the government or the state, rather than to their families and their religious traditions.

Pesta was particularly concerned about the National Sexuality Education Standards, which he implied (incorrectly) were part of the Common Core standards.[22] His slides were filled with examples from these standards of what he framed as egregious oversteps by the federal government designed, through the Common Core, to normalize the acceptance of LGBT people and to teach children that sexual activity was normal and acceptable outside of heterosexual marriage. At one point, he asked the audience, "Do you teach your kids about sex and homosexuality when they're five [years old]? Because that is what they're doing here."

That said, not all of the critiques I heard of the Common Core were about ideological concerns. Some just saw the methods of teaching associated with Common Core—particularly around math—to be unnecessarily confusing. In fact, when I first asked Danielle for examples of things she had seen from Common Core that concerned her, the first thing she said—with laughter—was "the math." She went on:

The new way that they're doing math, is absolutely ridiculous. Instead of just doing, like, forty-seven minus fifteen, and setting it up, you know, in the columns, like we were all taught when we were kids, they're now doing this, where you have to draw out these little diagrams. Okay, so it's called the new math. And what they're doing is they're making, what is otherwise a very simple math problem, into a ridiculously complicated math problem. And—I'd have to show you some of the examples on paper, because it makes no sense to me. But rather than doing, you know, setting it up with the two numbers, one on top of each other, lining up the ones column and the tens column, and putting a plus or minus sign and then the line, and showing how to borrow from the tens column and stuff, instead of doing it that way, what they're doing is saying things like, if you have, you know, forty-seven minus nine, if you take one away from the forty-seven to make the nine a ten, and then you have forty-seven left over, and then—it's complicated, like that. It's very bizarre.

Eva echoed Danielle's sense that the methods in the Common Core were strange and unnecessarily complicated, and told me that when she hired a friend who was a teacher to do some tutoring with her teenage daughter, she told the friend to do whatever she felt was best, as long as it was not "that Common Core bullshit."

The idea that these parents expressed that the Common Core was ridiculous, absurd, or just straight-up "bullshit" served to frame this attempt by the federal government to improve education as a giant farce. The federal government ends up, as a result, coming across both as incompetent and as overreaching into local schools, in a way that puts children's educations at risk. This sentiment was also something several parents expressed in regard to an earlier federal education reform, No Child Left Behind (NCLB). Robin, who was very liberal and nonreligious, conveyed this by referring to NCLB as "Every Child Left Behind," saying that it "was a disastrous program." Similarly, Alma, who was moderate and somewhat religious, said that "No Child Left Behind means no child gets ahead," because it required that public schools "cater to the lowest common denominator."

Conclusion: Are Homeschoolers and Government Natural Adversaries?

At the Christian homeschooling conferences that I attended, I frequently heard references to homeschoolers as being in danger, or "under attack," from a variety of enemies. Among the many "threats" and "enemies" I heard mentioned over the course of these conferences were homosexuality, the sexual revolution, sexual experimentation, atheism, the radical Left, biblically unsound "Christian" teachings, and of course, the devil himself. But just as frequently, homeschoolers were said to be under attack from various parts of the government, including Child Protective Services, public colleges and universities, public schools, the Common Core, the Texas state legislature, Washington, DC, politicians, and the government in general.

In the "battle" scenarios described at these conferences, the state was often portrayed as a huge part of the problem, and government encroachment into the spheres of religion and the family as perhaps the largest threat to homeschooling families. But the relationship between homeschoolers and the state may be better described as one of trepidation and skepticism than as one of outright distrust. In the discourse of government threat at these conferences, government often served as both problem and solution. According to the framework of social-movements scholar James Jasper, this indicates that government is understood as a place primarily inhabited by villains and their minions, but also (potentially) by heroes who could redeem the institution.[23] Activities that were recommended to conference attendees to combat these threats included lobbying elected officials to support parents' rights and pro-homeschooling laws, and supporting and voting for certain candidates for both state and national office. At one of the Texas Home School Coalition conferences, a Texas state senator was introduced by THSC president Tim Lambert as one of the most ardent supporters of homeschooling in the state legislature. Lambert also advocated for state financial support for homeschooling. Other politicians were also seen as being friends of homeschooling. For example, on the last day of the Great Homeschool Conventions conference, I was approached by someone with a clipboard asking me to sign a petition encouraging Ben Carson—who would be speaking at the conference later that night—to run for US president.[24] This made it clear that it was not government itself being portrayed in these spaces as the enemy, but rather, a secular, anti-Christian government that was perpetrating many of these "attacks" on homeschoolers.

That said, it was not only conservative Christian homeschoolers who were wary of government encroachment into their lives as homeschoolers. Parents across the political spectrum felt strongly that increased regulation would threaten their ability to homeschool their children in the ways they felt were best. Jacqui, who was moderate and nonreligious and very active in her local homeschooling community, felt strongly that there should be no government regulation of homeschooling, because "once the government gets their hands into your business, they just want more and more and more." Jacqui admitted that some children "fall through the cracks" because of this lack of oversight, but she argued that children also "fall through the cracks" in even the best public schools, so she did not think the extreme cases were enough of a reason to let the government into the homes of homeschoolers. Maria, who was liberal and somewhat religious, also felt that increased government oversight would be negative, saying, "No, just let us do this how we need to do this." Veronica, who was conservative and very religious, said, "I looooove Texas, you know, because I feel like as a parent, I have the freedom to teach my kids how I feel like they need to be taught. And some of the states, we've thought about moving now that my husband's been medically retired, and I'm like, oh, let me go look at the homeschool laws. And some of them are really strict." Veronica was one of several parents whom I interviewed who said that they would avoid moving to a state with stricter homeschooling regulations.

There was, however, a very small minority of parents whom I interviewed who did not express distrust or skepticism of the government. Maura, who was liberal and nonreligious, was one of the few in this group, and was the only parent who was openly critical of the anti-government stance that many of her fellow homeschoolers have. She told me, "I've been a little surprised, once I've got[ten] inside this world and taken a look around, by the number of people who are here because they have kind of anti-government views, which are—I guess that's a growing population, in recent years anyway. I hope that that doesn't continue to grow." Maura was not without her critiques of the government, but she was uncomfortable with the way so many homeschoolers seemed willing to write off all of its functions, saying, "I think despite corporate money in elections and all, it's still the will of the people being expressed, and the resources of the people being pooled to perform functions that can't really be performed any other way. Or at least not efficiently, or well. So I hope that it doesn't keep going in that direction, because I find myself pretty uncomfortable with that group."

With a few exceptions, though, parents across the spectrum of educational philosophies and motivations for homeschooling expressed a belief that the task of "fixing" public schools was such an immense problem that they did not feel they had any viable ideas about how to reform it, let alone the power to do so. Thus, although they had done it for a variety of reasons, these parents had given up on the government as an entity that they could trust to educate their children and had taken their children's education squarely into their own hands. As the next chapter will show, the mothers I interviewed, in particular, felt that attempting to work for change within schools—what they saw as the potential alternative to homeschooling—would be akin to "sacrificing" their own children's well-being and risking their own status as a good mother. In other words, these parents' views of government are very much intertwined with their views on motherhood.

6

Motherhood and the Gendered Labor of Homeschooling

On a hot September afternoon, I met Angie, a white, high-income, married mother of two teenage sons, Justin and Cody, at a cute, locally owned coffee shop about an hour and a half from Austin. Angie lived about fifteen minutes away, she had explained over e-mail, but in a somewhat rural area, and her house was hard to find, even using Google Maps. Angie had a striking face, with unusually light eyes, high cheekbones, and a stylish haircut, but she was dressed unassumingly in khaki capris and an oversized floral blouse. Based on the rapport I felt we had struck during our numerous e-mails exchanged leading up to the interview, I was surprised to find her soft-spoken and somewhat reserved.

After getting some hot drinks to compensate for the frigid air conditioning, we settled into a table near the coffee shop's entrance. Over the course of the next hour and a half, Angie touched on themes that, despite this being one of the earlier interviews I conducted, I had already become somewhat familiar with, and would come to hear repeated throughout subsequent interviews: that mothers did the lion's share of the homeschooling labor, that they did this almost by default, that their husbands (when they had them) were not well suited for the day-to-day work of homeschooling, and that homeschooling mothers made many sacrifices for their children.

I began the interview by asking Angie to tell me about her decision to homeschool. She confessed that it was not really much of a conscious decision, but was more something she fell into when she met some homeschooling families around the time that she was feeling uneasy about putting her older son, Justin, in school. She explained,

> When my son was kindergarten age, we had even gone to kindergarten round-up, and that's when it hit me that he just seemed so very young, to be sent off to what seemed like a full-time job, of 7:00 to 3:00 every

day. So what I did was put him in another year of preschool that had been designed for early fives. I had thought we would just kind of delay it another year. But by this time, we had met some homeschoolers, and it had started to enter my consciousness that there was an alternative. And by the end of that year it just—he still seemed too young to go away, all day, every day. To me, as a mother, it sort of felt like sending him off to the coal mines, you know? At home he can sit in my lap when he's upset or get all this one-on-one attention, and I felt like, how much one-on-one can he really get in an institutional setting? He's just going to be part of a little herd, and it didn't feel like what I wanted for him.

Angie explained that she figured at the time that she would just give homeschooling a try, and not necessarily commit to it for the long haul. But she came to feel, eventually, that her relaxed, play-based approach ended up precluding her putting her children in school at a certain point, since they would have been too far behind their peers in certain subjects. Still, she regularly checked in with her sons to see if they would prefer to go to public school, and they always responded that they preferred homeschooling.

One reason why Justin and Cody were happy with homeschooling was that they had developed a small community of homeschooling friends with whom they spent a fair amount of time. When I asked Angie how they met these other families, she said, "I met some parents through the La Leche League early on, the breastfeeding support [group]. There's a tendency for that sort of parenting to maybe lead into homeschooling." In fact, one of Angie's closest friends, who had two similar-aged children and who had been a big support to Angie when they first started homeschooling, came from this group. This friend's oldest son was Justin's best friend, and the two had just started college together, and were roommates.

Angie had a master's degree and had had a few years of work experience prior to having Justin, but decided to stay home with her sons, who were two years apart in age, while they were very young. She had intended to go back to work once Cody started kindergarten, but since Cody never went off to school, Angie never ended up going back to work. I asked her if she and her husband had consciously decided that she would be primarily in charge of the homeschooling labor, and she responded, "I always assumed that I would do the bulk of it, as far as research, choosing any curriculum, finding classes, but there were some areas that I thought he would need to be the expert." For example, there were some subjects—like high school math—that Angie thought her husband, an engineer, would be better able to cover, so she "expected that he would be there to help." And there were other things that her husband's interests were more suited for: "There were some things he just enjoyed more. He liked reading aloud, and I just never did. So he sort of took that over as his job when they were younger, and he's taught them a computer science class, and as far as anything athletic like coaching soccer and things like that, he definitely took the lead in that."

But, in general, Angie explained, it would not have worked for her husband to be the primary homeschooling parent, because of his more conformist temperament. She noted,

> He was not 100% supportive in the beginning. He is, um—I guess I had considered myself somewhat conformist, as I age I think I've become less and less so, but he tends to be *very* conformist, not rock the boat, "Why do you want to stand out, don't they need to learn to deal with bullies and get socialized," and all that. He was—this was very much a shock to his system, as far as going out and doing something kind of unheard of. He felt like they kind of lacked discipline, did not want to be hard workers, and so he wasn't happy with it for a few years.

I then asked Angie, "Did he try to convince you not to do it, or was it more just like, 'I'll support you, but it's not what I would choose?'" She responded, "Yeah, yeah, he didn't really try to convince me otherwise, but he just was never enthusiastic, always kind of halting, if there was any problem, 'Well, they could be in school,' kind of thing." She went on to explain that a year or two in, her husband coached Justin's soccer team, and he found that, at practice, Justin would easily follow directions, but the other children on the team would be goofing off. Through this experience, "It sort of dawned on him that, you know, for one thing our boys really aren't wild hooligans and undisciplined, and for another thing, when there is something they want to learn, they're there ready to do it. And the other kids were sort of burned out on listening, and waiting their turn, and stuff."

Despite feeling that she never really made a "conscious decision" to homeschool at the beginning, and that sticking with it was "like a commitment by default," Angie seemed pretty happy with how homeschooling had worked out for her family. Justin had recently started college as an engineering major, and had gotten an academic scholarship and acceptance into his university's honors college. And Cody seemed to be following in his brother's footsteps, also interested in pursuing an engineering degree. Her sons were bright, self-motivated, and pretty happy, even as teens; they had a great relationship with each other, and while "they realize themselves that they're not particularly cool," they had a tight-knit group of friends. Those benefits aside, Angie was one of the few mothers I spoke with who openly questioned how much she had sacrificed, personally, in order to homeschool:

> I think as I've gotten into my forties it's become a real concern that, gosh, I may really not be able to have a career at this point. My degree and my very limited work experience is twenty years out of date now. I'm really starting from scratch, and yet competing with people twenty years younger than me for something entry level. So it's possible that I really screwed myself over in that regard, and I tell [new homeschooling moms] now that if there's any way to just kind of keep your hand in the work world—there are a lot of women I know that really all they have wanted is to be a home maker, so it's not a concern for them. But if someone does feel like they want to return [to work], I tell them now, I wish I had just kept a little foot in the door. I have a friend who is an MD, family practitioner, and she has found a way to work, like, seven hours a week at a clinic, and keeps her license current and keeps current on all her continuing education and all that. And I just think that's really smart, because she's going to be able to make a really smooth transition back when her kids are grown. A friend of mine who's an attorney did not do that, and she moved to Texas and didn't ever take the bar here for this state, so it would just be too hard for her to go back at fifty to try to study and take the bar, so she'll probably just never go back to practicing law. It got too far out of date. So I think she and I both feel like keeping our hands in, in some way, might've been a good idea.

On the other hand, Angie noted, her husband, who had progressed quickly up the ranks of upper management in his company, had benefited from the fact that she was a stay-at-home mother. "If they said, 'We need you to go to Arkansas tomorrow to deal with this customer having a problem,' he was on the plane to Arkansas, and he didn't have to think about how long he might have to stay or anything. He always knew that I had everything handled and under control." Other couples they knew who juggled two careers while raising children did not have that luxury.

*   *   *

Though the idea that homeschooling is women's work came up time and time again in my interviews, this theme was echoed in other ways in my research, as well. For example, 97% of the over six hundred parents who took my survey were mothers, and the advice directed at "homeschooling mamas" *far* outnumbered that directed at dads at the conferences I attended. In this chapter, I explore the perspectives of my interview respondents on motherhood to understand why homeschooling is so overwhelmingly women's work, and what this tells us about gender and parenting in the school-choice era. I also contextualize the interview data with a discussion of how motherhood is framed within the larger homeschooling movement, using my observations at five homeschooling conferences and conventions to discuss the way the gendered nature of homeschooling labor is normalized within these spaces. I situate these discussions within the larger sociological literature on mothering ideologies, particularly the ideology of intensive mothering and neoliberal motherhood, and argue that the coupling of the ideology of intensive mothering with the neoliberal ideologies of school choice serves to depoliticize mothers who might otherwise focus their energies on creating social change.

Homeschooling Labor and Intensive Mothering Ideology

While the parents I interviewed for this project had notable differences in their religious and political beliefs, and these led to differences in their understandings of who children are, what childhood should look like, and what the ideal education was, they also had commonalities. Among the commonalities that I have already discussed include the sense of their children as unique and a lack of trust in the government to provide what their children need. In this chapter, I discuss a third common thread evident in my interviews: a commitment to intensive mothering ideologies. I argue that, in part, the trend of mothers giving up on government and taking on their children's education themselves is happening because many of these mothers feel that they are ultimately responsible, and held accountable, for ensuring the proper education and overall well-being of their child. Since, in their views, this responsibility does not rest with the government, with the local school system, or with society at large, if home education is what they believe to be the best option for their individual children, it is up to them, as mothers, to make it possible.

The term "intensive mothering" was first coined by sociologist Sharon Hays in her book *The Cultural Contradictions of Motherhood* to describe a parenting ideology characterized by three main tenets: first, that child care is primarily the responsibility of the mother; second, that parenting methods should be child-centered, expert-guided, emotionally absorbing, labor-intensive, and financially expensive; and third, that children are outside of market relations, and therefore decisions about child rearing should be made without reference to financial profitability or loss.[1] Hays argues that the logic of intensive mothering is the dominant parenting paradigm in the United States, and that, although this method is adapted and resisted by individual women, all mothers are aware of it and experience it as a power-laden discourse that shapes how they think about, feel about, and experience motherhood. Importantly, this ideology serves to obscure structural and institutional inequality, "suggest[ing] that all the troubles of the world can be solved by the individual efforts of superhuman women." As she succinctly argues, "Clearly, this places a tremendous and undue burden on women."[2]

The research for Hays's book was carried out in the early 1990s and was situated in the context of the growth in the number of working mothers who were trying to "do it all" by balancing a career and motherhood. While some scholars have (rightly) critiqued Hays's work for failing to understand how the contradictions of motherhood (between paid labor force participation and unpaid labor in the home) vary greatly by race and class,[3] researchers continue to note the relevance and centrality of the ideology of intensive mothering in the everyday lives of American mothers, whether or not they are able to come close to attaining its ideals. Jennifer Lois argues in her study of homeschooling mothers in the Portland, Oregon, area that the ideology of intensive mothering is exactly what makes homeschooling seem so sensible to the women whom she interviewed: they see the emotional, physical, and economic investment of homeschooling, and their corresponding sacrifices, as a way of performing "good motherhood."[4] More recently, Allison Pugh demonstrates that intensive mothering has only become *more* intensified under the increasing insecurity and divestment from the public provision of care that have come to be seen as hallmarks of the neoliberal state. Pugh argues that now, "Intensive mothers labor not only for their families but also on behalf of a system of insecure work and a neoliberal state, struggling to provide the care that seems to be receding elsewhere."[5] Over the last several decades, Pugh argues, Americans have seen the ideal of commitment erode in many aspects of their daily lives: of employers to their employees, of workers to their employers, and of spouses or partners to their marriages and other intimate relationships. As this ideal of commitment has eroded, some adults—especially women, but also some men—intensify their commitment to their children: "While some men view their care for children as optional, for many people immersed in insecure work, particularly women, children are commitment's final frontier."[6]

For most of the parents I interviewed, the erosion of this ideal of commitment also applies to the government and its treatment of public school children. As they see this erosion of commitment happening, they double down on the ideology of intensive mothering, emphasizing the primacy of the role of the individual mother in parenting in child-centered, expert-guided, emotionally absorbing, labor-intensive, and financially expensive ways, despite the expense to the family, which for many includes the loss of an income.[7]

These mothers explain their commitment, as mothers, to performing the labor of homeschooling in a variety of ways. They often reference the role of finances in making decisions about homeschooling, most frequently in how they refer to their husbands' higher earnings potential as the main reason why they, rather than their husbands, are the primary homeschoolers. Some mothers also call upon essentialized understandings of gender, in which they posit women as being more "naturally" suited for intensive child-rearing labor, to explain this decision. Other mothers resist the idea that homeschooling *should* be maternal territory, but, as Hays argues is the case, these mothers find they still must respond to cultural expectations of mothers in ways that shape their mothering experiences. I will discuss each of these explanations, after setting the stage with a discussion of how homeschooling is understood as mothers' work.

Homeschooling as Mothers' Work

I opened the previous chapter by describing a session at the 2014 annual conference of the Texas Home School Coalition, in which THSC president Tim Lambert and his wife, Lyndsay, split the session in half, covering both the "mom stuff" and the "dad stuff" of homeschooling. The "dad stuff" largely had to do with interfacing with the state—the subject of the previous chapter. The "mom stuff," on the other hand, was all of the day-to-day details related to homeschooling. While the idea that the labor of homeschooling was primarily mothers' work was not unique to these Christian spaces, this was a particularly prevalent theme that recurred throughout these conferences.

The overwhelming assumption of speakers, vendors, and participants at the four Christian homeschool conferences (three fundamentalist Protestant and one Catholic) that I attended over the course of my fieldwork for this project was that homeschooling families were made up of a heterosexual, married mother and father and their children, and that the mother was the family member who was responsible for homeschooling. In two different talks, Tim Lambert drew hearty laughter from the audience when he made the joke that dads saying "we homeschool" is like when dads say "we're pregnant"—yes, both parents are involved, but the mother is the one doing all of the work. The more practically oriented talks I attended, with titles such as "Help! I Have Preschoolers," "Getting It All Done," and "Organizing for Real Families," had mothers—or "homeschooling mamas," as they were often affectionately called—as their intended audience, with the presenters frequently referring to the audience as "all you moms." That mothers are presumed to do most of the work was reinforced by the occasional reference to "dad's role," as in a talk given by Tim Lambert called "So What's the Dad Supposed to Do?"

Motherhood was constructed at these conferences as being women's primary role, and service to the good of the family was seen as being a mother's primary responsibility. That mothers would inhabit this role was understood as being both natural and desirable. For example, in a talk designed to encourage mothers to "stay the course" with homeschooling, the speaker explained that as mothers, "we" intuitively know—and want—what is best for our children, and more specifically, we know that homeschooling is best for them. One reason it is best, she argued, is that moms are their children's best advocates, which in turn makes them their children's ideal teacher. In this argument, the speaker constructs mothering as natural—a capacity that women just have. She also explained that homeschooling is good for mothers, too. Homeschooling mothers get to see their children at their best times of day, not just in the mornings and evenings when everyone is tired, rushed, and cranky. They get to know their children's best selves, and in a deeper and more meaningful way than do moms whose children go to school. In this argument, it is assumed that this ability to spend more quality time with children is not just good for children but is something mothers will find rewarding. In this way, the speaker constructs intensive mothering as desirable.

Reinforcing the view that motherhood is both natural and desirable was a discourse of children as a blessing. One speaker talked about how, as Christians, "we" believe that all children are masterpieces made by God, and that we need to care for them as if this is true. Children are entrusted to their parents by God, according to this logic, and therefore motherhood is a divinely ordained role. And if all children are blessings, it follows that having many children means having many blessings. Before her presentation began, one speaker introduced herself individually to each audience member as they came into the room, asking them how many children they had and how long they had been homeschooling. When one woman said she had three children, the speaker responded, "What a fortunate mother," and later, when another mother said she had four children, she again told her she was a "fortunate woman." Interestingly, I did not hear her say this to anybody who told her they had only one or two children, so the message that came across was that one is especially blessed when one has many children. Those with a large number of children wore this as a badge of honor; and, this was especially played up in the introductions to speakers who had seven or more children. The speaker biographies in the conference programs frequently noted how many children a speaker had, including several that had seven or eight children, one who had fourteen, and, of course, Michelle and Jim Bob Duggar, who have nineteen children. Of the nineteen speakers listed in the programs of the two THSC conventions I attended, those who had their children mentioned in their bios had an average of 5.8 children per family.

However, despite this construction of motherhood as natural, desirable, and divinely ordained, and mothers of multiple children as especially blessed, there were also frequent acknowledgments throughout the conferences that mothering is very hard, often thankless work, and that the day-to-day lives of mothers are far from idyllic. One of the most frequently repeated messages at these conferences was that moms need a lot of encouragement—from their husbands, from their children, from God, and from each other—in order to continue to do the work of mothering. I heard frequent jokes about how often mothers think about quitting homeschooling, and how they would sometimes watch the school bus drive by in the mornings and long for their children to be climbing aboard. Thus, many of the talks served to remind mothers of the reasons why they homeschool, and to renew their conviction that homeschooling is an important and worthwhile endeavor. I heard several women at the THSC conferences talking about the annual "Homeschooling Moms' Winter Summit" that THSC cosponsors, and in one of my visits to the vendor area I was given a brochure about the summit and encouraged by the woman handing it to me to attend. She described it as a weekend to get away, to have your heart and soul refreshed, and to give you the strength and inspiration you need to finish out the homeschooling year.

One of the aims of these conferences, then, seemed to be the renewal of mothers' spirits, and their commitment to the practice of homeschooling. In fact, the insights of social movement scholars make it clear that these conference spaces are designed, in part, to remind homeschooling mothers of their important role in the family, and to deepen their commitment to the hard work that this role requires. One way in which the conferences accomplish this is to acknowledge the emotions that mothers often experience while homeschooling, such as frustration, isolation, and burnout, and to replace them with feelings of joy, community support, and a sense of being "blessed" or "fortunate." In her book about the role of emotion in the social movements formed at the start of the AIDS epidemic, Deborah Gould argues that "feeling and emotion are fundamental to political life ... in the sense that there is an affective dimension to the processes and practices that make up 'the political,' broadly defined."[8] More specifically, these conferences can be understood as rituals that, as social-movement scholar James Jasper explains, serve to make the meanings and frames of the movement "salient for participants," in part by "elicit[ing] emotions, such as awe, joy, or solidarity." Ritual spaces, such as these conferences, can elicit immediate, temporally short "reflex emotions," but more importantly in this context, they also impact "moods," which are more sustained feelings than reflex emotions, that, when positive, can leave participants "ready to redouble our efforts on behalf of the cause," and can be sustained for long periods of time after the ritual itself has ended.[9]

Though the mother's role was constructed as being responsible for the care and education of the children, the father was described as the head of the household, the one ultimately in charge, or, in an analogy I heard on multiple occasions, the "principal" of the homeschool in which mom is the teacher, mirroring the actual gender segregation typically seen in these occupations.[10] As mentioned before, the father was also constructed as being the bridge between the family and the state, in that any issue that required interfacing with the state was described as something the father should do. For example, one speaker noted that it is the father's responsibility to know the homeschooling laws and to make sure that they are being followed, with another speaker adding that this is not something with which mothers should be burdened. Fathers should also be responsible for keeping and managing all records related to the children's schooling, in case those records should ever be needed to substantiate their education to an outside authority.

Additionally, several speakers argued that fathers are accountable, in the eyes of God, for everything that goes on in the house, including everything that the children are taught by the mother.[11] One speaker used the analogy of sled dogs, with the father being the lead dog, and the mother being the second dog. It is the job of the lead dog, he explained, to follow the commands of the master (in this analogy, the master is God). It is the job of the second dog, however, to follow the lead dog. If the master commands the dogs to go left, and the lead dog goes right, the lead dog is in the wrong, but if the second dog attempts to go left, to follow the master's command instead of following the lead dog, that dog is also in the wrong. By this logic, if the mother teaches anything in the home that is, for example, not biblically correct, but she is following the leadership of her husband, then she is blameless before God, because it is the husband's duty to follow the commands of God, and the wife's duty to follow her husband. Similarly, at the Catholic conference I attended, one speaker brought up the concept of the "Cone of Obedience." The logic of the "Cone of Obedience" is that as long as you obey the person directly in charge of you, you are "covered." In other words, you are not held accountable before God for obeying someone who has God-given authority over you, even if your obedience means you act against God's will. If you sin because you were led into the behavior by someone with authority over you, that person is culpable. In the cone representing the family, the father is at the top of the cone, just underneath God—therefore, the speaker explained, the father is held accountable for anything that goes on in the family, including the homeschooling labor of the mother.

Therefore, the success of the homeschooling project ultimately rests in dad's hands: if the mother is struggling, it is up to the father to figure out how to help her. In this way, the father's role is also to support his wife. In one talk, the speaker suggested that, besides being the leader of the family, fathers are expected—by God and by their wives—to support their wives by praying for them, by praying with them, and by giving them time off when they need it, both to plan and also to rest. The speaker suggested, for example, that Sunday evenings were a good time for fathers to spend some time with their children, giving their wives a few hours to plan the week's lessons and to read or take a bubble bath or do something else by and for herself, so that she can start the week off feeling renewed and refreshed. This, of course, implied that, with the exception of those few hours on Sunday evening, mothers would spend the rest of the week in the presence of, and devoting her energy to, her children (and that mothers would experience time to do lesson planning as being refreshing and something "for herself").

Although the idea that mothers would do the bulk of the labor associated with homeschooling was clearly communicated at the Christian conferences that I attended, this concept was certainly not unique to religiously motivated homeschoolers. At the Texas Unschoolers conference, the one nonreligious conference I attended, there seemed to be an assumption that mothers were generally doing the bulk of the work involved in unschooling their children. However, this came across as a positive, rather than normative, assumption. In other words, this was assumed to be the way things currently *are*, but not necessarily the way things *should be*. And, while it seemed like mothers tended to be the ones more in charge of handling the details in most families, in general, the fathers I observed at the unschooling conference were very involved with their children, when compared to the fathers I observed at the other conferences. For example, a few parents whom I chatted with at the conference who had young children told me that they and their spouse were taking turns watching the children so that both could have the opportunity to attend talks. In families where there was a married mother and father, there seemed to be an assumption that even if the mother was at home with the children, the father would be involved in unschooling as much as possible. Nevertheless, there was still a separate "dads' chat" session on the schedule, implying that fathers generally have different experiences of unschooling than do mothers.

That mothers generally do the bulk of the homeschooling work was echoed across my interviews as well. For example, I asked Veronica, whom we met in chapter 3, whether moms did the bulk of homeschooling labor in the other families in the secular homeschool co-op she attends with her youngest son. She responded,

> Yes. We've had a few dads, which is really cool. We had one dad, his wife worked, he was a stay-at-home dad. And it was kind of weird for me at first, because I'd never been in a group where the dad was there. But he was really cool, you know. It was nice to get his perspective and stuff. Like, for my family, my husband, he supports me, [but says,] "You do that." And I've talked to him—of course, he's always worked, he's been in the military, so there was a lot of time I was by myself regardless. So now that he's retired, he's going to do, like, carpentry? And we're going to, you know, teach [our son] tools, and things that I don't know anything about. And [my husband] is excited. Because he can actually be part of it, whereas before it was always just, "Look what we did today, dad," and

"Oh, that's great." [...] I think the majority of the families, it's the woman doing most of it. But there are a few men that get involved. We had, it was really neat, we had one family, the husband taught a class, and the wife was able to teach a class, even though she worked. Don't know how she did it, I guess she just, you know, was able to make it work.

I asked this question of most of my respondents, and they all replied similarly: most had met, or had at least heard of, families where the father did more of the day-to-day homeschooling work, but everyone agreed that this was the exception. Aaron and Keith, the two dads whom I interviewed who were heavily involved in homeschooling their children, agreed that their level of involvement was not the norm in their communities. And in both of their cases, neither of them was exclusively in charge of homeschooling: they both shared the day-to-day homeschooling labor with their wives.

Homeschooling as an Extension of Mothering Philosophies and Practices

Many of the mothers I interviewed described homeschooling as feeling like a natural or logical extension of their mothering philosophies. Danielle recounted how "since Connor was born, I had just been doing what I thought was normal mom stuff, you know, pointing out letters of the alphabet and letting him watch Barney and taking those little teaching opportunities. When he would ask me a question, I would answer it, and we would go to the library, and we would watch PBS and things like that." Because of this "normal mom stuff" that she was doing, Connor was reading short books at the age of five, something the teachers said they would not expect of a child until the first grade. The teachers advised her to put Connor straight into first grade, but since he had just turned five, barely making the cut-off for kindergarten that year, Danielle felt that socially, skipping a grade would be a bad idea. However, just a couple of months into the school year, "He had come home so many times, frustrated and annoyed with school, and he was starting to develop the idea that school's boring, it sucks, I already know all this, why do I have to go." Danielle reasoned that, if it was her "normal mom" activities that had gotten Connor to the place where he was bored with how easy school was, then continuing this "normal mom" behavior in the form of homeschooling made sense.

For some of the mothers in heterosexual marriages that I interviewed, it seemed as though the idea that their husbands could be the primary homeschooling parent had never even crossed their minds. For these mothers, it seemed logical that they, rather than their husbands, would take on this work. This was especially notable in the case of Erica, whom we met in chapter 3 and who homeschooled her daughter, who had a life-threatening peanut allergy. Because she spoke of homeschooling as something *she* did, rather than, as many other moms did, describing it as something "we" did, I remember feeling surprised when she told me that homeschooling was initially her husband's idea. "He was actually the first one to bring up homeschooling," she said. "It took me longer to get on board with that. [. . .] And getting on board with it meant accepting that full responsibility. Versus, he trusted me with that responsibility early on, before I was ready to trust myself with that responsibility." While Erica's husband clearly thought that homeschooling was a good idea, he also thought of it as something for which Erica would be responsible. Rather than volunteer to do the work himself, he waited for Erica to come around to the idea. This did not seem to trouble Erica at all, indicating that she, too, accepted the logic that homeschooling would be something that she, rather than her husband, took responsibility for.

Part of the reason it seems logical to these mothers to take on most, if not all, of the labor of homeschooling is that they frame homeschooling as being an extension of what they already do as mothers. In other words, for most of these parents, parenting is already a gender-differentiated practice, where "mothering" and "fathering" involve gender-specific tasks. Despite women's increased participation in the paid labor force over the past several decades, child rearing is still largely understood in the United States (and elsewhere) as women's work.[12] It makes sense, then, that many parents would think of homeschooling as women's work. When Erin, who homeschooled her six children, spoke of the decision to homeschool, she included her husband when she framed homeschooling as an extension of their parenting practices. Interestingly, though, she switched to speaking just about herself as she continued talking:

When our oldest was born, the closer it got to—well, I think probably about the time he was three, we knew that homeschooling would be what we did. We just saw it as an extension of parenting, is how my husband described it. We've taught him to use a spoon, we've potty trained him, we've done all these things, why, at this point, do we give him to somebody else to finish the training, or to do more of the training? Why don't we just continue that? And so that was really what motivated us. I'm pretty much of a—if somebody gives me a suggestion of something to do, okay, I'll try to do that and see if I'm good at it or not. I'm willing to try things. So it flowed naturally from parenting. I taught him to read, I might as well teach him math and everything else too!

Erin switched from using "we" to using "I" when she went from talking about the initial decision to homeschool—a decision that she and her husband made together—to talking about the actual work of homeschooling, which was work that she did.

Some mothers understood homeschooling as their responsibility because they were already stay-at-home moms, or were intending to be, when they made the decision to homeschool. For example, when I asked Jasmine, who had only been homeschooling for a year because her children were still very young (almost five and two and a half, with baby number three on the way), whether she thought she would have stayed home with her children when they were little even if they had not homeschooled, she said, "Yes, I think so." She went on to explain that her husband was working a second job on top of his full-time job as a firefighter so that she could stay home with the children. "I had a very, very strong work ethic, through college, and I was going to go be fabulous. But then I decided, and I don't even remember when exactly, there's no specific time, that I wanted to be a mom, and I wanted to teach my kids. And that was going to be my full-time job." I asked Jasmine whether she felt that her husband minded being the one to work, and to work two jobs at that, so that she could stay home, and she responded,

> I think he's okay, I think he feels pretty balanced. He's a hard worker. He gets eight weeks of vacation a year that I have to *beg* him to take. I'm like, "Honey, it's there. Take it." He's like, "I'm not sick, why would I take a vacation day?" I would use every second! But I think he's good. I think he,

now that we've decided to do this, he's gung-ho. He's happy. I think he's glad that it's working for us, and that the bills are still getting paid, and that he's still able to be a present father and has been. I think he's good, I don't think he'd have it any other way right now.

And Jasmine, of course, also would not have it any other way. As a nurse, she still picked up occasional shifts so that she could keep her license, but, for the time being, she had no plans to work more than the minimum that was required yearly.

For some mothers, like Erin and Jasmine, who would have been stay-at-home mothers regardless, taking on the labor of homeschooling may have shifted their ideas about the specific *tasks* involved in mothering, but it did not otherwise involve a radical reprioritization of their mothering responsibilities, because they already saw it as being their top priority. For others, however, homeschooling meant sacrificing other roles in order to place mothering responsibilities at the forefront. Claudia, whom we met in chapter 2, had a career she enjoyed, and also worked as an army reservist, when she began to feel that God wanted her to homeschool. She had always planned on serving in the Reserves for twenty years so as to secure military retirement benefits, and at first, she tried to balance working and homeschooling, but after about a year, she made the decision to leave her career and the Army Reserves—thus sacrificing her retirement benefits—in order to prioritize homeschooling. Claudia told me, "Well I hung in there, as long as I could! And finally, it just came to a point where I couldn't balance it all. You know? And I had to just examine, what's my first priority? My first priority is my family." Since her husband was reluctant about homeschooling in the beginning—and, she reported, he "still wavers" about it—there had not been any discussion of which parent would be responsible for the labor of homeschooling: Claudia was the one who felt it was needed, so she was the one who gave up her career.

Gender Essentialism: Breastfeeding, Attachment Parenting, and Intensive Mothering

Some mothers, particularly those who were more conservative and religious, explained the division of homeschooling labor by drawing on essentialized notions of gender, explaining that women are "naturally" more nurturing, patient, and otherwise able to perform the labor of homeschooling. Others explained this in more individualized terms, referencing their personal temperaments, as if they just happened to be more interested in or comfortable with education or child rearing than their husbands but it could easily have been the other way around.

In particular, though, many mothers, both conservative and liberal, religious and nonreligious, made the connection between homeschooling and a particular parenting philosophy to which they subscribed: attachment parenting. Attachment parenting is a time- and energy-intensive parenting philosophy that emphasizes the importance for children's emotional development of forming a secure attachment to their parents early on in life. Parents who practice attachment parenting endeavor to be highly bonded to their children and responsive to their individual needs, through practices like extended breastfeeding, frequent holding of the baby (especially through "babywearing," or carrying a baby through the use of a wrap or other baby carrier), and cosleeping (sleeping in the same bed, or with the baby as close by as possible).[13] Sociologist Ana Villalobos argues that attachment parenting has become an increasingly popular practice in response to growing insecurity in other aspects of life.[14]

Many of the mothers whom I interviewed practiced attachment parenting. These mothers already believed in the importance of extended breastfeeding and forming a secure attachment with the child, which made homeschooling—something that would continue fostering that attachment—seem like a natural step. Holly, a middle-income, white, married mother of two teenage sons, first learned about attachment parenting when she was pregnant, and described how she learned about homeschooling from "that crowd":

> Well when I was pregnant with my first son who's now fifteen, I was active on a lot of pregnancy e-mail boards and trying to gather information, because I overanalyze everything. [Laughs] And I ran across some people that I clicked with, and they were talking about AP parenting, attachment parenting. And so that struck me as something that I wanted to do. And so over time, just hanging out with that crowd, they talked a lot about homeschooling as a natural extension of attachment parenting, so that's

what got me interested. And it worked out that I could stay home full-time with my kids, and so I mentioned to my husband, you know, this is a thing, and he was like, absolutely, do it. He didn't even have to think about it, it was just immediate, you know?

I later asked Holly if she and her husband had ever talked about the possibility of him staying home instead, and she replied, "No, it was always me." I then asked her why that was, and she said, "Well because of the—at the time, the attachment parenting, with extended nursing and all that stuff, that was never a question."

Holly was not the only parent to be introduced to the idea of homeschooling through the world of attachment parenting. Jacqui became introduced to the local homeschooling listserv, which she eventually ended up running, "because I was a member of an attachment parenting group here, [. . .] and lots of people who do attachment parenting go on to homeschool because it's sort of a natural progression." Dana, a white, bisexual, low-income, divorced mother of two, had heard of homeschooling before she had children, but was very resistant when her then husband, Todd, raised the idea. "He brought up homeschooling, and I was like, no way. [. . .] Because I'm thinking, sitting at home, at a desk, like, trying to be the teacher for my child." But later, she met a friend through an attachment parenting group who introduced her to the concept of unschooling. "She told me about it and I was like, 'Oh, like, just live with your child, and learning just happens. I could do that, that sounds awesome!'" Dana later echoed the same sentiment that Jacqui did, saying, "A lot of people who are into attachment parenting, you know, going to La Leche, and those kinds of things, then they go on to unschooling."

Natalie, a white, middle-income, married mother of three, also felt that unschooling, in particular, was "supported by attachment parenting ideas":

> We gravitated toward the unschooling philosophy, and we read a lot about that. [. . .] I think a lot of it was supported by attachment parenting ideas, too. I mean, we cosleep, we do extended breastfeeding, like, whatever else. I don't even know what else! You know, those ideas of paying attention to the actual person that is your child, not thinking of them

as just, like, an adult proto-type that will eventually become a person. It's like, no, this is a person right now, obviously, a person with needs and preferences and ideas, and, like, a learning machine, I mean. It just sort of grew out of that.

But it was not only the more progressive, unschooling parents who practiced attachment parenting. At the Christian homeschooling conferences I attended, I saw many babywearing mothers, and it was not at all uncommon to see mothers breastfeeding their babies during conference sessions (though mothers were encouraged, in the materials for these conferences, to use cover-ups while they did so, for the sake of modesty). Mindy, who was herself not religious but who knew a lot of religious homeschoolers, said that she had noticed that practices that used to be associated with "hippies" and liberals, like feeding children organic food,[15] giving birth at home or in a birthing center, and using a midwife or a doula instead of, or in addition to, a doctor, were increasing in popularity among religious people, who were coming to see these practices as "important to their faith" because they were closer to God's "plans" or intentions for parenting.

Because attachment parenting focuses so heavily on the bond between mother and child, supported through extended breastfeeding, it seemed to be almost by default in attachment-parenting families that homeschooling was seen as something that mothers, rather than fathers, would do. Carolyn explained the predominance of women doing homeschool labor in precisely this way: "The first, you know, one to three years of life, or more than that, depending on how you count life, are much more dependent on the mother's physical body. And it's really hard to work a full-time job and be pregnant and nurse and all of those things. There are so many obstacles against that. And so it's no surprise that the people who are going to throw up their hands first and be like, you know what, it's not worth it—are going to be the moms." Carolyn explained the greater investment of time that women have in the lives of their children by drawing on both biological and social explanations. On the one hand, she argued, women's parenting differs from that of men because women experience pregnancy, childbirth, and breastfeeding, and are therefore, by default, more *physically* invested in their children.[16] In addition to this, she noted that society (especially in the

United States, where national policies to support working parents are all but nonexistent) does not provide the support that mothers need to be able to continue to work while enduring the physical demands of motherhood.[17] This combination of factors, she concludes, causes women to be far more willing to leave their careers than men.

Parenting under Patriarchy

In addition to her discussion of why women are often more invested in child rearing, Carolyn also provided a more explicitly feminist analysis to explain why she, like so many other moms, did the bulk of the homeschooling labor. Carolyn described the decision that she, rather than her husband, would be in charge of the day-to-day work of homeschooling as being based primarily on financial considerations, noting that reversing these roles "was never an option" because "he's the financial provider." Carolyn put it to me quite bluntly that her husband made far more money working than she would be able to make, and his higher earnings potential was the primary consideration in determining how they divided paid and unpaid labor in their family. She also noted that in "every dad-driven homeschooling family I know, it's because the mom is the more financially stable."[18] This was also true for Maura, who said that her husband was initially more enthusiastic than she was about homeschooling, but that it was never a question that she would be the one to stay home with their daughter and do the homeschooling work "because he had the higher-paying job, so it made more sense for it to be me." When I followed up by asking if he would have wanted to do the homeschooling work if Maura had been the one with the higher-paying job, she replied, "Oh, absolutely, yeah."

But Carolyn also noted that it would be hard to reverse their roles in the family because her husband was less comfortable with unschooling. He was very invested in their children's education, she said, and as a self-professed computer geek, he loved playing educational computer games with them. But she did not feel as though he would be comfortable doing all of the day-to-day work of homeschooling. In saying this, Carolyn touched upon something that many other mothers also referenced: that they and their husbands have different aptitudes, which makes a stark division of labor, wherein their husbands work in the paid labor force and they "stay home" and homeschool the children, not only the most logical but also the easiest way of dividing things. Throughout my interviews, mothers referenced certain skills that their husbands had that allowed them to be "in charge" of certain subjects—usually math, science, or technology—but noted that they saw themselves as having the greater aptitude to be in charge of the whole endeavor, or, as Carolyn said, "primarily responsible for their education." Some parents drew on the gendered social world of their own upbringings to explain why this division of labor made sense, explaining that, as women who grew up in a society in which child care is seen as women's domain, they had far more experience working with children than their husbands did. A few referred to how, unlike their husbands, they babysat or were expected to help care for younger children when they were growing up, resulting in a skills gap that made them the far better "candidate" for the job of homeschooling.[19] Others described the difference in aptitudes and skills that they and their husbands had as being about personality differences—a rhetorical move that sociologist Arlie Hochschild calls the "reduction to personality,"[20] which serves to obscure the structural nature of the gender inequality in household labor.

Some mothers drew on several of these explanations in describing why they did the bulk of the homeschooling labor. Elena, a Latina, middle-income, married mother of two children, invoked both of these logics—the financial explanation and the appeal to gendered aptitudes—to explain the division of labor in her household. "Me working and then him doing homeschool was never an option. He has twelve years of military experience, I have—I don't have a degree to show for anything. I've never done real work for any extended period of time. I mean, I've had jobs, but I am not capable of being the breadwinner of the family. It's just not realistic." She then added, "He can make a lot more money, and that's really what it boils down to." But, like Carolyn, she was quick to note that her husband was still involved in their children's education. "He does a lot with them, like when they want to learn something that I feel ill equipped to teach, my husband will take over. Like chemistry, geometry—those kinds of, like, I can teach that, and that's fine, but I hate it. Like, with a passion. I'm not a math and science girl." This rhetorical move, where Elena referenced her husband's involvement and investment in *some* aspects of homeschooling, seemed to function as a way to explain away the gender inequality in their relationship. I interpret this strategy—one that I saw used commonly by the mothers I interviewed—as a form of impression management,[21] though whether women used it because they worried that I would judge them for their division of labor or to manage their own feelings of discomfort with the arrangement (or both) is unclear.

When I asked Elena whether she felt as though her husband wished he was able to be more involved in the day-to-day of homeschooling, she said, "Yes and no." He loved being around for the "fun stuff," she explained, like "zoo trips and park days and stuff like that." But, on the other hand, she said, "He cannot handle being around the kids for extended periods of time. He gets really cranky. Really, like, [heavy sigh], oh my god. And I'm like, 'Do you think they're putting on a show for you? Like, this is not special. This is how they always are. Like, why are you upset right now?' So I think we're built different." She then added that, when it came to the day-to-day operations, "I really don't think he'd be able to do it. I mean, and I think he knows that."

While some of the mothers I interviewed were not concerned about the gendered division of labor in their families, others expressed some ambivalence or even outright discomfort. Carolyn was one such mother. She identified as a feminist and was raising three sons, and thus she worried about the message their division of labor sent to their children. Her musings on the topic are worth quoting at length:

> It's funny, I was just talking to my girlfriend about that, about the idea—like, because it is true that my husband's and my roles in the family are pretty traditionally gender-drawn. And it has—like I can't know, you know, nature, nurture, whether it's because I was raised as a woman, born in the seventies, and how much of that is because of—but I was not raised with the expectation that I would be a stay-at-home mom. I was raised, actually, you know, very progressively. And I don't—I think [my husband and I] had a lot of conversations about staying home or not staying home and what that would mean, and it took me a lot of years to figure out the value in that and what I valued and where I saw value. And so that's definitely been sort of a personal journey, in trying to figure out what all of that means and what all of it is. But the counter to that is you know there'll be times where the kids, there'll be something physical that needs

to be done and they'll be like, well, we'll just wait for Daddy. And I'm like, "I am perfectly capable of doing this!" You know? "Daddy is not the one who built the damn chicken coop," like, right? So there are times where things will come out of their mouths where I'm like, "Whoa, how'd you get that idea?" Like, how did we do that? And on the other hand, like, he is the one who mows the lawn, and he is the one who, frankly, is much better at computers than I am. And a lot of the fix-it stuff I tend to put off on him. I don't know. I don't know what that's doing, that's part of the sort of pro-con, like, I am a strong and powerful woman and I am a force to be reckoned with, and I do a lot. You know, I was very independent. We do talk [with the kids] about the fact that I used to make money. And I used to make a good bit of it. And so our life and our lifestyle is about choices, and that right now, this is a choice that we're making. I've talked with my kids about the fact that, in fact, it's a complicated choice for women, because you know, when I left the workforce I was making a certain amount of money, and that is not what I can expect now, eight years out, and my value in the workforce goes down every year I'm out. Which means that my dependence on their father goes up, every year I'm out. And that's a trust, you know. But on the other hand, well, yeah, that's my husband, and I love him, and I trust him, right? Like at some point you leap off that bridge or you don't. And I leapt, and we're invested, and I believe that thirty years from now we'll be sharing a retirement, and it's fine.

Carolyn felt that she had to do a lot of work to counter the messages she had received during her feminist upbringing that being a stay-at-home mom was unfeminist. And yet, despite having done all of this work, she still seemed really conflicted, especially in light of evidence that her boys had internalized these traditional ideas about the gendered division of labor. One of the ways she attempted to deal with the anxiety this seemed to provoke was to be intentional and explicit in discussing with her children the decisions that she and her husband had made, including making sure that they understood the downsides, for her, of those decisions.

The narratives of these mothers make it clear that a set of social forces works in tandem to push mothers, rather than fathers, toward staying home, when parents decide that homeschooling is what is best for their children. The wage gap is an important piece of the puzzle. Men generally have higher earnings than women, particularly when women have spent any time out of the paid labor force caring for young children.[22] Women may also tend to have more experience with children and child care as a result of helping care for younger children as youths and young adults,[23] making them more likely than their husbands to have a skill set that lends itself to homeschooling and to being a stay-at-home parent.

The case of Robin, the only parent whom I interviewed who was in a same-sex marriage, is instructive here, as both her own skills and desires, and her earnings relative to her wife, played a role in their decision for Robin to be the primary homeschooling parent. Robin was their children's gestational parent, and though it was not initially her plan, she felt strongly, soon after giving birth to Hugo, her first child, that she did not want to go back to work full-time. She explained, "I have respect for women who work and all that, and I get that, but for me? I would've been miserable." That said, Robin had not left the paid labor force entirely; as a therapist, she maintained a small private practice, where she continued to see clients two evenings per week. When I asked Robin if being the stay-at-home parent was something that her wife would be interested in doing, Robin immediately said, "Oh, yeah"—a response that I only got from a couple of the mothers I interviewed who were married to men. I then asked her whether they had ever had a discussion about who would be the one to stay home, and we had the following exchange:

> ROBIN: Well, no. She's the one who has the more money-making job, and the benefits, for her and the kids, and that kind of stuff. I mean, she's involved, in that we don't have set hours or anything, so if something's happening—like sometimes he gets to math problems that I'm like, "Yeah, you're going to wait, until she gets home, and she's going to help talk you through this one because I never was able to do this when I was in school!" [. . .] I mean, the lion's share goes to me because I'm the one who's home. But I think it's a family effort. I don't think it's, like—I'm not the one "in charge" of it, in that way.
> KATE: Right, yeah. But in terms of the time?
> ROBIN: In terms of the time and in terms of the obsessively researching what's going to be the next thing that will actually fit? That would be me. [Laughs]

In some ways, Robin's explanation of their division of labor sounded a lot like other mothers' explanations. She talked about feeling a strong attachment to and desire to spend more time with her children after giving birth to them, she noted that her wife's higher-paying job and health insurance was a deciding factor, and she talked about how her wife's stronger math skills meant she was still called upon to help with certain subjects. But I also sensed that Robin felt she needed to justify "getting" to do the homeschooling labor, when it was also something that her wife wanted to do. This was definitely not something I heard in other interviews.

Not all parents divided the labor of homeschooling such that the bulk of it fell on one parent. But even the rare set of parents who strived intentionally to be equally involved in homeschooling struggled to make this a reality. Natalie and her husband decided to homeschool—and, more specifically, to unschool—before they had children. In fact, her husband first introduced the concept of unschooling to her while they were friends in college, years before they began dating. She described to me how she intentionally decided on a career where she could work from home, be her own boss, and make her own hours, so that she could breastfeed her children and avoid putting them in daycare. She also talked about how she and her husband worked really hard to be equal parents, and how this was becoming more of a reality in terms of daily time spent with the children after the birth of their third child, when her husband was also able to transition to working for himself, from home. Even so, she admitted, she took on a lot more of the responsibility for the behind-the-scenes activities, like reading and researching about unschooling, being active on message boards, and networking with other families. She did most of the thinking about homeschooling, specifically, and childrearing, more generally—what Lisa Wade has called the "invisible worry work of mothering,"[24] including reading, conducting research, and organizing the children's lives.[25]

Natalie and her husband both participated in the daily work of unschooling. From the way she described their days, I got the sense that if they were to participate in a time-use study wherein they tracked their daily activities,[26] it would show that they spent close to equal hours with their children. But it was clear to me that Natalie was still the one "in charge." She explained, "He was the one that gave me the idea first, but

I was the one that researched what people were doing. I'm probably still the decision maker about health stuff, food stuff, and whatever. I mean we both strongly identify as feminists, so we try to notice it, but, like, I don't know what else you can do at this point in history." Natalie was critical of the ideology that mothers *should* be the ones in charge of ensuring that their children are educated and well taken care of, that the mother should be the one tasked with researching things, knowing things, and making decisions. But she also saw her marriage, and herself, as being shaped and constrained by a society in which those tasks *are* seen as women's work, in which women have been better socialized to handle such details, and in which women are ultimately held accountable for their children's educations. Meanwhile, Natalie simultaneously resisted and embraced the logic of intensive mothering. She embraced the idea that child rearing should be time intensive, emotionally absorbing, labor intensive, and financially expensive, but rejected much of the "expert discourse" about education, relying instead on alternative experts who advocated for unschooling as the ideal way of raising and educating children, as well as embracing the tenets of attachment parenting. And so, while Natalie resisted the idea that it should be mothers who are primarily responsible for child rearing, she found herself unable to escape the reality that child-rearing decisions are ultimately seen as the responsibility of mothers in our society. The pressure this puts on homeschooling mothers can result in a lot of worry, fear, and doubt, something that another mother, Maria, described as a cross that she had to bear: "That constant checking in, for me personally—the 'Is this the best choice? Is this right choice? Am I missing something? Are there other possibilities?'—that's a personal cross that I bear, all the time." Yet in describing the weight of these decisions as a *personal* issue, Maria obscures the structural issue at hand: the fact that the weight of this cross is borne almost exclusively by women.

Homeschooling, Heteronormativity, and Neoliberal Motherhood: Implications for Gender Inequality

What does it mean that homeschooling labor is so strongly gendered? As my research revealed, homeschooled children do not live in an isolated world where they see only their parents' division of labor. Most of my respondents belonged to homeschool co-ops, play groups, or sports teams, and attended other formal and informal gatherings of homeschooling families, and these spaces were almost always inhabited by mothers—usually white and (heterosexually) married—and their children. Even children whose parents divide homeschooling labor relatively equally, or where the father is primarily responsible (something that was mentioned by many of my respondents, who all seemed to know a family, or know someone who knew a family, or had at least heard stories about a family with a full-time stay-at-home homeschooling dad), are embedded in homeschooling communities in which mothers are doing most of the work. At the homeschooling conferences I attended, the "homeschooling family" was often constructed as a two-parent, married, heterosexual couple in which the mother is in charge of the children's education. Whether this construction was normalizing, in the case of the Christian and Catholic conferences, or simply normative, in the case of the unschooling conference, it was nonetheless apparent in all of these spaces.

There is also reason to believe that practices within the broader homeschooling community might discourage participation from those whose families fall outside this norm. While my data are not observational and thus cannot show this directly, in general, my respondents portrayed homeschooling communities as being very gendered, heteronormative, and racialized, such that families who fall outside the norm often felt excluded from these communities, either implicitly or explicitly. A few of my nonwhite respondents remarked on the overwhelming whiteness of their homeschool groups and how that could make them feel uncomfortable at times, or make them wish that there were more minority mothers in the groups. Meanwhile, the single mothers I interviewed identified certain barriers to participation in some homeschooling groups, such as the tendency of such groups to meet only during traditional school hours, which can be inconvenient for those who work during the day and homeschool in the evenings, and group sign-up forms that ask for "mom's" and "dad's" information, suggesting that families were expected to have both. And Robin, the one married, lesbian mother whom I interviewed, spoke to me about constantly having to negotiate whether to "come out" in homeschooling spaces, or to just let people assume—as they tended to do—that her spouse was male. This was especially important to her as some of the homeschooling events they attended included parents with a variety of political and religious beliefs, and she expressed some discomfort with coming out in situations where there might be conservative Christians present, especially after experiencing a neighbor family refusing to let their (also homeschooled) children play with her children, because of their "alternative" family structure.

Thus, while some parents homeschool in part because of their discomfort with the implicit and explicit heteronormativity of public schools, their children still tend to do much of their socializing in heteronormative spaces, in which mothering is clearly associated with the labor of child care. Some parents worked to counter these messages by emphasizing the diversity of gendered and sexual expression with their children from a young age, with some including explicit lessons with their children about things like consent, same-sex sexuality, and deconstructing binary gender.[27] Other parents did not think that public schools emphasized heteronormativity enough and intentionally reinforced the gender division of labor with their children, preparing their children for expected heterosexual futures and to be good wives and mothers, or husbands and fathers, in their future families. What is unclear from this research, however, is how children themselves interpret, assimilate, and/or resist these messages. Future research on homeschooled children's perceptions about gender and sexuality will be important for understanding the degree to which these norms influence children's understandings of the possibilities they have for living gendered lives, especially in future relationships and family life.

Neoliberal Motherhood: What's Best for *My* Kid

Interestingly, one of the most important insights I gained over the course of this research about the importance of mothering ideologies within the homeschooling movement came from some conversations that I had with a homeschooling father, rather than a mother. Matt, who was the father of two young daughters, sought me out several times at the unschooling conference that I attended to chat about what he saw as a worrisome trend of individualism within the unschooling community. I felt as though he sought me out for these conversations in part because he thought I would be in a place to help him contextualize his own observations and in part because he had a hunch I would share in his concern about this trend, as someone whose job it is to look at the world from a scientific perspective.

Matt and his wife, Penny, came to the decision to unschool their daughters after having read books by psychologists and education critics—including Aflie Kohn, an outspoken critic of the testing culture in US education—that convinced them that unschooling was the ideal educational environment for all children (not just *his* children), as supported by scientific evidence.[28] Matt shared with me his concern about the tendency for people to say that they unschool because it is "what's best for our family," explaining the decision in terms of their own intuition or feelings about what their own children need. He contrasted this with how he and Penny chose to unschool because it is "what's best—period." He brought up two other, parallel parenting trends within the unschooling community to illustrate this difference: vaccination practices and food restrictions. Matt told me that, as far as he could tell, they were the only unschooling parents they know in Texas who vaccinate their children. In one conversation I had with Matt and Penny together, Matt asked his wife whether she agreed with this assertion, and after giving it some thought, Penny agreed; the only other families she could think of who had vaccinated their children did so before they came into unschooling and, according to Penny, they tended to express regret at having done so. Matt said that, as with the decision to unschool, his and Penny's decision to vaccinate was made on the basis of scientific evidence: they had read the scientific literature on vaccination and were convinced that vaccination is best, both for individual children and for society more broadly. Their friends, however, did not vaccinate because they felt it was best for their individual children not to be exposed to vaccines, but did not take the broader societal implications into consideration.[29] Matt also told me that many of their friends practice family-wide food restrictions, for example, on gluten—not because of diagnosed intolerance by any family members but because of a general sense that they and/or their children "just feel better" without certain foods. Matt and Penny both felt frustrated by the general disregard that they saw among their fellow unschooling parents for scientific evidence, and the tendency they observed for parents to trust their own "instincts" about their children over expert, research-based advice. I could tell by the way they each jumped in animatedly to finish each other's sentences as we spoke that this was a topic they had discussed with each other at length.

Matt's observations echoed my own perceptions, which I based on the frequency with which I heard phrases such as "what's best for our family" or "what's right for our family" both at the unschooling conference and in interviews with many homeschoolers—and not just those who practiced unschooling. This phrase indicates a belief that parents have a responsibility to do what is best for their family, or their children, even if what is best for their family is in conflict with what is best for society, as in the case of vaccination.[30] As Matt pointed out, it also relies on an understanding of the parent's intuition as the primary source of knowledge about what is right for the family, even when that contrasts with scientific findings or other expert recommendations. Yet, while these parents drew on a discourse of individualized, family-specific decision making about what is best for the family, there were clear trends across families as to what the parents had decided was right for their family, indicating that social forces beyond a parent's instincts were shaping these decisions. Further evidence of the social nature of these trends was the pressure that Matt and Penny felt to conform to them, for example, in the form of feeling intensely judged by other unschooling parents for willingly vaccinating their children.

I argue that the ideology of intensive mothering—and specifically, the form this ideology takes under neoliberalism—is the primary social force shaping this trend toward the individualization of child rearing. As I noted in chapter 4, Amy Shuffleton references the frequent refrain she hears from mothers as they discuss their children's schooling that "I just have to do what's best for my own child." But, she argues, this phrase is not an expression of selfishness or of irrational anxiety about the need to look out for their children's own best interest but rather, "Our national unwillingness to support children and families means that these mothers are accurately identifying a problem: if they do not tenaciously defend their own children's interests, those interests will go unaddressed."[31]

I saw Shuffleton's argument borne out in my own research time and time again. The mothers whom I interviewed had identified real problems in their children's schooling, whether they be rampant bullying, ineffective teachers, overcrowded classrooms, or unresponsive administrators. Many of these situations, discussed in detail in previous chapters, were obviously bigger than just the one child: for example, Tracy noted that many other parents had complained about how ineffective her son's math teacher was, and the bullying issues that Raya's and Shannon's sons experienced seemed to be schoolwide issues. Despite acknowledging this, however, none of these parents saw it as their responsibility to advocate for other children having the same experience, just their own.[32]

In fact, some parents went as far as to criticize, for neglecting their responsibility to their own child, mothers who would keep their child in public school while trying to make larger systemic changes. During my interview with Aspen, she asked me what motivated me to study homeschooling, and I explained that I felt that we can better understand how our society approaches public education by taking into account the perspectives of those who are opting out of it. Aspen responded that "you hear some stories from parents and it's hard to understand them *not* pulling their kids, based on the story." She went on to tell one such story:

> I have a friend of a friend, who I have known again since [my oldest] was three months old, so nine years. And her daughter started public school at one of the public schools that has the Spanish program—the dual language program. And this particular school, the principal is very rigid, and he didn't allow talking in the hallways. Or at lunch. Even for the five-year-olds. And her daughter started exhibiting behaviors, like, she started pulling her hair out, and she started having anxiety attacks, at five years old. And they didn't pull her. This, to me, I don't understand! It's like, um, there's a major problem! Your child is having health problems, mental health problems. That's taking it too far! You know? And it's hard to understand not pulling a child from a situation that's that stressful for them. I don't know, it's just—I guess I'm standing on a different side, you know? We're all looking at it from a different angle and she sees it one way and I see it a different way. Like, I would never let it get that bad, and then just take her to a psychologist. That would not be my answer; my answer would be to take her from the school.

Aspen went on to explain that she felt that this acquaintance did not pull her daughter from the school because she wanted to try to fix the larger issue, rather than just address the immediate problem of her daughter's stress. But Aspen thought that her friend's faith that such change was possible was misguided. "I think a lot of parents want to have faith in the school changing, and they believe that if they keep the kids in, and just fight for changes that it'll happen," she said. "But I don't think that's going to happen fast enough to help *your* kid."

Despite her criticism of this acquaintance, Aspen recognized that some parents did not have the luxury of pulling their children from school. She also acknowledged that if parents who might be able to fight for change pull their children instead, change may never happen. Still, she felt that her responsibility was to her own family, first and foremost. "I think it just depends on what you think your duty is," she said. "You know, is your duty to your family first, or to the people you've never met who don't have as much as you? And some people feel very strongly that your duty is to the greater good, and even if your family suffers that that's true, but that is not the way I view life. [. . .] That is not my number one duty. My duty is to my children." And Aspen certainly was not alone in expressing this idea. Other parents noted that homeschooling parents frequently hear criticism from those who believe that they should keep their children in school to make change from within. Some responded to this criticism as Julia did, with anger evident in her voice: "No. Fix the school. Fix the problem. And then we can talk about maybe sending my kids in there. But no, I'm not going to make sacrificial lambs out of my kids when I know, going into it, I would know that it's not optimum for them. That's a bad argument. That's a bad reason to send your kids to school."

The parents whom I interviewed varied in their assessment of whether change to public schooling was even possible. But those who thought it was, at least on a theoretical level, still expressed a deep lack of belief that they, as individual parents, had any power to make change. I argue that the broader neoliberal ideology that emphasizes individualization and personal responsibility leads these mothers to attempt individual-level interventions as their first line of defense against what are actually structural problems, and that when these (inevitably) fail, parents give up on "the system" entirely, rather than looking for other possible avenues of change. A common sentiment that I heard from the parents I interviewed was that if they could not change the situation for *one* child, how could they possibly change the situation for *all* children?

And even if such change were possible, many parents echoed Julia's sentiment that to put their children in a suboptimal learning environment would be to "make sacrificial lambs" of them—an image that is obviously intended to evoke an emotional response, perhaps even horror. Jamie was another parent who evoked this imagery of being unwilling to "sacrifice" her own child on the altar of social change. Jamie was a radical unschooler who believed that all learning should be child-led, and saw this ideal as starkly contrasted by the compulsory, standardized, and achievement-oriented nature of current public education. She told me, "I would love to see some of it change, but I'm not willing to go into it myself. I'm not going to offer up my child as a sacrifice just so I can—probably not [even] effect that much change, by myself. It's kind of pessimistic, but it's—my focus is on her, and that's where my energy goes." Jamie expressed a complex set of thoughts here. First, she saw the problems with her public school system as so big that, even if she did invest a lot of energy into working to change it, her effort would result in little improvement. But more importantly, her statement also revealed a belief that the work of changing public schools and the work of mothering are in conflict with each other. As a mother, she saw her primary responsibility as cultivating an environment in which her child could thrive, and she did not believe that public schools could offer that. She went so far as to say, "I don't think there's anything that I wouldn't do, to keep her out of that type of schooling. I am like, hardcore, adamantly against it." From this perspective, putting her daughter in school and dedicating her time to creating change from within would, in essence, be an abdication of her maternal responsibility, and would make her a bad mother.

Thus, despite her belief that change in the public school system is necessary because not all families have the means to homeschool, Jamie's understanding of her own maternal responsibility left her unable to imagine herself being a part of that change. And so, instead of working to change public education, Jamie and other liberal and progressive parents constructed a different understanding of social change that they felt was compatible with their parenting responsibilities. In order to ease the cognitive dissonance they felt as people who believed in public education in theory, but rejected public school for their own children, in practice, these mothers framed themselves as enacting social change at the most individual level, in how they raise their own children.

In short, Jamie, and other parents I interviewed, felt passionately about what public education in the United States could look like. But the mothering ideologies to which these mothers felt intensely accountable led them to limit their actions with regard to these visions to the sphere of their own families. In essence, they enacted their visions of a better way of educating children at the most local scale possible, by creating such an education only for their own children. In other words, neoliberal mothering ideologies politically neutralize these mothers, taking women who might otherwise be activists and circumscribing their activism in such a way that their ability to enact change is minimized.

Conclusion

Is Homeschooling a Problem?

In the spring of 2020 both the *Harvard Gazette* and *Harvard Magazine* published articles featuring Harvard Law School professor and child welfare expert Elizabeth Bartholet, in which Bartholet argues that homeschooling—and particularly, its lack of regulation—puts children at risk of maltreatment and abuse, and poses a threat to democracy.[1] These pieces, along with a planned "Homeschooling Summit" at Harvard Law School at which Bartholet was to be a featured speaker,[2] drew sharp criticism from advocates within the homeschooling community. In two of its weekly e-mail newsletters, the Alternative Education Resource Organization (AERO), which advocates for learner-centered educational approaches, referred to these articles and the summit as an attack on homeschooling from Harvard.[3] One of these newsletters included a link to an article that criticized the summit for its "one-sided approach to thumping on homeschool families across the country."[4]

Bartholet's opposition to homeschooling rests largely on two arguments: first, that homeschooling can allow parents to abuse and mistreat their children with little fear of being caught, as their children do not interact regularly with mandated reporters at school, and second, that the lack of regulation and oversight of homeschooling in the United States means that parents can, if they desire, deny their children a meaningful education.[5] While it is debatable whether such abuse is as widespread as Bartholet implies it is, there have certainly been high-profile cases of each of these phenomena. In early 2018, David and Louise Turpin, a California couple who had lived for many years in Texas and who "homeschooled" their thirteen children, were arrested and charged with torturing and abusing their children, who were found extremely malnourished and who were reported to be regularly kept chained and locked to their beds. The abuse was only discovered when one of the children managed to escape, as the family used homeschooling as a cover to isolate the children completely from the public.⁶ Just the next month, Tara Westover published her widely acclaimed memoir *Educated*, in which she talks about being "homeschooled" by her religious fundamentalist family, and how she missed out on having an actual education as a result.⁷

Stories like these, no matter how rare they may (or may not) be, compel us to ask, is homeschooling always in children's best interest? The Coalition for Responsible Home Education, which runs the project "Homeschooling's Invisible Children," documenting cases of abuse and neglect of homeschooled children, does not think so. "Current systems for detecting and preventing child abuse often assume that school-age children will attend school," they argue, and while "school attendance does not in and of itself prevent abuse or neglect . . . we also know that abusive parents can and sometimes do use homeschooling to conceal their mistreatment."⁸ Like Bartholet, the Coalition for Responsible Home Education is concerned about more than just physical abuse in homeschooling families. It also highlights the ways in which a lack of oversight of homeschooling—such as that which the Texas families I interviewed experience, and largely celebrate—can lead to cases of "educational neglect," where children do not receive enough of an education to be able to function as an adult in our society.⁹

Cases like these—and the attention drawn to them by child welfare experts such as Bartholet and organizations like the Coalition for Responsible Home Education—raise important questions about the rights of children and the role of education in a pluralist democracy. These are dramatic examples of heartbreaking abuse, mistreatment, and educational neglect, but there are also many less sensational examples that raise the same questions. In my observations at fundamentalist Christian homeschooling conferences, for example, I heard discussion of curricula based on "creation science," and was even given a free copy of a book, while perusing a display (complete with giant dinosaur head!) of materials from the Creation Museum,¹⁰ that outlined the "evidence"— primarily in the form of Bible verses—that dinosaurs and humanity coexisted on earth some six thousand years ago. During one of my interviews, I was taken aback to hear a mother describe how she uses the Bible not only to teach her children religion but also as their main history and science book. Is teaching children science in this way, which appears to be so clearly divorced from norms of the scientific community, a form of educational neglect? I also heard multiple speakers at the religious conferences I attended advocate for spanking children, or using what is known as "child training," with one speaking particularly wistfully as she recalled the days, when her now-adult children were young, when one could use a switch on one's children in public without fear of being reported to the authorities for doing so. While there is debate about the point at which corporal punishment crosses the line into abuse, it is not hard to see this, at the very least, as a worrisome trend in at least some corners of the homeschooling community of violating children's bodily integrity.[11]

One thing that each of these examples has in common is that they speak particularly to homeschooling practices among fundamentalist Christians. In fact, Bartholet's argument for banning—or at least strongly regulating—the practice of homeschooling rests on the understanding that homeschooling in the United States is primarily a religious practice. And while Bartholet is correct that the homeschooling lobby in the United States is predominantly made up of fundamentalist Christian organizations such as the Home School Legal Defense Association,[12] is she correct in her assertion that "many homeschooling parents are extreme ideologues"—primarily of the religious variety?[13] "Many" is a vague term, but it at least implies a majority, which, as I discussed in chapter 1, seems no longer to be true in the United States. And while the parents whom I interviewed for this project are not statistically representative of homeschooling parents, their perspectives make clear that, at least for some parents, the decision to homeschool is not at all guided by religious ideology. And in fact, the parents I spoke with were at least as likely, if not more likely, to invoke the ideology of neoliberalism in explaining their decision to homeschool as they were to invoke religious ideologies.

This is not to say that Bartholet does not raise important points about the implications for the growth of homeschooling for children's rights and well-being. But as I hope this book has made clear, there is a weakness to her argument, insofar as she paints homeschooling as being "about" a single thing, or as a single entity with more or less unified motivations, goals, and practices. What this book has shown is that homeschoolers hold some perspectives, like the idea of children as unique and deserving of individualized educations, largely in common, while they hold wildly divergent views on other topics, such as the rights and personhood of children.

In fact, a sizable minority of the parents whom I interviewed decided to homeschool, not because of their commitment to religious ideologies but due to real grievances with their schools, grievances that reflect broader problems that parents perceive schools as failing to address. Children being denied the special education services to which they are legally entitled (or at least, not getting them without significant time and energy spent by their mothers fighting the schools) is a legitimate problem. Children's mental health declining because of repeated teasing and tormenting from their peers is a legitimate problem. And it is a problem when children are bored in the classroom because their teachers—who are overwhelmed by too-large class sizes, lack sufficient mentoring due to seasoned teachers leaving the profession at increasing rates, and are pressured to teach to the test so that their schools can keep their funding—cannot give them the education they deserve. The parents of these children see that their children's interests are not being served. As my interviews revealed, these parents sometimes feel that they are left without much of a choice *but* to take what some may see as drastic steps, like quitting their jobs, withdrawing their children, and starting to homeschool.

What all of the parents I interviewed had in common—whether they felt that schools exposed their children to dangerous ideas about gender and sexuality, or felt that schools restricted children's bodily autonomy and gendered and sexual selves, or simply felt that schools were failing to provide the education their children need—was that they understood themselves as having the *choice* to homeschool their children. In reality, the rise of homeschooling is the outcome of a constellation of ideologies and social forces. But the common thread of the language of choice leads me to argue that if we were to attribute the recent growth of contemporary homeschooling primarily to one single ideology, it should not be to the ideology of fundamentalist Christianity but to the ideology of school choice.[14] Yet the ideology of school choice is one that Bartholet leaves unnamed, even as she invokes its logic when she notes that, in her view, there are "legitimate" reasons that parents might have for wanting to homeschool, including that "maybe the schools in their area are terrible."[15] Rather than asking, as Bartholet does, whether homeschooling is a problem, I propose that my research indicates that the more fruitful question should be, is school choice a problem?

Is School Choice a Problem?

School choice is an ideology that is best understood as part of the broader ideological construct of neoliberalism. Cultural critic Lisa Duggan has written that privatization and personal responsibility are the "key terms" of neoliberalism, and political scientist David Harvey—recognized as one of the foremost experts on neoliberalism—has argued that the concepts of individualism, liberty, freedom, and choice are central to its ideology.[16] Harvey argues that central to the United States' transition to neoliberalism was an "ideological assault" in which "independent 'think tanks' financed by wealthy individuals and corporate donors proliferated—with the Heritage Foundation in the lead—to prepare an ideological onslaught aimed at persuading the public of the commonsense character of neoliberal propositions."[17]

I argue that the growth of homeschooling, and the discourses that parents draw on to talk about homeschooling, are evidence that this mission has succeeded. The narratives I encountered in my research, and have presented in this book, demonstrate that parents across the political spectrum have, in fact, been persuaded to accept neoliberalism's key tenets as common sense. As an ideology, neoliberalism has made its way into the lexicon of everyday Americans, and it appears throughout their narratives of how they make decisions about how they raise their children. We see the concept of individualism clearly in the discourse of the unique child and the argument that children need individualized education. We see the concept of personal responsibility in the rhetoric that mothers use to describe their prioritizing of their own children's and families' needs over the needs of the community. Privatization is invoked in how mothers take on roles that were previously understood as public goods—such as their children's education—and describe themselves as better qualified than public school teachers to take on that task. And the concepts of liberty and freedom are central to parents' desire to keep the state out of their family lives through a lack of regulation of homeschooling. Finally, we see the language of choice, of course, in how parents talk about the importance of having options for their children's education, even while at the same time they feel these options are largely not good enough. What this book makes clear is that the implications of the "neoliberal turn" extend far beyond government, the economy, and our civil institutions, and into the day-to-day lives of families.

What is particularly insidious, however, is that these parents' decisions are, in part, a direct result of the undermining of public institutions, such as public education, and the shredding of the social safety net, which have contributed to parents' dissatisfaction with public school and to the growing insecurity that leads to the doubling down of women's commitment to intensive motherhood.[18] Thus, these parents are forced into the "choice" of homeschooling, in part, as a direct result of neoliberal policies; accordingly, the ideological, political, and economic components of neoliberalism have created a feedback loop that serves to further rationalize neoliberalism and strengthen its ideological grip on individuals and families. This ideological grip has profound consequences for inequality along the lines of gender, race, class, and age.[19] I made the case in chapter 6 for how neoliberal motherhood ideals reinforce gender inequality by making mothers primarily responsible for making the sacrifices required to carry out the day-to-day labor of homeschooling. But an analysis of homeschooling as a case of school choice makes clear that there are other implications of school choice for inequality, as well.

Implications of School Choice for Racial and Class Inequality

In her incisive analysis of race, segregation, and neoliberal education reform, Noliwe Rooks demonstrates that the logic of school choice, which has become part and parcel of neoliberal education reform, actually began to emerge prior to the neoliberal turn in the United States, alongside the process of the racial desegregation of public schools. In response to desegregation orders, Rooks notes, some southern states "instituted so-called Freedom of Choice plans under which families and students could opt to attend the public school of their choice," while others created voucher systems that allowed white students to attend segregated private schools using taxpayer funds—what became known as "segregation academies."[20] Scholars have demonstrated that these private schools were often dominated by evangelical Christian families, and indeed that many private Christian schools began as segregation academies.[21] It is perhaps unsurprising, then, that the rise of homeschooling among the Christian Right coincided with the closing of many segregation academies just as desegregation in American schools reached its peak.[22]

In other words, the logic of school choice emerged in the United States as an explicitly white-supremacist project, though these racist origins were obscured when the mantle of school choice was taken up by neoliberalism through the use of the race-neutral language of freedom and choice. Nevertheless, Rooks argues that, while the *language* of school choice has been made race neutral, the *practice* of school choice remains far from deracialized. Rooks argues that most white parents claim they would be comfortable sending their children to desegregated schools, but that their numbers "decrease when whites are asked about *how* to achieve racial integration. They do not support busing or any program that would deny their children access to the school of their choice."[23] This happens, in part, because parents know that schools are not providing equal educations. While Rooks argues that policies are needed that would work to "aggressively integrate our classrooms" in order to move toward equality,[24] I argue that the roadblocks to achieving such equality are not just found in policy makers and the for-profit school-reform ventures Rooks describes in her book. Individual parents—white parents—who actively seek educational advantage for their children through school choice policies, at the expense of increased equality, are also part of the problem.

In her insightful book on the experiences of white children with racial privilege, sociologist Margaret Hagerman argues that white families are one site at which racism is reproduced, "intentionally and unintentionally, overtly and subtly, through big decisions and everyday choices."[25] She locates one source of this reproduction of inequality in the competing roles that parents face as parents to their own children, and as citizens of a larger society:

> American families are located within a society structured at its most fundamental core by intersecting forms of inequality, and parents of race-

and class-privileged children are faced with a difficult paradox: in order to be a "good parent," they must provide their children as many opportunities and advantages as possible; in order to be a "good citizen," they must resist evoking structural privileges in ways that disadvantage others. Decisions about navigating this paradox are part of a complex, ongoing, everyday process of parenting, a process that is filled with many other challenges, day-to-day trials, and unintentional missteps.[26]

This paradox that race- and class-privileged parents face is not inevitable. Rather, as I have demonstrated in this book, it is the result of this current constellation of hegemonic neoliberal ideologies that tells mothers that the only way to be "good mothers" is to do everything they can to ensure the success of their own children, even when this comes at the expense of other children. In this way, the mothering ideology that many of the mothers I interviewed for this project invoke when describing their decision to homeschool—the ideology that says they must not "sacrifice" their own child for the good of a larger whole—functions as a form of opportunity hoarding, helping to maintain segregated, and highly unequal, educational experiences.[27]

One way that we can better understand how this paradox of the "good parent" versus the "good citizen" is the result of a specific set of ideologies, rather than an inevitability, is by looking to alternate, resistant mothering ideologies. For example, in her classic sociological work *Black Feminist Thought*, Patricia Hill Collins presents the practice of "other-mothering" as one of the ways in which Black mothers in the United States have historically practiced mothering quite differently from white mothers.[28] Because of racialized patterns of labor force participation (both unpaid, under slavery, and [under]paid, after slavery), Black mothers historically did not have the luxury of "opting out" of the labor force to raise their children, and thus communal child-rearing practices such as "other-mothering" have always been common in Black communities. In other words, for many Black mothers, there is less of a clear distinction between their own children and "other people's children."[29] The same is true of other women of color and poor women (including some poor white women), who are far more likely than their white and middle-class counterparts to rely on extended family and others in their communities to contribute to the labor of raising children, and to offer the same to others.[30] Under this particular set of ideologies and practices—which stand in opposition to the dominant ideologies invoked by the mothers in my research—the paradox of ensuring "what's best for my kid" at the expense of "other people's children" would be rendered less of a paradox, and perhaps even be completely illegible.

That said, it is important to remember that, while the majority of homeschooling families are white, as discussed in chapter 1, numbers of nonwhite homeschoolers are on the rise. And like the parents whom I interviewed who chose to homeschool when they found their public schools—which had been stripped of the ability to function optimally due to neoliberal education reforms—insufficient for their children, there is evidence that nonwhite parents also choose homeschooling because of very real grievances with schools. For some, like Kamilah and Jasmine, whom I interviewed for this study, the decision to homeschool was motivated in part by the actual or anticipated experiences of their Black children in majority-white schools that could or did hurt their self-esteem and threaten their safety. For others, like a family that I met at an unschooling event, homeschooling allows them to expose their children to more (and more accurate) Black history, literature, and art than they would get in public schools. For these parents, homeschooling acts as a form of "racial protectionism,"[31] which is needed as a result of both school segregation and the lasting influence of white supremacy on school curricula.

What this makes clear is that, while homeschooling began growing in part out of explicit white supremacy, its continued growth is better understood as, at least in part, a more indirect result of the racialized legacy of school choice. For those who are concerned about the welfare of homeschooled children, then, banning or increasing regulation of the practice would likely be ineffective—and politically impossible—without a robust rethinking of the delivery and funding of public education in the United States.

Implications of School Choice for Gender, Sexuality, and Children's Rights

As I have demonstrated in this book, neoliberal discourses of individualism and choice have bolstered the now-ubiquitous concept of the unique child. However, while this understanding of childhood has allowed and even encouraged parents of diverse political orientations to opt for homeschooling as the ideal educational choice for their children, it would be a mistake to take this as evidence that childhood, under neoliberalism, is uncontested. One of the central contributions of this book has been to demonstrate that we cannot fully understand the influence of neoliberal ideas on children, education, and the family without taking gender and sexuality into account. When we do so, we see that the nature of childhood in the United States under neoliberalism is still very much contested.

Despite the similar, child-intensive parenting practices employed by most of the parents in this study, the point about which parents disagreed most dramatically was the nature of childhood. Although both of the views of childhood discussed in chapter 2 require the intensive involvement of parents, particularly mothers, to ensure that the unique needs of each child are met, we should not let this similarity obscure the fact that there are also important differences in the parenting practices of homeschooling parents. Some parents maintain a strict and authoritarian hierarchy within the family, imposing and enforcing a certain understanding of morality and character upon their children, while other parents attempt to make the home as nonhierarchical a space as possible, giving children a say in what they learn and do, without attempting to restrict access to "forbidden" knowledge. Whereas the former parenting style emphasizes disciplining children through obedience to the parents, the latter emphasizes allowing and encouraging children to develop a sense of personal autonomy—and to respect others' autonomy—from an early age. There are clearly implications for these different parenting styles in terms not only of these children's access to sex education but also in their sexual subject formation and understanding of concepts like consent and bodily autonomy.

More fundamentally, there are consequences to children of being treated only as future adults, who are currently a blank slate to be inscribed upon by their parents. As gender theorist Judith Butler argues, "The reification of the child's body as passive surface would thus constitute, at a theoretical level, a further deprivation of the child: the deprivation of psychic life."[32] In this sense, the ideologies of childhood that the parents I interviewed hold, and the messages that they communicate to their children as a result of these ideologies, cannot be reduced to being understood as two neutral, equally viable options—they are models of childhood that have political consequences, and the potential to produce radical differences in children's lives.

Some of the parents I interviewed saw certain expressions of gender and sexual identity—particularly those that are transgender, gender nonconforming, and nonheterosexual—as sinful or as signs that a person lacks character or virtue. Statistically speaking, it is highly likely that some of these parents were raising children who would one day—or may already—identify outside of the confines of their parents' cisnormative and heteronormative expectations, as we have seen an increased rate in recent years of children "coming out" as lesbian, gay, bisexual, transgender, queer, or otherwise nonheterosexual/noncisgender, and at increasingly younger ages.[33] Research has shown that family acceptance is a key ingredient to the mental and physical health of LGBTQ youth, and that family rejection can hamper positive identity development.[34] I share Bartholet's concern about such children, as I find disturbing the relative isolation of these children, whose social worlds are primarily made up of other religious homeschoolers, from adults who might counter their parents' messages. Similarly, girls in these communities face a barrage of messages about their future only having meaning as a wife and mother, and about their subordinate position in relation to their future husbands, again, without a broader school community to offer alternate messaging. Further research that directly studies the experiences of the children within homeschooling families is certainly needed to fully explore these implications of this isolation.[35]

More broadly, my research raises questions about parents' rights and children's rights, and whether these two are fundamentally in conflict. At the Christian homeschooling conferences I attended, the importance of parents' rights, vis-à-vis the state, was a central theme, and this was echoed in many of my interviews with conservative Christian homeschooling parents. According to this argument, parents—not the state—are given authority by God (and, some argue, the US Constitution) to raise their children as they see fit. With this authority comes responsibility, as God charges parents with providing the best possible education and faith-formation environment for their children, which, due to increasing secular influence on public schools, often means homeschooling.

On the other hand, with the unschooling parents I interviewed, and at the unschooling conference, discussion revolved less around the rights of parents and more around the rights of children. Parents were understood as having the responsibility to protect their children's right to autonomy and self-determination. Whereas the fundamentalist parents and conference speakers constructed children as belonging to their parents (or, as one said, "on loan" to their parents, from God), for the unschooling parents and conference speakers, children were constructed as individual people, belonging primarily to themselves. Thus, while parents have a responsibility to their children to ensure that their autonomy is respected (as much as possible, in a society that does not widely acknowledge children's rights), children do not belong to their parents: they are their own people. When it comes to the lived experiences of children, these are not perspectives of neutral difference. But the dominance of the school-choice paradigm enables these perspectives to coexist, and the nature of childhood and children's rights to remain contested, by allowing parents to pull their children out of school and opt for homeschooling, instead, when they find that their understanding of childhood is not that which schools prioritize.

Conclusion

I return, then, to the question raised by Bartholet and others, with which I opened this chapter: is homeschooling a problem? As a feminist, antiracist sociologist who is committed not just to studying race, gender, class, and sexuality inequalities but to eradicating them, I would answer by saying, "Perhaps, but not (only) for the reasons you think." Homeschooling is just one example of a larger phenomenon in which, enabled by the neoliberal logic of school choice, (some) parents are allowed, encouraged, and enabled to pull their children out of educational environments that they are dissatisfied with—whether due to larger problems with underfunded or violent schools, or due to ideological differences of opinion. School choice reinscribes gender inequality, placing an incredible burden on mothers as they face the expectation that they sacrifice all to manage their children's education, and depoliticizing them in the process, as they are forced to ration their energy by devoting it to their own children, rather than to the common good of all children. School choice also exacerbates racial and class inequalities by deepening school segregation, as race- and class-privileged parents utilize the option of pulling their children out of underfunded public schools, leaving underprivileged children behind. Finally, school choice allows parents who disagree with the principles of inclusivity and democratic pluralism to remove their children from public schooling, leading some children to be denied an education that affirms their autonomy and promotes their ownership of their bodies and their identities. Thus, while a radical reimagining of our nation's priorities, with the rights of children at the core, is needed if we are to protect the children who are made vulnerable by some homeschooling parents, that would not be enough. We also need to resist and dismantle the encroachment of neoliberal logics and policies in all areas of American lives—including, and especially, into the family.

ACKNOWLEDGMENTS

Writing a book is a paradoxical experience: it involves an incredible amount of solo work, yet it can't be done well without a *lot* of support. This is true of any book, but I suspect it's especially true for first books. The community of people that got me to this point extends back in time to long before I began this project, so I have many people, without whom this book never would have existed, to thank here.

First, thank you to my many academic mentors. My entering academia at all would never have happened without Jane Crosthwaite, my undergraduate advisor at Mount Holyoke College, who believed in me long before I believed in myself. Jane thought that I had important things to say, and first pushed me to find my scholarly voice. My mentors at Harvard Divinity School, notably Farid Esack and Susan Abraham, further nurtured this voice, giving me the confidence to continue my academic training. Christine Williams, my advisor and dissertation chair at the University of Texas at Austin, always had more confidence in me than I have ever felt I deserved; my attempts to live up to her belief in me have made me the scholar I am today. Rob Crosnoe, Gloria González-López, Sofian Merabet, and Deb Umberson saw value in my work and gave valuable feedback and encouragement. Other faculty at UT–Austin, especially Simone Browne, Mary Kearney, and Shannon Cavanagh, shaped my thinking in ways that are reflected throughout this book.

I'm incredibly grateful for the support of the UT–Austin Urban Ethnography Lab. Members of the lab provided feedback on pieces of writing that became some of the earliest drafts of chapters of this book, and the lab provided me with the funding to attend my very first homeschooling convention many years ago, as I was just starting to explore my interest in this topic.

At each of the academic institutions I've been a part of, I've had colleagues and friends whose support has been incredibly important to me.

My friends from Mount Holyoke—Anna Allen, Emily Drazen, Alexis McDermott, Meghan Mead, and Leigh Quarles—worked alongside me in the library as I worked on some of my first pieces of academic writing, and to this day are huge sources of support, though that happens now mostly via Marco Polo and group texts. Jeremie Bateman, Rebecca Fullan, Jacob Lau, and Kori Pacyniak were foremost among those at HDS who encouraged me to undertake bold work. My colleagues in the Sociology Department at UT–Austin shaped and challenged my thinking on the topics that are central to this book, served as sounding boards for ideas, helped me create tables and figures, and talked through ideas over coffee, wine, or margaritas; these include Anima Adjepong, Claude Bonazzo, Letisha Brown, Shantel Buggs, Thatcher Combs, Beth Cozzolino, David Glisch-Sánchez, Erika Grajeda, Carmen Gutierrez, Kathy Hill, Kristine Kilanski, Michelle Mott, Pamela Neumann, Emily Paine, Marcos Pérez, Brandon Robinson, Katie Rogers, Vivian Shaw, Lynnette Short, Chelsea Smith, Amanda Stevenson, Allyson Stokes, and so many more.

I'm especially grateful to my very own flamboyance of feminists, the women of Fem(me) Sem 2.0, who started out as grad school colleagues but have become trusted advisors and dear friends. Caity Collins, Megan Neely, and Katie Sobering not only gave detailed feedback on sections of this book at every stage but also provided crucial emotional support and an untold number of pep talks.

I'm grateful to all of my current colleagues at the University at Albany, SUNY, in the Departments of Sociology and Women's, Gender, and Sexuality Studies. Special thanks are due to Jaime Galusha, who may not realize the contribution she has made to this book, but without whose assistance on so many administrative tasks I never would have found the time to write! My intellectual community at UAlbany has supported me in countless ways; I'm especially grateful to Joanna Dreby, Zoya Gubernskaya, Joanne Kaufman, Karyn Loscoco, Zawadi Rucks Ahidiana, Barbara Sutton, Laura Tetrault, and Francisco Vieyra for their support, advice, and friendship throughout this process, and to Erin Baker, HoKwan Cheung, Teniell Trolian, and the rest of the Women who Get Tenure and Drink, for camaraderie and much-needed breaks from writing. The gender and sexualities graduate students at UAlbany have been a part of many conversations that helped me to clarify the ideas in this book. I'm especially grateful to the founding members of the Gender Collective—Ian Callahan, Mairead Carr, Elizabeth Harwood, Jaime Hsu, Griffin Lacy, and Sara Querbes—who push me to be a clearer writer and a more critical scholar.

Thank you to the many sociologists who have encouraged me and provided bits of wisdom as I worked on this project, including Amy Best, Tristan Bridges, Megan Carroll, D'Lane Compton, Cati Connell, Tina Fetner, Jessica Fields, Clare Forstie, Jaime Hartless, Angela Jones, Simone Kolysh, Emily Mann, CJ Pascoe, Carla Pfeffer, Amy Stone, Stacy Torres, Salvador Vidal-Ortiz, Michael Yarborough, and many, many others.

A huge thanks to my editor, Ilene Kalish, whose excitement about this book has carried me through the process of writing and revising it, and to Alexia Traganas, Sonia Tsuruoka, and the entire editorial and production team at NYU Press for turning my manuscript into an actual book.

I would also like to thank all of my respondents, from those who took my survey to those who sat down with me, often inviting me into their own homes, to talk about their homeschooling experiences. I'm especially grateful to the Texas Unschoolers for welcoming me so warmly into their conference space.

I am so lucky to have a wide support network of family and friends across the country who have carried me through the process of researching and writing this book. I especially want to thank Jena DiPinto, Jen Petro-Roy, and Pam Styles, who are among my biggest cheerleaders; I'm so glad to have them as my chosen family. I am also eternally grateful for the encouragement and inspiration given to me by the McIntosh/Jehn family—Janet, Tom, Tobias, and Theo.

There aren't words strong enough to express just how grateful I am for the constant support of my family. Thank you to my mother, Nancy Lane, and my father, Joseph Long, for being my biggest cheerleaders throughout my life, and to my stepmother, Jessica Long, my stepfather, Joe Principato, and my in-laws, Renée and Richard Strait, and Dan Averett and Deborah Dannelley, for enthusiastically joining in the cheering. Renée and Richard deserve special thanks for literally putting a roof over my head while I was doing much of the research for this book. Thank you to my siblings and siblings-in-law—Maureen Long and Tony Fiorini, Patrick and Danielle Long, Betsy and Justin Hirsch, Maeve

Long, and Alexis Averett—and my niblings—Avery McBride, Connor and Caitlin Long, Patrick and Caroline Fiorini, and Nathaniel and Caleb Hirsch—for being a constant source of joy in my life. A special thank you to Tony for taking the gorgeous cover photo for the book, and to Patrick and Caroline for being willing (and, frankly, adorable) models! I'm so lucky to have the support of a huge extended family of aunts, uncles, cousins, and step-everythings; thank you to all of these folks in the extended Lane, Long, Hughes, Martin, and Brownfield families. I am especially grateful for the honorary grandparental figures in my adult life, Charlie Long and Blondie and Charlie Brownfield. Their support as I worked on this project meant the world, and I wish they were here to see the book in print. I miss them all so much.

Last, but certainly not least, my biggest thank you goes to my biggest supporter of all: my wife, Sanden Averett. For believing in me, cheering me on, bragging about my work, and reading and giving feedback on every draft and revision of the book, I could never thank you enough. Thanks for being my person.

APPENDIX

Methodology

STUDY DESIGN: THE USES OF MIXED METHODS FOR RESEARCHING UNDERSTUDIED GROUPS

For this research, I employed a three-part mixed-methods approach.[1] The data gathered include a survey of 676 currently homeschooling parents in Texas, transcripts of qualitative in-depth interviews with a subsample of forty-four of these parents (and two of their spouses) and fieldnotes from these interviews, and fieldnotes from participant observation at five homeschooling conferences held throughout Texas. Because there is little sociological research on homeschooling, the combination of these three methods of data collection allowed me to analyze how the meanings of homeschooling in Texas are produced at the cultural, institutional, and interactional levels of analysis.[2]

The first component of the data collection employed survey methodology to address the specific research question about the correlation between motivations for homeschooling and beliefs about childhood gender and sexuality. I created an online survey using the online survey software Qualtrics. The survey's target population was parents who currently homeschool one or more of their children and who reside in Texas. In addition to demographic questions, the survey asked questions about the family, including each child's educational history and measures of parent-assessed child well-being; homeschooling experiences and approaches; motivations for homeschooling; and political and social views, including, for example, views on same-sex marriage, abortion, school prayer, and sex education. The survey was not intended to provide statistically generalizable information about homeschooling parents in the state of Texas; rather, it allows comparison between, for example, politically conservative and politically liberal parents, and religious and nonreligious parents.

I recruited respondents for the survey primarily by distributing a call for participants through contact with various homeschooling organizations, co-ops, and support groups in Texas. Through extensive Internet research, I identified 218 such organizations that had existing websites and/or contact e-mail addresses, ranging from town- and even neighborhood-specific to statewide groups, with about 60% of these organizations claiming a specifically religious (usually [Protestant] Christian, though occasionally Catholic or LDS [Mormon]) mission or membership. I e-mailed each of these organizations, introducing myself, explaining the purpose of my project, and requesting that they send a call for participants, which I included at the bottom of the e-mail, to their membership list or listserv, or to post the call on their group's website or Facebook page. The survey was administered between July 2014 and April 2015, with the majority of responses occurring during the first two months of data collection, and yielded a total of 676 completed surveys (more detail on the survey methodology, including sample characteristics, can be found below). Survey respondents came from 74 of the 254 counties in Texas (see figure A.1 for geographical distribution of survey responses).

Because the main research questions of this project are questions about meaning- and decision-making processes in the everyday lives of homeschooling families, the second and third components of the research design used qualitative research methods. Using the sample of survey respondents, who indicated at the end of the survey whether they would like to be contacted for a follow-up interview, I created a purposive sample of forty-four parents to be interviewed in person, using semistructured, in-depth interviewing techniques. The purpose of these interviews was to elicit the narratives of homeschool parents regarding how and why they made the decision to homeschool, their homeschooling approaches, and the advantages and disadvantages they see to homeschooling over traditional or public schooling (see interview guide below).

I chose potential interview respondents by creating a spreadsheet of all possible respondents (based on their having indicated on the survey their willingness to participate) and their demographic characteristics and location. Due to logistical constraints on doing in-person interviews in such a large state, the vast majority of my respondents lived within

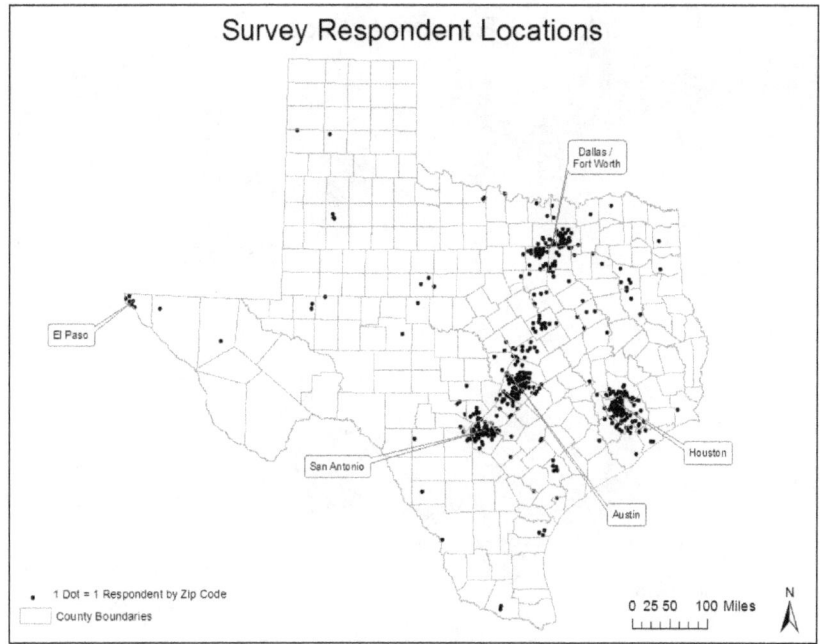

Figure A.1: Survey Respondent Locations (by Zip Code)

an hour and a half drive of at least one of Texas's major cities, including Austin, Dallas, Fort Worth, Houston, and San Antonio (see figure A.2 for geographical distribution of interview respondents). I selected interview respondents in such a way as to collect as diverse a sample as possible (see table A.1 for a comparison of the interview and survey samples). I was particularly interested in having a representation of various political views (conservative, moderate, and liberal) and degrees of religiosity, and thus attempted to initiate contact with roughly equal numbers of conservative and liberal, and religious and nonreligious, respondents: of the forty-four focal interviewees, one quarter (eleven respondents) identified as politically moderate, while 39% (seventeen respondents) identified as conservative or very conservative, and 36% (sixteen respondents) identified as liberal or very liberal. Half of the sample identified as not very or not at all religious, and half identified as somewhat or very religious. It is important to note that in two of the forty-four interviews I conducted, the focal respondent opted to have their spouse take part in the interview as well. Because the survey included some spousal data,

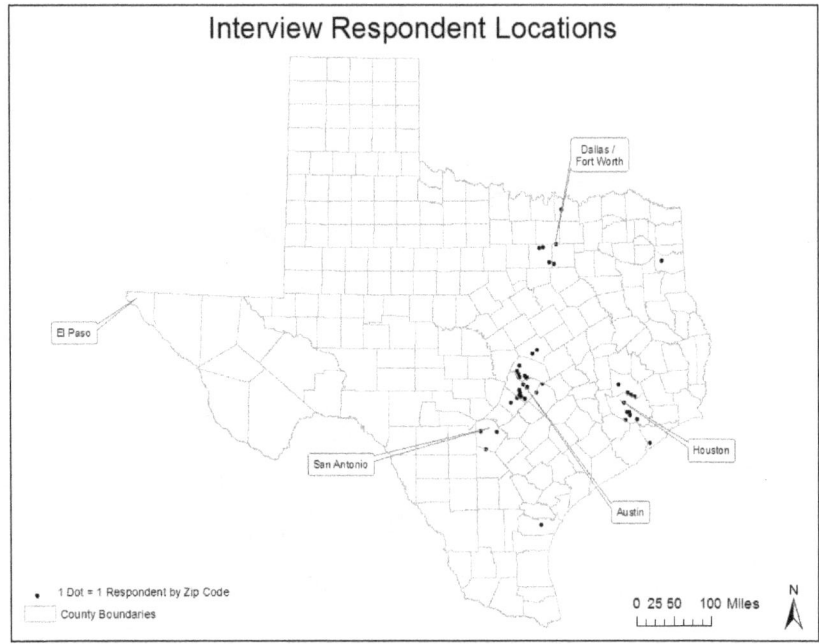

Figure A.2: Interview Respondent Locations (by Zip Code)

I was able to include these spouses in some, but not all, of the demographic totals. Thus, some of these demographics (race, education level, gender, sexual orientation) include all forty-six interviewees, while others are only for the household (income level and marital status, n=44), and others only for the focal respondent (political views and religiosity, n=44).

I also reached out specifically to respondents who, in one or more ways, were not the normative homeschooler, including racial and ethnic minorities, sexual minorities, men, single mothers, and those with low income and/or education. The majority of homeschooling parents in the United States are white (68%) and well educated (69% have at least some college education or a college degree or higher, while 20% have high school diplomas or the equivalent and 11% did not complete high school),[3] and my survey respondents were even more overwhelmingly white (84%) and well educated (31% had completed high school but had not attended or had not completed college, 49% had a college degree, and 20% had graduate degrees). Of my interview respondents, only one respondent had no education past high school, while fourteen had some college, twenty-four had a college degree, and seven had graduate or professional degrees (see table A.1 for comparison of the interview and survey samples).

It was especially important to include nonwhite parents and the parents of nonwhite children in this study. Scholars have noted that race is central to the experience of gendered discipline and violence of public school students in the United States[4] and is central to parents' perceptions of their children's school environment and peer influence;[5] therefore, diversity of race and other demographic characteristics is important in the effort to uncover a wide range of homeschooling motivations and experiences. As a result of these recruiting efforts, the interview sample is more diverse than the survey sample on a number of measures. Thirty-one of my interview respondents were white, seven were Latina, three were Black or African American, one was Asian American, and four identified themselves as mixed race or as having more than one race/ethnicity. Respondents were given an "other" category, in which they were allowed to self-identify, for questions regarding race, gender, and sexual orientation. There are benefits and drawbacks to this method: on the one hand, it allows respondents some flexibility within which they can identify themselves in ways that feel meaningful to themselves, but on the other hand, it makes comparison across groups harder, and it is often difficult to interpret the meaning behind certain self-identifications, such as those who identified as mixed race.

Forty-three of the respondents were women, while only three were men, and forty respondents identified as heterosexual while six (all women) identified as lesbian, gay, or bisexual. While I did not set out to survey and interview primarily mothers, the fact that it was overwhelmingly mothers who responded to my survey and thus were interviewed for this project makes it clear that homeschooling, like healthcare decisions, is largely what Jennifer Reich refers to as a "maternal terrain."[6] Thirty-nine of the households included married couples, and five respondents were single mothers. (See table A.1 for a comparison between the survey and interview samples.)

Of the forty-four households represented in the sample, I classified nine as low income, twenty-seven as middle income, and six as high income. On the survey, respondents were asked to indicate their total household income for the previous year, and were given eight categories of income ranges to choose from. To simplify these income brackets into something that is easier to make sense of in the analysis of the interview data, I used the Pew Research Center's income calculator, which calculates whether a given family is in the low-, middle-, or high-income brackets in the United States relative to household size. For each of my interview respondents, I used the midpoint of the income bracket they selected (e.g., $50,000 for the $40,000–$59,999 bracket) and the size of their particular household (self, spouse [if any], and number of children) and classified each family as low, middle, or high income. This means that some families in the same income bracket on the survey are classified differently; for example, a family of three or four in the $40,000–$59,999 range would be classified as middle income, where a family of five or more in the same bracket would be classified as low income.[7] For the two interviewees who did not provide household income data, I estimated their income level on the basis of my observations of them and their homes during the interview.

I audio recorded each of the in-depth interviews, and transcribed them myself in order to gain intimate familiarity with the interviews as an important first step in the data-analysis process. I then assembled the interview transcripts and fieldnotes from the interviews and used a multistage process of coding to analyze the data, using the qualitative coding software MaxQDA. I first engaged in open coding to identify salient themes; next, I used a focused coding process to group and further refine these themes.[8] Throughout this process I regularly wrote memos concerning themes, questions, and insights that arose from my analysis of the data. This writing played an important role in my analysis, as it provided me with the opportunity to explore ideas and refine my thinking about what I was seeing in the interview data. This allowed me to go back to the data with fresh questions about my analysis, with an eye toward looking for examples of, and exceptions to, the patterns I saw emerging.

The third component of the data collection entailed participant observation at various homeschooling conferences and conventions. I attended five such events—three large, explicitly fundamentalist Christian homeschooling conferences, one small Catholic homeschooling conference, and one small conference of unschoolers—throughout the state of

Texas between August 2013 and April 2015. At these conferences I acted as a participant observer in order to better contextualize the discourses and experiences of homeschooling families as part of larger social movements and discourses. At each conference I participated as a regular registrant, attending various talks, workshops, and special events/performances, and "window shopping" among the vendor areas.

At the three largest conventions, I was largely a "stealth" observer, mostly due to the fact that the conferences were so large that it was easy to move about without much interaction with others. If asked casually by other participants (very uncommon) or by salespeople in the vendor areas (more common), I usually said that I was not a homeschooler, but was interested in learning more about it; if pressed for more information I was willing to offer that I do not currently have any children, and that I was doing research on homeschooling. The few times I interacted with speakers at the conferences, I introduced myself as a scholar studying homeschooling. Because the Catholic conference was much smaller, I expected a larger degree of interaction with other attendees, but actually experienced very little, and these interactions were similarly superficial to those I experienced at the larger conferences.

At the unschooling conference, which was much more community oriented, I e-mailed the conference organizer before I registered, introducing myself and asking if she thought it would be okay to attend. She responded enthusiastically. Because interactions at this conference were more frequent and personal, I was very open about being a researcher with everyone that I met at this conference, including introducing myself to the entire group at the pancake breakfast the first morning (when all individuals and families were invited to introduce themselves). Though I worried that introducing myself as a researcher would make people wary of being around me, I found the opposite to be true: after introducing myself, I was rarely alone for the rest of the conference, as multiple parents sought me out specifically at meals, talks, and breaks to ask questions about my research or offer their own perspectives. Overall, I found the unschooling community to be incredibly welcoming.

With the exception of the Catholic conference, each conference had concurrent sessions and activities from which to choose; when presented with multiple sessions, I looked specifically for sessions that dealt with gender and/or sexuality in some way, as well as for sessions that were about homeschooling more broadly. The talks I attended at the Texas Home School Coalition (THSC) conferences included "Raising Dangerous Sons in a Safe and Mediocre World," "Ten Things to Teach Your Daughter before She Graduates," "Have You Heard about the Common Core?" and "Two Parents, One Purpose." Talks I attended at Great Homeschool Conventions (GHC) included "Child Abuse in the Homeschool World," "The Minds of Girls: Effective Strategies for Teaching Girls," "The Emotional Lives of Boys," "Characteristics of a Lady," and "The Problem with Modern Secular Education." In general, I tended to stay away from more teaching-specific talks that dealt with topics such as teaching math to kindergartners or various approaches to teaching reading. At each of these conferences, whenever possible, I took handwritten notes on the content of the sessions during the talks, also noting things like the size of the room and the number of people attending. At the end of each day—or during breaks, when available—I either typed or audio recorded (and later transcribed) fieldnotes of my impressions of the people in the audience, of the speakers, of the content of the talks, and of any relevant interactions that took place. I then compiled all of my fieldnotes into MaxQDA and engaged in a coding practice similar to that which I undertook with my interview transcripts (see above).

POSITIONALITY AND ACCESS TO THE HOMESCHOOLING COMMUNITY

There are several aspects of my own identity, embodiment, and experience that I believe both facilitated and hindered my ability to recruit and build rapport with the participants needed for this study. Though I am not a parent myself, I have found both in this and in my previous research that, generally, parents are quite willing to speak with me about their children. I have extensive experience working with children and parents as a childcare provider, and I found that this experience was helpful in building rapport with parents and children alike. Additionally, the parents I was interviewing were part of a population that cares a lot—perhaps far more than is typical—about education, so the fact that I was a researcher affiliated with an institution of higher education, rather than, say, a journalist, likely increased the investment some of my respondents felt in the project. Many of my respondents asked about my own educational trajectory and how I became interested in studying homeschooling, and some used that as a way to talk about their own experiences in college and beyond, and what they would study if they could go back and do it all over again. Though I explained to all of my respondents that this was research for a book I planned to write, a few insisted on referring to it as a "class project," with one respondent remarking, "I bet you're the only student in your class studying this!"

At the start of this project, I anticipated that my identity as an openly queer woman might cause me some difficulty in accessing the more fundamentalist religious subset of the population of homeschooling parents, in that it might hinder some parents from participating in the interview portion of the project. While I do not see it as necessary or even appropriate to "reveal" my sexuality to my respondents, because I have in the past, for example, written and published essays and blog posts that deal with sexuality and religion, it is not out of the realm of possibility that potential respondents could, through a simple Google search, find this information on their own. I took some basic steps to make such a search slightly more difficult, such as making my social media accounts private and/or not associated with my full name, but in this day and age, there is only so much one can do to make oneself hard to find online. Of course, it is impossible to know whether anybody did Google me and opt not to participate in the survey or in an interview because of my own sexuality or my "liberal" views on gender and sexuality. That said, I was surprised to find myself, on a few occasions, in the homes of conservative fundamentalist Christian mothers, who spoke to me about their own views on LGBTQ people with what felt to me like an expectation that I would agree with them. Perhaps the fact that I was genuinely interested and even invested in the topic of homeschooling, which for them was experienced as an explicitly Christian phenomenon, led them to assume that I was also a conservative Christian. I often left these interviews feeling uncomfortable and even sad, but as a researcher, I was also grateful that these respondents felt willing to be honest with me about their beliefs.

Other aspects of my identity and embodiment, however, certainly facilitated my access to the homeschooling community. Because homeschooling is a predominantly white phenomenon, and homeschooling spaces, such as the conferences I attended, are very white spaces, my whiteness likely allowed me access both to this field, and to my respondents, that I might not have had otherwise. My whiteness, my relatively gender-normative presentation of self, and my level of education and middle-class status all allowed me to blend in easily at the homeschooling conferences that I attended; not sticking out in the crowd allowed my presence at these conferences to go unquestioned. I did replace my rainbow phone case with a plain teal one while at the religious conferences so as to not signal queerness, and made sure that the clothing I wore would not stand out too much. Some, though certainly not all, religious homeschoolers tend to have an expectation that women will dress "modestly," but it is not exactly hard to keep relatively covered up spending the entire day in a freezing cold, overly air-conditioned conference center! My age surely also played a role in facilitating my access to both the conference spaces and my interview respondents; being in my early thirties during this fieldwork, I was within the normative age range of parents at the conferences I attended, and was also within the age range of my interview respondents, who ranged from their midtwenties to their early sixties. My gender, as well, likely aided in my access to the field—given that homeschooling is a highly female-gendered domain, my presence as a woman did not disrupt this norm in any way.

ISSUES OF TRUST IN STUDYING THE HOMESCHOOLING COMMUNITY

According to homeschooling researcher Joseph Murphy, "Resistance on the part of some of the homeschool community to engage with researchers is legendary."[9] I went into this project aware that developing trust with members of this community would be important to the overall success of the project. Further complicating matters was the fact that the homeschooling community includes people from both extreme ends of the political and ideological spectrum, which itself raised some interesting methodological challenges. In my recruitment materials, and in my interactions with study participants, I had to walk a fine line between appearing knowledgeable about homeschooling and not appearing to clearly favor one approach or the other. One way this came up was in how I constructed my survey questions around gender identity and sexual orientation. If I asked about gender as if gender is a binary with only two options, male and female, I risked alienating queer and transgender parents, and would sacrifice my ability to capture any variation in transgender/cisgender identity. However, if I included more than two gender categories, or asked specifically about transgender or nonbinary identities, I risked "signaling" to more conservative respondents that I had a "liberal," inclusive agenda. In other words, doing this research highlighted that there are methodological difficulties in asking "inclusive" questions, when being inclusive is itself seen as a political act—and where being seen as political risks alienating potential respondents. In the end, I opted to ask how the respondent "identifies their gender," offering three choices for gender: "male," "female," and "other (please specify)." This definitely ended up causing limitations in my analysis, as I do not actually know whether any of my respondents are transgender, because transgender respondents with a binary identity would likely have simply chosen male or female. I also asked for respondents' sexual orientation, giving four options: "straight or heterosexual," "gay or lesbian," "bisexual," and "other (please specify)." I did get some feedback, in the form of a handful of angry-sounding e-mails, that the very fact that I *asked* about sexual orientation caused some people to opt out of the survey, as they felt it was evidence of a liberal, pro-gay agenda. In my fieldwork at fundamentalist conferences, I came to see that gender identity is even more heated a topic within some segments of the homeschooling community than is sexual orientation. Had I included a question about transgender/cisgender identity on the survey, I have little doubt that it would have systematically eliminated a group of my respondents.

I have no way of knowing the characteristics of those who did not take the survey, and whether my various identities, including my sexual identity and feminist identity, played any role in these decisions. It is likely, however, that there were external factors that systematically shaped who did and did not respond to the survey. Several of my respondents revealed to me that my survey had been the subject of (sometimes heated) discussion on the homeschool Facebook pages, message boards, and listservs to which they belonged, and in which my call for participants was posted. These respondents described a general sense of suspicion about my intentions, and a fear that I would use the results to stereotype homeschoolers in certain ways. Interestingly, this was the case with both religious and secular pages and groups.

I also received some direct critical feedback about the project in the form of e-mails from people who had taken (or had started, but did not complete) my survey, accusing me of having a certain agenda or bias in my research. Most of these concerns were in response to the survey questions about social beliefs and ideas about gender and sexuality. For example, one e-mail I received read, "If the survey is about the motivation of homeschoolers, why does it have questions about homosexuality? Please provide the rationale for including these questions. Thank you." At first I assumed that this e-mail was presuming a pro-gay bias on my part, but when I responded to the e-mail with an explanation, the person then responded with a lengthier e-mail, part of which informed me that "you are creating a lot of discussion regarding the motives behind the questions on the survey. Concerns have been expressed that you may be attempting to portray homeschoolers as right winged, intolerant homophobes." An e-mail from another survey respondent was less clear about what they thought my bias was, but accused me of being "disingenuous" in how I was presenting my project: "It seems that your (Kate's) research and papers up to this point all revolve around child sexuality and gender identification. I am wondering how switching to the topic of homeschooling fits in with previous and ongoing work. It appears that your reason for researching homeschooling is disingenuous." Yet another e-mail read as follows: "Your gay liberal slant on homeschooling is disgusting. Many of us are female professionals (straight and proud to be mothers) that educate for academic reasons. I resent your liberal gay or anti gay [sic] slant. This is Texas thank GOD. We live in Texas to get away from this liberal garbage. I am an airline pilot for a major airline that doesn't have to put up with this type of generalization. Get on with your life! And live with the rest of Texas!" This e-mail was very clearly accusing me of having a liberal and (less clearly) pro-gay agenda. I received several such e-mails, including some that indicated that others were having conversations about the purpose of these questions, which prompted me to write the following blog post on the project website explaining the purpose of these questions, which I posted on July 23, 2014:

> SURVEY QUESTIONS AND CONCERNS
> Since I launched the survey less than a week ago I have gotten a lot of responses and a lot of helpful feedback. I am so grateful to those who have taken the survey, forwarded the call for participants, and taken the time to send really thoughtful questions and comments.

Several of the questions that have come up have been about the types of questions on the survey and how they relate to the motivations of the study, and since I imagine these are concerns held by others as well, I wanted to share some reflections that I hope will help clarify people's questions and concerns about the project.

~ ~ ~ ~ ~ ~ ~ ~ ~ ~

Concern #1: You can't possibly learn enough (or anything at all) about homeschooling from this survey!
I completely agree. As a researcher, I believe that a lot of questions or topics—at least the ones that are most interesting—can't be adequately covered by just one method of studying them. The survey is just one part of the overall study—it plays a small, but crucial role.

Part of why the survey is needed is that there just isn't that much research done on homeschooling. One of the few sources of nationally representative data on homeschooling is the report "Parent and Family Involvement in Education, from the National Household Education Surveys Program of 2012," which was published in 2013 by National Center for Education Statistics, which is part of the U.S. Department of Education (you can read the report here).[10] While basic statistics about who homeschools and why don't tell us much about the on-the-ground experience of homeschooling, they do help serve as a backdrop for further research. The survey is short and very basic, not because I think I can learn what I need to from such a short, basic survey, but because I think it can serve as a jumping off point for the rest of the project.

I think that the best way to learn about the social world is to be a part of it—to interact with people and learn from them. That's why the real heart of this study will be the in-person interviews that I do with homeschoolers throughout the state of Texas. It's in these interviews that I will be able to gain a much more rich, detailed, and nuanced understanding of homeschooling. I like to think of the survey as the scaffolding on which the study is built—the story of the study will need this scaffolding to stand, but the scaffolding alone can't tell the story.

Concern #2: The survey doesn't ask the right questions/provide enough response categories.
I've gotten a lot of feedback that the response categories (the "answers" you can choose from for various questions) aren't adequate, or that they

don't capture the things that are important to/reflective of the experiences of a lot of homeschoolers. This feedback is invaluable to me, as it can be extremely helpful in figuring out how to interpret the survey data as well as how I can shift my thinking as the project moves forward.

Some people say that writing surveys is a science, while others say it is an art—I'm not sure which side I fall on, but I definitely think that there is no such thing as a perfect survey. In part, that's because, as I said above, there are lots of things about the social world that you just can't capture by asking multiple choice survey questions. But there are other reasons, too. For example, some of the questions on my survey are exact replicas, or slightly-altered versions, of questions that other researchers have previously used. Re-asking these questions can be really useful, even if the questions themselves aren't perfect, because it lets us compare our findings to other surveys and see what may be changing over time—for example, it used to be assumed that almost all people who homeschooled did so for religious reasons, but recent studies have shown that this isn't the case. If I didn't ask questions about potential religious motivations, I wouldn't be able to add to this bigger conversation.

Some of the questions definitely seem like they are built on outdated assumptions about homeschooling, but by asking these questions and capturing the "other" responses—the things you tell us are missing from the response categories—we (as researchers) will actually be able to say whether these assumptions are outdated, and if they are, construct better ways of asking such questions in the future.

Concern #3: Based on the questions, it seems like you're trying to portray homeschoolers as _____.

We all know that there are various stereotypes out there about homeschooling—that all homeschoolers are very religious, that homeschooling always looks like a mom at the front of the room with a bulletin board and a stack of workbooks and some bored kids, that homeschool children have poor social skills. If I thought that these stereotypes were true—that is, if I thought that all homeschool families looked the same and thought the same and had the same experiences—I wouldn't be doing this research. One of the reasons that I am studying homeschooling is that I believe that people come to homeschooling for many different reasons, and that they go about it in many different ways—in short, that homeschoolers are a diverse and complex group. Part of why I ask questions about political, social, and religious beliefs is to test this theory—that there is great diversity within this movement. I'm sure many of you will think "well obviously there is—you could've just asked one of us and we'd have told you that we're diverse!" But, for better or for worse, that's not how things work in the research world—I need to be able to back up any claims that I make about the diversity of homeschoolers with data gathered from the responses of lots of people. Thus, to be able to dispel any of the stereotypes that exist about homeschooling, I have to ask questions about these very stereotypes.

I will admit that some of the feedback I've gotten on these types of questions has been hard to hear. I hate knowing that I have offended anyone, and I am truly sorry that this has been the case. I want to assure you that my goal with this study is not to portray homeschoolers in a negative light. In fact, my goal isn't really to portray homeschoolers in any particular way at all, but rather, to demonstrate that homeschoolers have a complex and valuable perspective on bigger questions about education, how our society values children, what children need, and who can or should provide it. I don't want this project to be a voyeuristic look at homeschooling—I want it to be about what homeschooling can tell us about our larger society.

Concern 4: The survey doesn't ask anything about the success of homeschool students.

My advisor has had to remind me countless times as I have been preparing to start this research, "you can't do everything." There are so many interesting questions I could ask, so many different angles from which I could approach this project, that I could spend years trying to do it all and still only scratch the surface. I've had to rein in my ideas multiple times in order to make this a project that I can do—and hopefully, do well—in the amount of time I have to complete [the project].

I think that researching the success of homeschool students is a worthwhile endeavor, one that would also help to dispel some of the persistent myths about homeschooling. But that would be a whole other project. The central goal of this project is to be able to better understand how and why parents make the decisions that they do about their children's education, and I've chosen to study that by focusing on parents who have decided to homeschool. I think that homeschooling parents will have a lot to say about what children need to thrive, and about why homeschooling was the option they chose from among many options to provide that for their kids.

~ ~ ~ ~ ~ ~ ~ ~ ~ ~

Your feedback about the project is very valuable to me, so please know how much I appreciate it and that I am taking it to heart as I shape the trajectory of this project. Several people have said that I need to spend more time with homeschoolers to get a better sense of who you are and what you do, and I completely agree—over the next few months I will be looking for and taking any opportunity I can get to meet homeschoolers and hear your stories.

I'm looking forward to having my eyes opened to the richness and complexity of homeschooling families. I am thankful for the generosity of all of you who are willing to help me on this journey.

As with previous research that I have conducted with LGBTQ parents—another nontraditional, often marginalized group of parents—many of my interview respondents asked me "screening questions" before we started the interview. Frequent questions included whether I was a parent, whether I was "in favor of" homeschooling, and whether I planned to homeschool my own children someday. My usual answers to these questions were (1) that I am not a parent, but have spent a lot of time with young children as a childcare provider and an aunt, (2) that homeschooling is a very broad phenomenon, so it is hard for me to say I am "pro-homeschooling" in all its forms, but that I do not consider myself anti-homeschooling, and (3) that I honestly do not know whether I would homeschool my own children, if I have them, someday, but that doing this research has definitely made me consider that question. I even had a thirty-minute phone conversation with the woman who manages one of the largest homeschooling listservs in Texas, in which she asked me these types of screening questions in order to decide whether she would be willing to send my call for survey respondents to the list (apparently, I passed the test, as she sent the announcement out the next day).

I found that my background in the study of religion as well as my experience growing up in a Catholic community with occasional forays into evangelical Christianity (via youth group and Bible study participation with evangelical friends) were assets in building rapport with the more conservative and religious families. I am conversant with, if not fluent in, some of the particular cultural discourses of both Catholic and evangelical Protestant Christianity. By way of example, I attended my first homeschooling conference in the summer of 2013, the annual conference of the Texas Home School Coalition. The THSC is Texas's largest statewide homeschool organization and is explicitly fundamentalist in its ideological leanings. Most of the presentations at the conference began with prayer, and there were frequent references to Bible verses or popular Christian authors or preachers. Because of my past experiences, I understood many of these references, and I felt comfortable interacting with and interpreting the presentations. In interviews, participants would ask me questions such as whether I was familiar with a particular Bible verse or story, or a particular theological concept, and I could honestly answer yes to most of their questions. It is likely that my ability to converse about religion gave these participants a certain sense of ease with me, as if I were "one of them."

On the other hand, I also anticipated that my queer identity would serve as an asset in building rapport with the subset of the population of homeschooling parents who may be homeschooling lesbian, gay, bisexual, transgender, or gender-nonconforming children, who may be more likely to speak with a researcher whom they feel is sympathetic to and supportive of their children's identities. However, none of the parents whom I interviewed explicitly mentioned LGBTQ identity or gender nonconformity as reasons for homeschooling their children, though what I interpreted as veiled references to such were made by a few parents who were concerned that their sons would be bullied due to being very "sensitive" or "emotional" boys. That said, I do believe that my queer and feminist identities influenced my access to the liberal/progressive parents, particularly to unschoolers, as I found that these respondents tended to perceive me as someone who was very open to alternative education. In general, I felt that the majority of my interview respondents, regardless of their political and religious beliefs, assumed that I agreed with them on their critiques of public schools, regardless of what those critiques were.

TABLE A.1: Comparison of Interview and Survey Respondent Characteristics

	Interview Sample[a]	Survey Sample[b]
	n (percent)	n (percent)
Gender		
Male	3 (7%)	15 (2%)
Female	43 (93%)	651 (97%)
Race		
White	31 (67%)	562 (84%)
African American or Black	3 (7%)	12 (2%)
Hispanic or Latino/a	7 (15%)	22 (3%)
Asian or Asian American	1 (2%)	2 (0%)
Native American/American Indian	0 (0%)	0 (0%)
Mixed race/More than one selected	4 (9%)	60 (9%)
Orientation		
Straight or heterosexual	40 (87%)	641 (97%)
Gay or lesbian	2 (4%)	4 (1%)
Bisexual	4 (9%)	15 (2%)
Education Level		
Some high school	0 (0%)	1 (0%)
High school diploma or GED	1 (2%)	20 (3%)
Some college or associate's degree	14 (30%)	188 (28%)
College diploma	24 (52%)	324 (49%)
Master's or professional degree	5 (11%)	112 (17%)
Doctoral degree	4 (2%)	22 (3%)

Table A.1 (cont.)

Yearly Income		
Under $20,000	3 (7%)	18 (3%)
$20,000–$39,999	3 (7%)	44 (7%)
$40,000–$59,999	10 (23%)	87 (14%)
$60,000–$79,999	2 (5%)	96 (15%)
$80,000–$99,999	10 (23%)	114 (18%)
$100,000–$149,999	7 (16%)	185 (29%)
$150,000–$199,999	2 (5%)	55 (8%)
$200,000–$499,999	5 (11%)	37 (6%)
$500,000 or above	0 (0%)	6 (1%)
Marital Status		
Married	39 (87%)	629 (94%)
Partnered (not legally married)	0 (0%)	10 (2%)
Divorced	2 (5%)	16 (2%)
Widowed	0 (0%)	4 (1%)
Single (not partnered/never married)	3 (7%)	9 (1%)
Political Views		
Conservative	17 (39%)	335 (50%)
Moderate	11 (25%)	181 (27%)
Liberal	16 (36%)	149 (22%)
Religiosity		
Nonreligious	22 (50%)	178 (27%)
Religious	22 (50%)	490 (73%)

[a] n=46 for gender, race, orientation, education level, n=44 for all others

[b] n=676

TABLE A.2: Interview Respondent Characteristics

Respondent	Gender	Race/Ethnicity	Sexual Orientation	Education Level
Veronica	Female	White	Heterosexual	Some college
Maria	Female	Hispanic or Latina	Heterosexual	Some college
Maura	Female	White	Heterosexual	College diploma
Sharon	Female	White	Heterosexual	College diploma
Aspen	Female	White	Heterosexual	High school diploma/GED
Erin	Female	White	Heterosexual	Some college
Monica	Female	Hispanic or Latina	Heterosexual	Some college
Holly	Female	White	Heterosexual	Some college
Angie	Female	White	Heterosexual	Master's degree
Cynthia (Donald)	Female (Male)	White (White)	Heterosexual	Some college
Alma	Female	Hispanic or Latina	Heterosexual	College diploma
Julia	Female	White	Heterosexual	College diploma
Margaret	Female	White	Bisexual	College diploma
Janice	Female	White	Heterosexual	Some college
Virginia	Female	White	Heterosexual	Doctoral degree
Melinda	Female	White	Heterosexual	College diploma
Jacqueline	Female	White	Heterosexual	Master's degree
Wendy	Female	White	Heterosexual	Some college
Vanessa	Female	White	Heterosexual	College diploma
Carolyn	Female	White	Bisexual	College diploma
Shannon	Female	Mix*	Heterosexual	Some college
Kelly	Female	White	Gay or lesbian	College diploma
Jenny	Female	White & Hispanic or Latina	Heterosexual	Some college
Allison	Female	White	Heterosexual	Master's degree
Elena	Female	Hispanic or Latina	Heterosexual	Some college
Aaron	Male	White	Heterosexual	College diploma
Catherine	Female	White & Hispanic or Latina & Native American	Heterosexual	College diploma
Claudia	Female	African American or Black	Heterosexual	College diploma
Raya	Female	Asian or Asian American	Heterosexual	Master's degree
Keith (Kamilah)	Male (Female)	White (African American or Black)	Heterosexual	College diploma
Tracy	Female	White & Asian or Asian American & Native Hawaiian	Heterosexual	College diploma
Danielle	Female	White	Heterosexual	College diploma
Jasmine	Female	African American or Black	Heterosexual	College diploma
Mindy	Female	White	Heterosexual	College diploma
Robin	Female	White	Gay or lesbian	Master's degree
Ruth	Female	White	Heterosexual	College diploma
Sonya	Female	White & African American or Black & Native Amer.	Heterosexual	Some college
Jamie	Female	White	Bisexual	Some college
Eva	Female	Hispanic or Latina	Heterosexual	Some college
Anita	Female	Hispanic or Latina	Heterosexual	College diploma
Erica	Female	White	Heterosexual	College diploma
Mia	Female	White	Heterosexual	College diploma
Natalie	Female	White	Heterosexual	College diploma
Dana	Female	White	Bisexual	College diploma

* Self-identification
** Estimated income level; respondent did not provide response to income question.

TABLE A.2 (cont.)

Spouse's Education Level	Income Level	Political Views	Religiosity	# of Children
Some college	Low	Conservative	Very religious	5
Master's degree	Low	Liberal	Somewhat religious	3
College diploma	Middle	Liberal	Not at all religious	2
High school diploma/GED	Middle**	Very conservative	Very religious	1
College diploma	Middle	Very conservative	Not at all religious	2
Some college	Low	Very conservative	Very religious	6
Some college	Middle	Moderate	Not very religious	2
High school diploma/GED	Middle	Very liberal	Not very religious	2
College diploma	High	Liberal	Not at all religious	2
College diploma	Middle	Very conservative	Very religious	2
College diploma	Middle	Moderate	Somewhat religious	2
High school diploma/GED	Middle	Moderate	Not at all religious	3
Some college	Middle	Moderate	Not at all religious	2
Some college	Middle**	Very conservative	Very religious	4
Doctoral degree	High	Conservative	Somewhat religious	4
N/A	Middle	Moderate	Somewhat religious	2
College diploma	Middle	Moderate	Not at all religious	3
High school diploma/GED	Low	Conservative	Very religious	5
Some college	Low	Moderate	Not very religious	4
College diploma	Middle	Very liberal	Not at all religious	3
Some college	High	Moderate	Not at all religious	2
N/A	Middle	Very liberal	Not at all religious	1
Some college	Middle	Liberal	Not at all religious	2
N/A	Middle	Conservative	Very religious	2
Some college	Middle	Conservative	Very religious	2
College diploma	Low	Very conservative	Somewhat religious	3
Some college	Middle	Very liberal	Not at all religious	1
Some college	Middle	Conservative	Very religious	3
Master's degree	Middle	Liberal	Somewhat religious	2
Doctoral degree	High	Moderate	Not very religious	3
Some college	High	Conservative	Very religious	2
Doctoral degree	High	Conservative	Somewhat religious	2
Some college	Middle	Moderate	Very religious	2
N/A	Low	Very liberal	Not at all religious	1
Master's degree	Middle	Very liberal	Not at all religious	2
Master's degree	Middle	Conservative	Very religious	3
Some college	Middle	Very conservative	Very religious	9
College diploma	Middle	Very liberal	Not at all religious	1
Some college	Middle	Very liberal	Somewhat religious	1
College diploma	Middle	Conservative	Very religious	4
Some college	Middle	Liberal	Not at all religious	1
High school diploma/GED	Low	Very liberal	Not at all religious	2
College diploma	Middle	Liberal	Not at all religious	3
N/A	Low	Moderate	Not at all religious	2

Interview Guide

1) Decision to homeschool:
   - Why did you decide to homeschool? (Possible prompts: Was it your first choice of schooling method? Did your children attend other schools first? Did you know other people who homeschooled? What would you say was the most important reason to homeschool?)

2) Homeschool experiences/approaches:
   - There is a lot of variation in the approaches taken to homeschooling. What does homeschooling look like for your family? (Prompts: Do you use a formal curriculum? Do you interact with other homeschool families? Do you teach your child(ren) entirely yourself, or do you use tutors, coaches, or homeschool group classes?)

3) Perspectives on traditional/public education:
   - Did your child(ren) ever attend public schools or any other more traditional school?
     - If yes: What do you think are the advantages of homeschooling? What did you like/not like about the public school?
     - If no: Would you ever consider sending your child to public school? Why or why not?
   - What do you think is currently good about American public education? What do you think is not good?
   - What does an ideal school look like to you? Is homeschooling the ideal, or can you imagine another type of school that would be ideal, if it existed? What does this look like?

4) Sex education:
   - How do you handle sex education as a homeschool parent? What do you think it is important for kids to learn/know about sexuality? What resources do you draw on to help you teach your children about sexuality?

5) Future of homeschooling:
   - What do you think homeschooling as a movement will look like in 20 years? What do you think public acceptance of homeschooling will look like?

6) Sources:
   - What books/articles/blogs etc. have been influential to you or important in shaping your approach to homeschooling?
   - What books would you recommend to a friend who is thinking about starting homeschooling?

7) Is there anything that is important to you about your homeschool experience that I haven't asked you about, that you would like to tell me?

NOTES

INTRODUCTION

1. Isenberg, "What Have We Learned about Homeschooling?"; Murphy, *Homeschooling in America*; McQuiggan, Megra, and Grady, "Parent and Family Involvement in Education."
2. Stevens, *Kingdom of Children*.
3. McQuiggan, Megra, and Grady, "Parent and Family Involvement in Education"; Noel, Stark, and Redford, "Parent and Family Involvement in Education."
4. Spring, *The American School*; Smith, *The Ideology of Education*.
5. Smith, *The Ideology of Education*; Spring, *The American School*; Stevens, "The Normalisation of Homeschooling in the USA."
6. Murphy, *Homeschooling in America*, 2.
7. Duggan, *The Twilight of Equality?*; Harvey, *Brief History of Neoliberalism*. For more detail on the neoliberalization of education, see chapter 4 of this book.
8. Joseph Murphy, in *Homeschooling in America*, argues that homeschooling, once a deviant practice, "is [now] thriving because the essential pillars of society that made it anathema for over a century are being torn down and replaced with scaffolding that supports homeschooling" (54). Murphy concludes that homeschooling is perhaps the most radical expression of the privatization of education.
9. Ariès, *Centuries of Childhood*; Cook, *The Commodification of Childhood*.
10. Zelizer, *Pricing the Priceless Child*.
11. Angelides, "Feminism, Child Sexual Abuse, and the Erasure of Child Sexuality."
12. Homeschooling merges what are generally considered two separate institutional contexts: education and the family. Theorists of gender and childhood emphasize the importance of the institutional context to how children experience and understand gender and sexuality, arguing that gender differs in salience by context. Chodorow, *The Reproduction of Mothering*; Messner, *It's All for the Kids*; Thorne, *Gender Play*.
13. Ferguson, *Bad Boys*; Pascoe, *Dude, You're a Fag*; Thorne, *Gender Play*.
14. Elliott, *Not My Kid*; Pascoe, *Dude, You're a Fag*; Thorne and Luria, "Sexuality and Gender in Children's Daily Worlds"; Thorne, *Gender Play*.
15. Fields, *Risky Lessons*; Pascoe, *Dude, You're a Fag*.
16. Elliott, *Not My Kid*.
17. Zelizer, *Pricing the Priceless Child*.
18. Hays, *The Cultural Contradictions of Motherhood*.

19 For a thoughtful discussion on the various definitions of ideology, see Eagleton, *Ideology*. Here I favor Eagleton's sixth definition of ideology, which sees ideologies as systems of ideas and beliefs that "arise . . . from the material structure of society as a whole" (30). In this vein, revealing the ideologies that structure people's behaviors can help us to understand the material structure of society.
20 Taylor, "Re-Examining Cultural Contradictions."
21 Hays, *The Cultural Contradictions of Motherhood*.
22 Lois, *Home Is Where the School Is*; Murphy, *Homeschooling in America*.
23 Rutherford, *Adult Supervision Required*.
24 Rutherford, *Adult Supervision Required*.
25 Reich, "Neoliberal Mothering and Vaccine Refusal"; Reich, *Calling the Shots*.
26 See appendix for interview guide and more detail about the collection and analysis of the interview data.
27 Eagleton, *Ideology*.
28 Isenberg, "What Have We Learned about Homeschooling?"; Stevens, "The Normalisation of Homeschooling in the USA."
29 Some states require parents to submit curricula and regular progress reports to state or local school officials for review and monitoring, require yearly standardized testing, or even require regular contact with state-certified teachers or tutors. Other states, however, have few, if any, regulations concerning home education.
30 Klicka, "HSLDA—Legal Memorandum on Homeschooling in Texas."
31 THSC, "Leeper Case Decisions."
32 As of 2012, over 7 million of Texas's 26.4 million residents were children under the age of eighteen. It is estimated that approximately 3.2% of school-age children nationwide are homeschooled; if this is representative of the rate in Texas, that would put the number of children in Texas who are currently homeschooled at over two hundred thousand. See US Census Bureau, "Texas QuickFacts from the US Census Bureau," accessed February 27, 2014. quickfacts.census.gov; and Noel, Stark, and Redford, "Parent and Family Involvement in Education."

CHAPTER 1. HOMESCHOOLING IN THE UNITED STATES

1 It is true that many prominent figures in American history were educated, at least in part, at home. As Wilhelm and Firmin note, "The first colonists home educated their children out of necessity, since settlement schools were not yet established" (306). However, many scholars, including Gaither and Murphy, argue that there is not a clear through line between these early Americans and today's homeschoolers. Wilhelm and Firmin, "Historical and Contemporary Developments in Home School Education"; Gaither, "The History of Homeschooling"; Gaither, *Homeschool*; Gaither, "Homeschooling in the USA"; Murphy, *Homeschooling in America*.
2 Murphy, *Homeschooling in America*; Gaither, "Homeschooling and the Home School Legal Defense Association"; Gaither, "The History of Homeschooling."

3 Gaither, "Homeschooling and the Home School Legal Defense Association"; Hess and Okun, "Home Schooling"; Gaither, *Homeschool*.
4 Gaither, "The History of Homeschooling."
5 The most well known and influential of Holt's early writings are *How Children Fail* and *How Children Learn*.
6 Gaither, "Homeschooling and the Home School Legal Defense Association."
7 Gaither, "Homeschooling and the Home School Legal Defense Association."
8 Gaither, "Homeschooling and the Home School Legal Defense Association."
9 Murphy, *Homeschooling in America*; Stevens, *Kingdom of Children*.
10 Wilhelm and Firmin, "Historical and Contemporary Developments in Home School Education."
11 Research on the diffusion of homeschooling legislation carried out by Tal Levy demonstrated that states with higher degrees of school segregation had a decreased likelihood of adopting pro-homeschooling legislation, while states with a larger presence of Christian fundamentalists had an increased likelihood of passing homeschooling legislation. While there are other possible explanations for this finding, one potential explanation that Levy proposes is that homeschooling advocates may have been more likely to push for such legislation when responding to school desegregation (levels of which peaked in the 1980s, when much of this legislation was passed). Historian Randall Balmer argues that contrary to the popular belief that the rise of the religious Right can be traced to the Supreme Court ruling on abortion in *Roe v. Wade*, the driving force behind its rise was actually school desegregation. Thus, it makes sense that homeschooling, as a practice popularized by the religious Right, would have these racially motivated undertones. Levy, "Homeschooling and Racism"; Balmer, "The Real Origins of the Religious Right."
12 Gaither, "Homeschooling and the Home School Legal Defense Association"; Gaither, "The History of Homeschooling."
13 Gaither, "Homeschooling and the Home School Legal Defense Association."
14 Gaither, "Homeschooling and the Home School Legal Defense Association."
15 While many scholars (e.g., Hess and Okun, Kolenc) have noted that all three of these cases were important to the eventual legalization of homeschooling, Krause argues that *Yoder* was actually less important, as almost every legal case mounted by homeschoolers that cited *Yoder* as precedent failed due to the extremely limited case upon which that decision was based. Hess and Okun, "Home Schooling"; Krause, "Homeschooling: Constructing or Deconstructing Democracy"; Kolenc, "Legal Issues in Homeschooling."
16 Wilhelm and Firmin, "Historical and Contemporary Developments in Home School Education."
17 THSC, "Leeper Case Decisions"; Krause, "Homeschooling: Constructing or Deconstructing Democracy."
18 Krause, "Homeschooling: Constructing or Deconstructing Democracy."

19 My interviews with parents who lived in or near Texas's cities supported this notion of a bifurcated movement. In these cities, there was a large enough population of homeschoolers that it was easy for families to limit their interactions with those who had very different philosophical approaches to homeschooling. For example, most of the homeschool co-ops to which my respondents described belonging were either religious co-ops, which required parents to sign a statement of faith to join, or were explicitly secular co-ops. There were some self-identified Christian homeschoolers who belonged to secular co-ops, but these parents spoke of explicitly valuing openness to multiple worldviews with their children—in other words, their approach to homeschooling did not strike me as being fundamentalist in orientation. The handful of families I interviewed who lived in smaller towns or more rural areas, however, were more likely to talk about interacting with families who had very different beliefs than they did, because the homeschooling population in these areas was too small for it to be divided into different factions. Because religious homeschooling seemed to be the dominant form in these locations, secular homeschooling parents spoke about the discomfort they sometimes experienced fitting into more explicitly faith-based groups.
20 Murphy, *Homeschooling in America*.
21 Templeton and Johnson place homeschooling regulations in US states into four tiers: high, moderate, low, and no regulation. They classify ten US states (Alaska, Connecticut, Idaho, Illinois, Indiana, Michigan, Missouri, New Jersey, Oklahoma, and Texas) and two US territories (Guam and Puerto Rico) in the lowest tier (no regulation). See Templeton and Johnson, "Homeschool Learners."
22 Klicka, "HSLDA—Legal Memorandum on Homeschooling in Texas."
23 The Home School Legal Defense Association, a conservative Christian organization dedicated to the rights of homeschooling parents across the United States and worldwide, maintains a comprehensive database of homeschooling regulations across all fifty states and many other countries. See, for example, Home School Legal Defense Association, "New York Homeschool Law."
24 Templeton and Johnson classify six US states as high regulation (Massachusetts, North Dakota, New York, Pennsylvania, Rhode Island, and Vermont). The majority of US states fall into either the moderate regulation (twenty states and two US territories) or low regulation (fourteen states and one US territory) tiers. Templeton and Johnson, "Homeschool Learners."
25 The Coalition for Responsible Home Education, for example, is a group of homeschool alumni who advocate for greater oversight of homeschooling. See Coalition for Responsible Home Education, "Homeschooling & Educational Neglect." Other groups, such as the Texas Home School Coalition, argue that any regulation of homeschooling is an encroachment on parents' rights. See Pace, "THSC Speaks Out against Regulation."
26 See, for example, Jones, "The Turpins Won't Be the Last." Responding to the nationally publicized case of David and Louise Turpin, whose thirteen severely

malnourished and physically abused children were rescued from their California home in early 2018, Jones argues that California's lack of oversight of homeschool families (requiring them to register with the state, but not much else) enabled the couple's severe abuse.

27 Templeton and Johnson, "Homeschool Learners."
28 Murphy has an extensive discussion of research into the different types of homeschooling in chapter 6 of his book. See Murphy, *Homeschooling in America*.
29 Murphy, *Homeschooling in America*.
30 Templeton and Johnson, "Homeschool Learners."
31 Templeton and Johnson, "Homeschool Learners."
32 For a thorough discussion of "eclectic" and other types of homeschooling approaches, see Templeton and Johnson, "Homeschool Learners."
33 Parents of high school–age homeschoolers frequently noted the importance of creating transcripts for their children to use if and when they applied to college, which raised questions about what "counts" as a class or credit, particularly given that the context of learning could often look quite different for homeschoolers than for their public-school peers.
34 Lubienski, Puckett, and Brewer, "Does Homeschooling 'Work'?"
35 Hess and Okun, "Home Schooling"; Lubienski, Puckett, and Brewer, "Does Homeschooling 'Work'?"; Murphy, "The Social and Educational Outcomes of Homeschooling."
36 Hess and Okun, "Home Schooling."
37 Hess and Okun, "Home Schooling."
38 Data from the NCES estimate that the percentage of school-aged children in the United States being homeschooled increased from 1.7% in 1999 to 2.7% in 2007 and to 3.3% in 2016. See Bielick, "1.5 Million Homeschooled Students in the United States in 2007"; McQuiggan, Megra, and Grady, "Parent and Family Involvement in Education."
39 Murphy, *Homeschooling in America*.
40 Isenberg, "What Have We Learned about Homeschooling?"; Ray, "Homeschooling Rising into the Twenty-first Century"; Murphy, *Homeschooling in America*.
41 McQuiggan, Megra, and Grady, "Parent and Family Involvement in Education."
42 DiPerna, "Moms and School Survey."
43 Murphy, *Homeschooling in America*.
44 Murphy, *Homeschooling in America*; Templeton and Johnson, "Homeschool Learners."
45 Hess and Okun, "Home Schooling."
46 McQuiggan, Megra, and Grady, "Parent and Family Involvement in Education"; Noel, Stark, and Redford, "Parent and Family Involvement in Education."
47 Bielick, "1.5 Million Homeschooled Students in the United States in 2007."
48 Noel, Stark, and Redford, "Parent and Family Involvement in Education"; McQuiggan, Megra, and Grady, "Parent and Family Involvement in Education."
49 Fields-Smith, "Homeschooling among Ethnic-Minority Populations."

50 Redford, Battle, and Bielick, "Homeschooling in the United States: 2012"; McQuiggan, Megra, and Grady, "Parent and Family Involvement in Education."
51 Mazama and Lundy, "African American Homeschooling and the Quest for a Quality Education"; Ray, "African American Homeschool Parents' Motivations for Homeschooling."
52 Fields-Smith, "Homeschooling among Ethnic-Minority Populations."
53 Mazama and Lundy, "African American Homeschooling as Racial Protectionism"; Fields-Smith and Kisura, "Resisting the Status Quo"; Ray, "African American Homeschool Parents' Motivations for Homeschooling."
54 Mazama and Lundy, "African American Homeschooling and the Question of Curricular Cultural Relevance"; Mazama and Lundy, "African American Homeschooling and the Quest for a Quality Education"; Fields-Smith, "Homeschooling among Ethnic-Minority Populations."
55 Fields-Smith, "Homeschooling among Ethnic-Minority Populations."

CHAPTER 2. WHAT IS CHILDHOOD?

1 Perhaps nowhere is the salience of this question more evident than in current debates about transgender children in schools: what names and pronouns to call them by, what bathrooms they should use, or even whether children can "know" their own gender. Here are a sampling of recent news and opinion pieces covering aspects of this debate: Orso, "Philadelphia May Soon Require All Charter Schools, Youth Organizations to Accommodate Trans Kids"; Sullivan, "When the Ideologues Come for the Kids"; Bracho-Sanchez, "Transgender Teens in Schools with Bathroom Restrictions"; Packer, "When the Culture War Comes for the Kids"; Truong, "In a Virginia School, a Celebration of Transgender Students in a Kindergarten Class."
2 Cook, *The Commodification of Childhood*; Ariès, *Centuries of Childhood*.
3 Zelizer, *Pricing the Priceless Child*.
4 Fields, *Risky Lessons*.
5 Chodorow, *The Reproduction of Mothering*; Messner, *It's All for the Kids*; Thorne, *Gender Play*.
6 Chodorow, *The Reproduction of Mothering*; Elliott, *Not My Kid*; Martin, "Normalizing Heterosexuality"; Martin and Luke, "Gender Differences in the ABC's of the Birds and the Bees."
7 Ferguson, *Bad Boys*; Pascoe, *Dude, You're a Fag*; Thorne and Luria, "Sexuality and Gender in Children's Daily Worlds"; Thorne, *Gender Play*.
8 Elliott, *Not My Kid*.
9 Martin and Luke argue that parents of pre-school-age children talk about sexuality with their children in gendered ways, and that, in part, this is evidence that children are socialized to the idea of a sexual double standard, in which girls are expected to maintain a higher standard of sexual purity than boys, beginning very early in childhood. Janice's comment here indicates that even parents who expect

abstinence from sons as well as daughters understand the stakes of protecting daughters' innocence to be particularly high. See Martin and Luke, "Gender Differences in the ABC's of the Birds and the Bees."

10 See, for example, Martin, "Normalizing Heterosexuality"; Martin and Kazyak, "Hetero-Romantic Love and Heterosexiness in Children's G-Rated Films"; Renold, "'Coming Out'"; Renold, "Presumed Innocence."

11 In speaking about the desire to delay the transition from child to adult as long as possible, these parents engage, and reify, the adult/child binary, which is an ideological construction used to demarcate children and adults as separate and different populations. See Elliott, *Not My Kid*.

12 Thanks to the family's reality TV success, Michelle Duggar made a name for herself, both within and outside fundamentalist Christian circles, as something of an expert on Christian child rearing. One year after I attended Michelle's talk at the THSC convention, however, her status as an expert in raising virtuous children was called into question when news broke that the Duggars' eldest child, Josh, had, as a teenager, molested several girls, including some of his sisters. The incidents in question occurred in 2002, before the family's first television special was ever filmed, and was "handled" by the family's church community, with the involvement of at least one law enforcement officer. It was not until media outlets broke the story open in 2015 that the family's then popular reality television show, *19 Kids and Counting*, was canceled.

13 Schalet, *Not under My Roof*.

14 Maria is identifying a theme in one of several competing discourses about adolescent girls' sexuality, exemplified by psychologist Deborah Tolman's finding that girls' experience and understanding of their own sexuality and sexual desire is very much shaped by their social location and experiences. See Tolman, "Doing Desire."

15 For a discussion of how this hierarchy within schools impacts children's relationships with one another in negative, even violent ways, see Klein, *The Bully Society*.

16 Scholars of sexuality have long noted the use of two prominent, contrasting discourses about (particularly) women's/girl's sexuality: a "danger discourse," which focuses on the risks associated with sex (such as pregnancy, STIs, and sexual violence) and a "pleasure discourse," which focuses on sexual desire, gratification, and joy. For an excellent discussion of the ways these discourses feature in US children's sexual educations, see Fields, *Risky Lessons*.

17 Robertson, *Growing Up Queer*, 6.

18 Ahmed, *Queer Phenomenology*, 23.

19 "Compulsory heterosexuality" is a term used to describe the way in which heterosexuality is both assumed and enforced in patriarchal, heteronormative societies. The term was popularized by feminist scholar Adrienne Rich in a now-classic essay, first published in 1980. See Rich, "Compulsory Heterosexuality and Lesbian Existence."

CHAPTER 3. EDUCATING THE UNIQUE CHILD

1 Zelizer, *Pricing the Priceless Child*.
2 Stevens, *Kingdom of Children*, 185.
3 For a discussion of how diagnoses of "invisible disabilities" often overlap, see Blum, *Raising Generation Rx*.
4 Blum, *Raising Generation Rx*, 249.
5 As Allison explained to me, all but one of the kindergarten classes met in a very large room with half-walls delineating where each class was. While this made the classrooms feel much less restrictive, she explained, it also made the environment loud and very distracting, especially for students with attention difficulties.
6 Reich, "Neoliberal Mothering and Vaccine Refusal."
7 Blum, *Raising Generation Rx*, 4.
8 Blum, *Raising Generation Rx*, 4.
9 Blum, *Raising Generation Rx*.
10 As noted in the introduction, Texas is one of several states that does not require homeschooled students to take any form of standardized test or assessment. While most of the parents I spoke with were against changing this, a few did note that they saw the merit in having at least some oversight to keep what they saw as the minority of homeschooled children who were not actually being educated from falling through the cracks. Whether and to what degree homeschooling should be regulated is a hot topic of debate among Texas homeschoolers, and among homeschoolers nationally; for a summary of this debate, see Michels, "A House Divided."
11 Public schools in the United States are required under the Individuals with Disabilities Education Improvement Act of 2004 (IDEA) to develop an IEP for students with disabilities. See *Wikipedia* contributors, "Individualized Education Program." For the official definition of the Individualized Education Plan, see Section 300.320 of Title 34 of the Code of Federal Regulations: US Government Publishing Office, "Code of Federal Regulations: Title 34—Education."
12 See Rutherford, *Adult Supervision Required*; Reich, *Calling the Shots*.
13 Michel Foucault argues that schools are a space in which children's docile bodies—bodies "that may be subjected, used, transformed, and improved"—are trained, or "disciplined," such that they internalize the very means of their own domination. As education theorist Nirmala Erevelles notes, critical education theorists have used this concept "to describe how bodies are inscribed by the dominant cultural practices of schools" through processes in which students learn how to experience their bodies—much like the "cookie cutter" analogy Allison used above. Erevelles writes that in schools, "Students learn the importance of disciplining their bodies so as not to distract from the 'mental efforts' of the mind. In an attempt to control these 'disruptive excesses' of unruly bodies, schools have developed elaborate practices that support" the disciplining of students' bodies. Children who, for one reason or another, cannot or do not "control [their]

disruptive excesses" thus become a problem to be managed, as they cause a rupture in these processes—including "the rigid organizing of classroom space and time, the overriding emphasis on discipline, and the careful monitoring of the curriculum"—that support the disciplining of all students' bodies and thus the functionality of the classroom environment. In short, like Mia's son Joey, Ethan was an unruly, as opposed to docile, body in the classroom. Foucault, *Discipline and Punish*, 136; Erevelles, "Educating Unruly Bodies," 33.

14 Reich, "Neoliberal Mothering and Vaccine Refusal," 685.
15 Reich, "Neoliberal Mothering and Vaccine Refusal," 679.
16 Pugh, *The Tumbleweed Society*, 157.
17 Zelizer, *Pricing the Priceless Child*, 10.
18 Zelizer, *Pricing the Priceless Child*, 222.
19 Hays, *The Cultural Contradictions of Motherhood*.
20 Reich, "Neoliberal Mothering and Vaccine Refusal"; Blum, *Raising Generation Rx*; Cairns, Johnston, and MacKendrick, "Feeding the 'Organic Child'"; Villalobos, *Motherload*.
21 Hays, *The Cultural Contradictions of Motherhood*; Zelizer, *Pricing the Priceless Child*.
22 Roberts, *Killing the Black Body*.

CHAPTER 4. VIEWS OF EDUCATION

1 Harvey, "Neoliberalism as Creative Destruction."
2 Rooks, *Cutting School*.
3 Maranto et al., *School Choice in the Real World*; Spring, *The American School*; Stevens, "The Normalisation of Homeschooling in the USA."
4 Duggan, *The Twilight of Equality?*, x.
5 Duggan, *The Twilight of Equality?*, 14.
6 Cairns, Johnston, and MacKendrick, "Feeding the 'Organic Child'"; Reich, "Neoliberal Mothering and Vaccine Refusal"; Wilson and Yochim, "Mothering through Precarity."
7 Rutherford, *Adult Supervision Required*.
8 Davies and Bansel, "Neoliberalism and Education"; Smith, *The Ideology of Education*.
9 Connell, "The Neoliberal Cascade and Education"; Davies and Bansel, "Neoliberalism and Education"; Gabbard and Atkinson, "Stossel in America."
10 Connell, "The Neoliberal Cascade and Education," 108.
11 Connell, "The Neoliberal Cascade and Education"; Davies and Bansel, "Neoliberalism and Education."
12 Baltodano, "Neoliberalism and the Demise of Public Education."
13 Smith, *The Ideology of Education*.
14 Baltodano, "Neoliberalism and the Demise of Public Education"; Connell, "The Neoliberal Cascade and Education."

15 Brown, "Neo-Liberalism and the End of Liberal Democracy"; Davies and Bansel, "Neoliberalism and Education."
16 Baltodano, "Neoliberalism and the Demise of Public Education."
17 Connell, "The Neoliberal Cascade and Education," 107–8.
18 Baltodano, "Neoliberalism and the Demise of Public Education"; Connell, "The Neoliberal Cascade and Education"; Gabbard and Atkinson, "Stossel in America"; Endacott et al., "Robots Teaching Other Little Robots."
19 Griffith and Smith, *Mothering for Schooling*.
20 Shuffelton, "How Mothers Divide the Apple Pie."
21 Migliaccio and Raskauskas, *Bullying as a Social Experience*.
22 Migliaccio and Raskauskas, *Bullying as a Social Experience*, 5.
23 Klein, *The Bully Society*; Payne and Smith, "LGBTQ Kids, School Safety, and Missing the Big Picture"; Pascoe, *Dude, You're a Fag*; Pascoe, "Notes on a Sociology of Bullying"; Salmivalli, "Bullying and the Peer Group."
24 Renold, "'If You Don't Kiss Me, You're Dumped'"; Renold, "Presumed Innocence"; Pascoe, *Dude, You're a Fag*; Pascoe, "Notes on a Sociology of Bullying."
25 Renold, "Learning the 'Hard' Way."
26 Klein, "An Invisible Problem"; Klein, *The Bully Society*; Payne, "Sluts."
27 Renold, "'If You Don't Kiss Me, You're Dumped'"; Pascoe, *Dude, You're a Fag*.
28 Payne and Smith, "LGBTQ Kids, School Safety, and Missing the Big Picture"; Payne and Smith, "Gender Policing."
29 Cairns, Johnston, and MacKendrick, "Feeding the 'Organic Child'"; Reich, "Neoliberal Mothering and Vaccine Refusal."
30 See Lareau, *Unequal Childhoods*.
31 Reich, "Neoliberal Mothering and Vaccine Refusal," 681.
32 Gorman and Sandefur, "'Golden Age,' Quiescence, and Revival."
33 Gorman and Sandefur, "'Golden Age,' Quiescence, and Revival."
34 Timmermans and Oh, "The Continued Social Transformation of the Medical Profession"; Light, "Health-Care Professions, Markets, and Countervailing Powers."
35 Ozga, "Deskilling a Profession"; Endacott et al., "Robots Teaching Other Little Robots."
36 Chakraborty, "Deskilling of the Teaching Profession."
37 Davies and Bansel, "Neoliberalism and Education"; Forrester, "Professional Autonomy versus Managerial Control."
38 Chakraborty, "Deskilling of the Teaching Profession"; Forrester, "Professional Autonomy versus Managerial Control"; Moloney, "Teaching to the Test"; Wong, "Control and Professional Development."
39 Moloney, "Teaching to the Test"; Endacott et al., "Robots Teaching Other Little Robots"; Allington, *Big Brother and the National Reading Curriculum*.
40 See Endacott et al., "Robots Teaching Other Little Robots"; and Weiner, "A Lethal Threat to U.S. Teacher Education." The most thorough and compelling analysis I have read of Teach for America (TFA) and other "alternate credentialing" programs can be found in Rooks, *Cutting School*. Rooks's discussion of such pro-

grams lays out in clear detail the links between TFA, privately managed charter schools, and the hedge fund industry, making it clear just how profitable—for a select few—the school choice "industry" is.
41 Forrester, "Professional Autonomy versus Managerial Control," 139.
42 Endacott et al., "Robots Teaching Other Little Robots"; Forrester, "Professional Autonomy versus Managerial Control."
43 Moloney, "Teaching to the Test."

CHAPTER 5. GIVING UP ON GOVERNMENT

1 Dalton, "The Social Transformation of Trust in Government."
2 "The ANES Guide to Public Opinion and Electoral Behavior."
3 Cook and Gronke, "The Skeptical American."
4 Sheingate, "Why Can't Americans See the State?"
5 Sheingate, "Why Can't Americans See the State?," 2.
6 Sheingate, "Why Can't Americans See the State?," 11.
7 Sheingate, "Why Can't Americans See the State?"
8 Rudolph and Evans, "Political Trust, Ideology, and Public Support for Government Spending."
9 Rudolph and Evans, "Political Trust, Ideology, and Public Support for Government Spending," 668.
10 In other chapters, I note participants' race, socioeconomic status, sexual orientation, and marital status when I first introduce them. I break with this convention in this chapter, because the focus of the chapter, views of government, makes it helpful to know the participants' political views and levels of religiosity, as reported on the survey taken by each interviewee. Political views are described as very conservative, conservative, moderate, liberal, or very liberal, based on responses to the question, "How would you describe your political views?" Religiosity is based on responses to the question, "How important is religion in your life?" Respondents are reported as very religious if they responded "very important," somewhat religious if they responded "somewhat important," not very religious if they responded "not that important," and nonreligious if they responded "not at all important."
11 I am not sure to what electoral "controversy" Danielle was referring here, as Obama handily won both the popular vote and the electoral college over Republican opponent John McCain in the 2008 presidential election (Obama received 52.93% of the popular vote, compared to McCain's 45.65%, and Obama secured 365 electoral college votes, which was well over McCain's 173 as well as the 270-vote threshold needed to win the election). It is possible that she was referring to what has become known as "birtherism," or the (false) belief, as propagated by Donald J. Trump, that President Obama was not born in the United States. See *Wikipedia* contributors, "2008 United States Presidential Election"; Kessler, "Birtherism and the Deployment of the Trumpian Mind-Set."

12 Kamilah was the parent who filled out the survey, and she identified herself there as moderate. While Keith did not fill out the survey, he referred to himself as a liberal during the interview.
13 It is important to note that not all Christians are against teaching evolution in school, and in fact, many Christians believe in evolution. Similarly, not all Christians believe that the Bible condemns homosexuality. For more, see Baker, "Acceptance of Evolution and Support for Teaching Creationism in Public Schools"; Thomas and Olson, "Evangelical Elites' Changing Responses to Homosexuality."
14 It is worth noting that the words "under God" were not actually added to the Pledge of Allegiance until 1954. See Lipka, "5 Facts about the Pledge of Allegiance."
15 The idea behind "creation science" is that the tools of science can be used to demonstrate that the biblical worldview is true. The creation museum, for example, uses dinosaur fossils prominently in its exhibits, but argues that, because the earth is only some seven thousand years old, dinosaurs and man coexisted on the earth. The museum's website boasts that it employs "real creation scientists," who have PhDs and "teach about anatomy, astronomy, biology, geology, and more from a biblical worldview." See "Creation and Science."
16 For a discussion of the recent increase in opposition by conservative/fundamentalist Christians to the involvement of scientists and scientific perspectives in public debates, see Evans, "The Growing Social and Moral Conflict between Conservative Protestantism and Science."
17 According to a 2013 report by the Pew Research Center, about 33% of Americans reject the idea of evolution, but this rate varies widely by religious denomination, with 64% of white evangelical Protestants, 50% of Black Protestants, and 15% of white mainline Protestants rejecting evolution. Pew Research Center, "Public's Views on Human Evolution."
18 Golding, *Lord of the Flies*.
19 Rudolph and Evans, "Political Trust, Ideology, and Public Support for Government Spending."
20 The Common Core is a set of common academic standards for the United States. Common Core was implemented in 2010 at the federal level with the cooperation of most US states, and as of August 2015, it had been adopted by forty-two US states and several US territories. Common Core Standards Initiative, "Development Process: Common Core State Standards Initiative." The implementation of Common Core has been controversial, with several states who had initially adopted the standards rejecting and replacing them. Criticisms of the Common Core standards have been widespread and multiple, from the content of the standards and the "new" pedagogical methods to the financial interests of some of the parties involved in their design and implementation. Robelen, "Common Core." Interestingly, Texas is one of the states that has *not* adopted the Common Core standards.
21 Freedom Project USA, "Who We Are."

22 The National Sexuality Education Standards: Core Content and Skills, K–12, is a document that was published in 2012 by the Future of Sex Education Initiative (FoSE) and the *Journal of School Health* and was compiled by representatives of a number of organizations. It is intended to lay out minimum curricular standards for comprehensive sexuality curricula. While the FoSE website notes that the standards are currently in use in thirty-two states, I can find no evidence that the federal government has required its adoption. See Future of Sex Education Initiative, "National Sexuality Education Standards Core Content and Skills"; "What Is FoSE"; Barr et al., "Improving Sexuality Education."

23 We can understand the frequent use of the metaphor of homeschooling as being under attack as a "frame," which social movements scholar James Jasper, in *Protest*, defines as "a kind of underlying metaphor that includes diagnosis of a problem, suggests solutions, and hopefully motivates action" (50). In this case, the diagnosed problem is that Christianity is under attack from secular, science-oriented, and sexually liberal forces, and that public schools are a main site at which this battle is taking place. Frames, Jasper explains, are intimately connected to, and help to produce, collective identities: "If frames tend to diagnose the problems that need to be fixed, collective identities suggest the group that is supposed to fix them" (51). Character tropes, such as heroes, villains, victims, and minions, shape the moral arc of this metaphor. The homeschooling community is cast here as both the victim and the hero of this battle story; more specifically, its children are cast as the victims, and the parents as the heroes who save their children from the villain—in this case, the government and those who determine the national education agenda—and its minions, the public schools and those who work in them, including "bystanders" who do nothing to stop the attack.

24 Ben Carson, a retired neurosurgeon known for his conservative social views, did, in fact, enter the large pool of Republican primary candidates for the 2016 presidential election, but suspended his campaign shortly after Super Tuesday, announcing that he would become the new chairman of My Faith Votes, a national organization that seeks to encourage Christians to vote. Carson would later go on to become President Donald Trump's secretary of Housing and Urban Development. See Kopan, "Ben Carson Ends Campaign."

CHAPTER 6. MOTHERHOOD AND THE GENDERED LABOR OF HOMESCHOOLING

1 Hays, *The Cultural Contradictions of Motherhood*; see also Zelizer, *Pricing the Priceless Child*.
2 Hays, *The Cultural Contradictions of Motherhood*, 177.
3 Taylor, "Re-Examining Cultural Contradictions."
4 Lois, *Home Is Where the School Is*.
5 Pugh, *The Tumbleweed Society*, 168.
6 Pugh, *The Tumbleweed Society*, 9.
7 Hays, *The Cultural Contradictions of Motherhood*.

8 Gould, *Moving Politics*, 3.
9 Jasper, *Protest*, 60.
10 Department for Professional Employees Research Department, "School Administrators"; Hegewisch et al., "Separate and Not Equal?"
11 See Pevey, Williams, and Ellison, "Male God Imagery and Female Submission."
12 Hays, *The Cultural Contradictions of Motherhood*; England, "Emerging Theories of Care Work"; Collins, *Making Motherhood Work*; Sanchez and Thomson, "Becoming Mothers and Fathers"; Ridgeway, *Framed by Gender*; Yavorsky, Kamp Dush, and Schoppe-Sullivan, "The Production of Inequality."
13 Sears and Sears, *The Attachment Parenting Book*.
14 Villalobos, *Motherload*.
15 For more on the association of organic food with mothering philosophies, see Cairns, Johnston, and MacKendrick, "Feeding the 'Organic Child.'"
16 Of course, it is not only women who experience pregnancy and childbirth, and not all mothers give birth to their children. See Charter et al., "The Transgender Parent"; and Walks, "Chestfeeding as Gender Fluid Practice" for more on the experiences of transgender and nonbinary people with pregnancy and breastfeeding/chestfeeding. That said, the majority of people who give birth do identify as women/mothers, so Carolyn is correct in her assertion that pregnancy and breastfeeding, and the social meanings that we give to these practices, do play a role in shaping larger patterns of gender inequality. See Averett, "Queer Parents, Gendered Embodiment, and the De-Essentialization of Motherhood" for a thorough discussion of the literature on the relationship between mothering and gender inequality.
17 Collins, *Making Motherhood Work*; Stone, *Opting Out?*
18 Of the forty-four interviews I conducted, in only one family (Keith and Kamilah) did the father do more of the day-to-day homeschooling labor than the mother. In this case, although both parents were employed, Keith worked from home and had far more flexibility in his work, whereas Kamilah worked outside the home. However, as a physician working at a hospital, Kamilah did not work a typical nine-to-five schedule. This resulted in her being able to be involved with the day-to-day parenting work to a higher degree than she might have had she had a more typical work schedule.
19 For more on how the first jobs that many American youth hold—babysitting, for many girls, and paper routes or mowing lawns, for boys—contribute to gender inequality later in life, see Besen-Cassino, *The Cost of Being a Girl*.
20 Hochschild, *The Second Shift*.
21 Goffman, *The Presentation of Self in Everyday Life*.
22 Hegewisch et al., "Separate and Not Equal?"; Correll, Benard, and Paik, "Getting a Job"; Benard and Correll, "Normative Discrimination and the Motherhood Penalty"; Gough and Noonan, "A Review of the Motherhood Wage Penalty."
23 Besen-Cassino, *The Cost of Being a Girl*.
24 Wade, "The Invisible Worry Work of Mothering."

25 Sociologist Susan Walzer was among the first to describe the phenomenon of gender inequality in the thinking work of parenting. See Walzer, "Thinking about the Baby."
26 The American Time Use Survey is a widely used, ongoing national study that uses the time diary method and is often used in research that demonstrates the changing, but ongoing, nature of gender inequality in household labor in the United States. For more on the study and its measures, see Frazis and Stuart, "Where Does the Time Go?"; and Phipps and Vernon, "Twenty-four Hours." For an excellent visualization of gender inequality in household labor, see US Bureau of Labor Statistics, "American Time Use Survey."
27 See Averett, "The Gender Buffet."
28 See, for example, Kohn, *The Case against Standardized Testing*; Kohn, *Punished by Rewards*—the latter of which is perhaps Kohn's most famous book, and certainly the book of his that was most frequently recommended to me by unschooling parents over the course of this research.
29 In her research on mothers and "vaccine refusal," Jennifer Reich argues that this practice is, in fact, one in which mothers see themselves as the ultimate experts on their own children. She also argues that vaccine refusal acts as a symbolic form of boundary making that creates community through the avoidance of "others" who might expose their children to disease. Reich, "Neoliberal Mothering and Vaccine Refusal"; Reich, *Calling the Shots*.
30 Reich, "Neoliberal Mothering and Vaccine Refusal"; Reich, *Calling the Shots*.
31 Shuffelton, "How Mothers Divide the Apple Pie."
32 This is consistent with Reich's finding in her study of vaccine refusal that parents prioritize the needs of their individual child over the needs of the many, seeing it as unethical to "sacrifice" their own child's well-being. See Reich, *Calling the Shots*.

CONCLUSION

1 Mineo, "Law School Professor Says There May Be a Dark Side of Homeschooling"; O'Donnell, "The Risks of Homeschooling."
2 The summit, "Homeschooling Summit: Problems, Politics, and Prospects for Reform," was scheduled to be held June 18–19, 2020, but was postponed due to the COVID-19 pandemic. At the time of this writing, the event had yet to be rescheduled. See Harvard Law School, "Homeschooling Summit: Problems, Politics, and Prospects for Reform."
3 AERO, "Harvard Attack on Homeschooling?"; AERO, "Harvard Attacks Homeschooling Again!"
4 Bufkin, "Harvard to Host Event Aimed at Criminalizing Homeschooling."
5 Bartholet, "Homeschooling"; Mineo, "Law School Professor Says There May Be a Dark Side of Homeschooling." There are some clear flaws in Bartholet's argument, at least as it is presented in the interview with Mineo, including that she implies that the majority of homeschoolers are religious ideologues and that she implies that we know that abuse in the homeschooling community is widespread,

which we do not (for the same reason that we do not know, as she notes, that homeschooled students are "successful," educationally; because homeschoolers are a hard-to-access, uncounted, and understudied group, we simply do not have good representative data on many aspects of homeschooling). That said, I agree with Bartholet's assertion that stricter oversight of homeschoolers would at least mitigate some of the potential abuse, mistreatment, and educational neglect that certainly does take place in the homeschooling community. I also agree with her assessment that the strict protection of parents' rights and the general lack of acknowledgment of children's rights under US law means that implementing such oversight would be difficult.

6 I place the term "homeschooled" in scare quotes here because it is not clear that the Turpins were actually providing any sort of education for their children. That said, they used the guise of homeschooling as a means of getting away with abusing their children. See Rios, "A California Couple Abused Their 13 Kids."
7 Westover, *Educated*.
8 Homeschooling's Invisible Children, "Some Preliminary Data on Homeschool Child Fatalities."
9 Coalition for Responsible Home Education, "Homeschooling & Educational Neglect."
10 "Creation and Science."
11 For an excellent discussion of the debate in the United States about the use of corporal punishment, see Demby, "Is Corporal Punishment Abuse? Why That's a Loaded Question."
12 The Home School Legal Defense Association, or HSLDA, is an organization that provides legal support for homeschooling families and lobbies for parents' right to homeschool, both in the United States and worldwide. They are an explicitly Christian organization, as are their offshoot organizations, such as Generation Joshua. Generation Joshua is a teen-focused program that, according to its website, "wants America to be a beacon of biblical hope to the world around us. We seek to inspire every one of our members with faith in God and a hope of what America can become as we equip Christian citizens and leaders to impact our nation for Christ and for His glory." See Homeschool Legal Defense Association, "Our Related Organizations and Strategic Partners"; Generation Joshua, "About."
13 Mineo, "Law School Professor Says There May Be a Dark Side of Homeschooling."
14 Throughout this book, I have demonstrated that the narratives of homeschooling parents are constructed through and around a variety of ideologies about childhood, motherhood, education, and the state. The language these parents use amounts to ideologies, I argue, because they are "organized around a set of ideas, normative claims, and value structures that have an emotional component influencing their usage and appeal" and are internalized by these parents in a way that gives meaning to their experiences. Johnston and Taylor, "Feminist Consumerism and Fat Activists," 944; see also Fegan, "'Ideology' after 'Discourse'"; Ferree and Merrill, "Hot Movements, Cold Cognition."

15 Mineo, "Law School Professor Says There May Be a Dark Side of Homeschooling."
16 Duggan, *The Twilight of Equality?*; Harvey, "Neoliberalism as Creative Destruction"; Harvey, *Brief History of Neoliberalism*.
17 Harvey, "Neoliberalism as Creative Destruction," 31.
18 Villalobos, *Motherload*.
19 This entrenchment of inequalities is not an accidental side effect of neoliberalism. As David Harvey has argued, the story of neoliberalism in the United States has always been a story of the restoration of power to class elites. See Harvey, "Neoliberalism as Creative Destruction."
20 Rooks, *Cutting School*, 101–2; see also Grady and Hoffman, "Segregation Academies."
21 Grady and Hoffman, "Segregation Academies"; Dowland, *Family Values and the Rise of the Christian Right*; Bagley, "School Desegregation"; Gaither, "Why Homeschooling Happened."
22 Levy, "Homeschooling and Racism."
23 Rooks, *Cutting School*, 12–13.
24 Rooks, *Cutting School*, 3.
25 Hagerman, *White Kids*.
26 Hagerman, *White Kids*, 207.
27 "Opportunity hoarding" is a term used to describe the phenomenon in which privileged members of a society (those whom a stratified system has endowed with power to control resources) monopolize a resource, keeping others from accessing it. See Massey, *Categorically Unequal*.
28 Collins, *Black Feminist Thought*.
29 This particular insight arose for me while hearing Patricia Hill Collins speak during an invited session at the 2018 annual meeting of the American Sociological Association. In asking the audience to reflect on our embodied commitments to resisting white supremacy, she called out those who can turn their back on "other people's children." Collins's words during this panel have informed my thinking on white motherhood, perhaps more than any other single text. Collins, "Former ASA Presidents Reflect on Race and Emotion."
30 Sarkisian and Gerstel, *Nuclear Family Values, Extended Family Lives*.
31 Mazama and Lundy, "African American Homeschooling as Racial Protectionism."
32 Butler, *Undoing Gender*.
33 Dunlap, "Changes in Coming Out Milestones across Five Age Cohorts."
34 Durwood, McLaughlin, and Olson, "Mental Health and Self-Worth in Socially Transitioned Transgender Youth"; Olson et al., "Mental Health of Transgender Children"; Simons et al., "Parental Support and Mental Health among Transgender Adolescents"; Bregman et al., "Identity Profiles in Lesbian, Gay, and Bisexual Youth"; Ryan et al., "Family Acceptance in Adolescence and the Health of LGBT Young Adults."
35 While I am not aware of any academic research on this topic, my less-scientific explorations of the issue have led me to believe that my hunch about the potential

damaging effects of the isolation of children in fundamentalist homeschooling communities has weight. In particular, the "ex-vangelical" movement, which took off on social media in 2018, has done a lot to expose the negative experiences of the gendered, sexual, and racialized messages within these communities. For anyone interested, I recommend spending some time perusing the tags #exvangelical and #exposechristianhomeschooling on social media.

APPENDIX

1. This research was approved by the Institutional Review Board at the University of Texas at Austin.
2. This approach was modeled after the methodological approaches taken by Mignon Moore, in her study of Black sexual-minority women, and Mark Padilla, in his study of gay sex tourism. Both Moore and Padilla employed a mixed-methods approach that included quantitative survey data, interviews, and participant observation in order to create multifaceted data about understudied groups and phenomena. See Moore, *Invisible Families*; Padilla, *Caribbean Pleasure Industry*.
3. Noel, Stark, and Redford, "Parent and Family Involvement in Education."
4. Ferguson, *Bad Boys*.
5. Elliott, *Not My Kid*.
6. Reich, "Neoliberal Mothering and Vaccine Refusal."
7. Fry and Kochhar, "Are You in the American Middle Class?"
8. Emerson, Fretz, and Shaw, *Writing Ethnographic Fieldnotes*.
9. Murphy, *Homeschooling in America*, 14.
10. Noel, Stark, and Redford, "Parent and Family Involvement in Education."

BIBLIOGRAPHY

AERO. "Harvard Attack on Homeschooling." E-mail newsletter, April 25, 2020.
———. "Harvard Attacks Homeschooling Again!" E-mail newsletter, May 16, 2020.
Ahmed, Sara. *Queer Phenomenology: Orientations, Objects, Others*. Durham, NC: Duke University Press, 2006.
Allington, Richard L., ed. *Big Brother and the National Reading Curriculum: How Ideology Trumped Evidence*. Portsmouth, NH: Heinemann, 2002.
Angelides, Steven. "Feminism, Child Sexual Abuse, and the Erasure of Child Sexuality." *GLQ: A Journal of Lesbian and Gay Studies* 10, no. 2 (January 1, 2004): 141–77. https://doi.org/10.1215/10642684-10-2-141.
Ariès, Philippe. *Centuries of Childhood: A Social History of Family Life*. New York: Knopf, 1962.
Averett, Kate Henley. "Queer Parents, Gendered Embodiment, and the De-Essentialization of Motherhood." *Feminist Theory* (forthcoming).
———. "The Gender Buffet: LGBTQ Parents Resisting Heteronormativity." *Gender & Society* 30, no. 2 (April 2016): 189–212. https://doi.org/10.1177/0891243215611370.
Bagley, Joseph Mark. "School Desegregation, Law and Order, and Litigating Social Justice in Alabama, 1954–1973." PhD diss., Georgia State University, 2014.
Baker, Joseph O. "Acceptance of Evolution and Support for Teaching Creationism in Public Schools: The Conditional Impact of Educational Attainment." *Journal for the Scientific Study of Religion* 52, no. 1 (March 1, 2013): 216–28. https://doi.org/10.1111/jssr.12007.
Balmer, Randall. "The Real Origins of the Religious Right." *Politico Magazine*, May 27, 2014. www.politico.com.
Baltodano, Marta. "Neoliberalism and the Demise of Public Education: The Corporatization of Schools of Education." *International Journal of Qualitative Studies in Education* 25, no. 4 (June 1, 2012): 487–507. https://doi.org/10.1080/09518398.2012.673025.
Barr, Elissa M., Eva S. Goldfarb, Susan Russell, Denise Seabert, Michele Wallen, and Kelly L. Wilson. "Improving Sexuality Education: The Development of Teacher-Preparation Standards." *Journal of School Health* 84, no. 6 (2014): 396–415. https://doi.org/10.1111/josh.12156.
Bartholet, Elizabeth. "Homeschooling: Parent Rights Absolutism vs. Child Rights to Education and Protection." *Arizona Law Review* 62, no. 1 (2019). https://doi.org/10.2139/ssrn.3391331.

Benard, Stephen, and Shelley J. Correll. "Normative Discrimination and the Motherhood Penalty." *Gender & Society* 24, no. 5 (October 1, 2010): 616–46. https://doi.org/10.1177/0891243210383142.

Besen-Cassino, Yasemin. *The Cost of Being a Girl: Working Teens and the Origins of the Gender Wage Gap.* Philadelphia: Temple University Press, 2018.

Bielick, Stacey. "1.5 Million Homeschooled Students in the United States in 2007." Issue Brief. National Center for Education Statistics, 2008. https://doi.org/10.1037/e609712011-006.

Blum, Linda M. *Raising Generation Rx: Mothering Kids with Invisible Disabilities in an Age of Inequality.* New York: NYU Press, 2015.

Bracho-Sanchez, Edith. "Transgender Teens in Schools with Bathroom Restrictions Are at Higher Risk of Sexual Assault, Study Says." *CNN Health* (blog), May 6, 2019. https://www.cnn.com/2019/05/06/health/trans-teens-bathroom-policies-sexual-assault-study/index.html.

Bregman, Hallie R., Neena M. Malik, Matthew J. L. Page, Emily Makynen, and Kristin M. Lindahl. "Identity Profiles in Lesbian, Gay, and Bisexual Youth: The Role of Family Influences." *Journal of Youth and Adolescence* 42, no. 3 (March 1, 2013): 417–30. https://doi.org/10.1007/s10964-012-9798-z.

Brown, Wendy. "Neo-Liberalism and the End of Liberal Democracy." *Theory & Event* 7, no. 1 (2003): 1–43. https://doi.org/10.1353/tae.2003.0020.

Bufkin, Ellie. "Harvard to Host Event Aimed at Criminalizing Homeschooling." *Townhall*, April 22, 2020. townhall.com.

Butler, Judith. *Undoing Gender.* New York: Routledge, 2004.

Cairns, Kate, Josée Johnston, and Norah MacKendrick. "Feeding the 'Organic Child': Mothering through Ethical Consumption." *Journal of Consumer Culture* 13, no. 2 (July 1, 2013): 97–118. https://doi.org/10.1177/1469540513480162.

Chakraborty, Sarbani. "Deskilling of the Teaching Profession." In *Sociology of Education: An A-to-Z Guide,* edited by James Ainsworth. Thousand Oaks, CA: Sage, 2013. https://doi.org/10.4135/9781452276151.n106.

Charter, Rosie, Jane M. Ussher, Janette Perz, and Kerry Robinson. "The Transgender Parent: Experiences and Constructions of Pregnancy and Parenthood for Transgender Men in Australia." *International Journal of Transgenderism* 19, no. 1 (2018): 64–77. https://doi.org/10.1080/15532739.2017.1399496

Chodorow, Nancy J. *The Reproduction of Mothering: Psychoanalysis and the Sociology of Gender.* 2nd ed. Berkeley: University of California Press, 1999.

Coalition for Responsible Home Education. "Homeschooling & Educational Neglect." Accessed March 24, 2020. responsiblehomeschooling.org.

Collins, Caitlyn. *Making Motherhood Work: How Women Manage Careers and Caregiving.* Princeton, NJ: Princeton University Press, 2019.

Collins, Patricia Hill. *Black Feminist Thought: Knowledge, Consciousness, and the Politics of Empowerment.* New York: Routledge, 2000.

———. "Former ASA Presidents Reflect on Race and Emotion." Presented at the American Sociological Association Annual Meeting, Philadelphia, August 12, 2018.

Common Core State Standards Initiative. "Development Process: Common Core State Standards Initiative." Accessed March 17, 2016. www.corestandards.org.

Connell, Raewyn. "The Neoliberal Cascade and Education: An Essay on the Market Agenda and Its Consequences." *Critical Studies in Education* 54, no. 2 (2013): 99–112. https://doi.org/10.1080/17508487.2013.776990.

Cook, Daniel Thomas. *The Commodification of Childhood: The Children's Clothing Industry and the Rise of the Child Consumer*. Durham, NC: Duke University Press, 2004.

Cook, Timothy E., and Paul Gronke. "The Skeptical American: Revisiting the Meanings of Trust in Government and Confidence in Institutions." *Journal of Politics* 67, no. 3 (August 2005): 784–803. https://doi.org/10.1111/j.1468-2508.2005.00339.x.

Correll, Shelley J., Stephen Benard, and In Paik. "Getting a Job: Is There a Motherhood Penalty?" *American Journal of Sociology* 112, no. 5 (March 1, 2007): 1297–1339. https://doi.org/10.1086/511799.

"Creation and Science." Creation Museum. Accessed September 29, 2019. creationmuseum.org.

Dalton, Russell J. "The Social Transformation of Trust in Government." *International Review of Sociology* 15, no. 1 (March 2005): 133–54. https://doi.org/10.1080/03906700500038819.

Davies, Bronwyn, and Peter Bansel. "Neoliberalism and Education." *International Journal of Qualitative Studies in Education* 20, no. 3 (May 1, 2007): 247–59. https://doi.org/10.1080/09518390701281751.

Demby, Gene. "Is Corporal Punishment Abuse? Why That's a Loaded Question." *NPR. Org* (blog), September 19, 2014. https://www.npr.org/sections/codeswitch/2014/09/19/349668828/a-decision-about-your-children-thats-also-about-your-parents.

Department for Professional Employees Research Department. "School Administrators: An Occupational Overview." *Department for Professional Employees—AFL-CIO*, 2014. dpeaflcio.org.

DiPerna, Paul. "Moms and School Survey: Nationwide Public Opinion on Schooling." Polling Paper. The Friedman Foundation for Educational Choice, 2012. files.eric.ed.gov.

Dowland, Seth. *Family Values and the Rise of the Christian Right*. Philadelphia: University of Pennsylvania Press, 2015.

Duggan, Lisa. *The Twilight of Equality? Neoliberalism, Cultural Politics, and the Attack on Democracy*. Boston: Beacon Press, 2003.

Dunlap, Andy. "Changes in Coming Out Milestones across Five Age Cohorts." *Journal of Gay & Lesbian Social Services* 28, no. 1 (January 2, 2016): 20–38. https://doi.org/10.1080/10538720.2016.1124351.

Durwood, Lily, Katie A. McLaughlin, and Kristina R. Olson. "Mental Health and Self-Worth in Socially Transitioned Transgender Youth." *Journal of the American Academy of Child & Adolescent Psychiatry* 56, no. 2 (February 1, 2017): 116–23.e2. https://doi.org/10.1016/j.jaac.2016.10.016.

Eagleton, Terry. *Ideology: An Introduction*. London: Verso, 1991.

Elliott, Sinikka. *Not My Kid: What Parents Believe about the Sex Lives of Their Teenagers*. New York: NYU Press, 2012.
Emerson, Robert M., Rachel I. Fretz, and Linda L. Shaw. *Writing Ethnographic Fieldnotes*. Chicago: University of Chicago Press, 1995.
Endacott, Jason L., Ginney P. Wright, Christian Z. Goering, Vicki S. Collet, George S. Denny, and Jennifer Jennings Davis. "Robots Teaching Other Little Robots: Neoliberalism, CCSS, and Teacher Professionalism." *Review of Education, Pedagogy, and Cultural Studies* 37, no. 5 (October 20, 2015): 414–37. https://doi.org/10.1080/10714413.2015.1091258.
England, Paula. "Emerging Theories of Care Work." *Annual Review of Sociology* 31, no. 1 (2005): 381–99. https://doi.org/10.1146/annurev.soc.31.041304.122317.
Erevelles, Nirmala. "Educating Unruly Bodies: Critical Pedagogy, Disability Studies, and the Politics of Schooling." *Educational Theory* 50, no. 1 (March 1, 2000): 25–47. https://doi.org/10.1111/j.1741-5446.2000.00025.x.
Evans, John H. "The Growing Social and Moral Conflict between Conservative Protestantism and Science." *Journal for the Scientific Study of Religion* 52, no. 2 (June 1, 2013): 368–85. https://doi.org/10.1111/jssr.12022.
Fegan, Eileen. "'Ideology' after 'Discourse': A Reconceptualization for Feminist Analyses of Law." *Journal of Law and Society* 23, no. 2 (1996): 173–97. https://doi.org/10.2307/1410415.
Ferguson, Ann Arnett. *Bad Boys: Public Schools in the Making of Black Masculinity*. Ann Arbor: University of Michigan Press, 2000.
Ferree, Myra Marx, and David A. Merrill. "Hot Movements, Cold Cognition: Thinking about Social Movements in Gendered Frames." *Contemporary Sociology* 29, no. 3 (2000): 454–62. https://doi.org/10.2307/2653932.
Fields, Jessica. *Risky Lessons: Sex Education and Social Inequality*. New Brunswick, NJ: Rutgers University Press, 2008.
Fields-Smith, Cheryl. "Homeschooling among Ethnic-Minority Populations." In *The Wiley Handbook of Home Education*, edited by Milton Gaither, 207–21. New York: Wiley, 2016.
Fields-Smith, Cheryl, and Monica Wells Kisura. "Resisting the Status Quo: The Narratives of Black Homeschoolers in Metro-Atlanta and Metro-DC." *Peabody Journal of Education* 88, no. 3 (2013): 265–83. https://doi.org/10.1080/0161956X.2013.796823.
Forrester, Gillian. "Professional Autonomy versus Managerial Control: The Experience of Teachers in an English Primary School." *International Studies in Sociology of Education* 10, no. 2 (July 2000): 133–51. https://doi.org/10.1080/09620210000200056.
Foucault, Michel. *Discipline and Punish: The Birth of the Prison*. 2nd ed. New York: Vintage Books, 1995.
Frazis, Harley, and Jay Stuart. "Where Does the Time Go? Concepts and Measurement in the American Time Use Survey." In *Hard-to-Measure Goods and Services: Essays in Honor of Zvi Griliches*, edited by Ernst R. Berndt and Charles R. Hulten, 73–97. Chicago: University of Chicago Press, 2007.
Freedom Project USA. "Who We Are." Freedom Project Academy, 2016. www.fpeusa.org.

Fry, Richard, and Rakesh Kochhar. "Are You in the American Middle Class? Find Out with Our Income Calculator." *Pew Research Center* (blog), December 9, 2015. http://www.pewresearch.org/fact-tank/2015/12/09/are-you-in-the-american-middle-class/.

Future of Sex Education Initiative. "National Sexuality Education Standards Core Content and Skills, K–12. A Special Publication of the Journal of School Health." 2012.

Gabbard, David, and Terry Atkinson. "Stossel in America: A Case Study of the Neoliberal/Neoconservative Assault on Public Schools and Teachers." *Teacher Education Quarterly* 34, no. 2 (2007): 85–109.

Gaither, Milton. *Homeschool: An American History*. Rev. 2nd ed. New York: Palgrave Macmillan, 2017. https://doi.org/10.1057/978-1-349-95056-0.

———. "Homeschooling and the Home School Legal Defense Association." In *Encyclopedia of Educational Reform and Dissent*, edited by Thomas Hunt, James Carper, Thomas Lasley, and C. Raisch. Thousand Oaks, CA: Sage, 2010. https://doi.org/10.4135/9781412957403.n209.

———. "Homeschooling in the USA Past, Present, and Future." *Theory and Research in Education* 7, no. 3 (November 1, 2009): 331–46. https://doi.org/10.1177/1477878509343741.

———. "The History of Homeschooling." In *The Wiley Handbook of Home Education*, edited by Milton Gaither, 7–31. New York: Wiley, 2016. ebookcentral.proquest.com.

———. "Why Homeschooling Happened." *Educational Horizons* 86, no. 4 (2008): 226–37.

Generation Joshua. "About." Accessed May 30, 2020. generationjoshua.org.

Goffman, Erving. *The Presentation of Self in Everyday Life*. Garden City, NY: Doubleday, 1959.

Golding, William. *Lord of the Flies*. London: Faber and Faber, 1954.

Gorman, Elizabeth H., and Rebecca L. Sandefur. "'Golden Age,' Quiescence, and Revival: How the Sociology of Professions Became the Study of Knowledge-Based Work." *Work and Occupations* 38, no. 3 (2011): 275–302. https://doi.org/10.1177/0730888411417565.

Gough, Margaret, and Mary Noonan. "A Review of the Motherhood Wage Penalty in the United States." *Sociology Compass* 7, no. 4 (2013): 328–42. https://doi.org/10.1111/soc4.12031.

Gould, Deborah B. *Moving Politics: Emotion and Act Up's Fight against AIDS*. Chicago: University of Chicago Press, 2009. www.press.uchicago.edu.

Grady, Marilyn, and Sharon Hoffman. "Segregation Academies Then and School Choice Configurations Today in Deep South States." *Contemporary Issues in Educational Leadership* 2, no. 2 (2018): 1–25. https://doi.org/10.32873/unl.dc.ciel.1009.

Griffith, Alison I., and Dorothy E. Smith. *Mothering for Schooling*. New York: RoutledgeFalmer, 2005.

Hagerman, Margaret A. *White Kids: Growing Up with Privilege in a Racially Divided America*. New York: NYU Press, 2018.

Harvard Law School. "Homeschooling Summit: Problems, Politics, and Prospects for Reform—June 18–19, 2020." Child Advocacy Program, November 4, 2019. cap.law.harvard.edu.

Harvey, David. *Brief History of Neoliberalism*. Oxford: Oxford University Press, 2005.
———. "Neoliberalism as Creative Destruction." *Annals of the American Academy of Political and Social Science* 610, no. 1 (March 2007): 21–44. https://doi.org/10.1177/0002716206296780.
Hays, Sharon. *The Cultural Contradictions of Motherhood*. New Haven, CT: Yale University Press, 1996.
Hegewisch, Ariane, Hannah Liepmann, Jeff Hayes, and Heidi Hartmann. "Separate and Not Equal? Gender Segregation in the Labor Market and the Gender Wage Gap." Briefing Paper. Washington, DC: Institute for Women's Policy Research, September 2010.
Hess, Frederick M., and Joleen R. Okun. "Home Schooling." In *Encyclopedia of Education*, edited by James W. Guthrie, 3:1060–63. New York: Macmillan Reference USA, 2003. Gale Virtual Reference Library. link.galegroup.com.
Hochschild, Arlie Russell. *The Second Shift*. 2nd ed. New York: Penguin Books, 2003.
Holt, John. *How Children Learn*. New York: Pitman, 1964.
Holt, John Caldwell. *How Children Fail*. New York: Dell, 1964.
Home School Legal Defense Association. "New York Homeschool Law." Accessed April 24, 2018. hslda.org.
———. "Our Related Organizations and Strategic Partners." Accessed May 30, 2020. hslda.org.
Homeschooling's Invisible Children. "Some Preliminary Data on Homeschool Child Fatalities." Accessed March 24, 2020. hsinvisiblechildren.org.
Isenberg, Eric J. "What Have We Learned about Homeschooling?" *Peabody Journal of Education* 82, no. 2–3 (2007): 387–409. https://doi.org/10.1080/01619560701312996.
Jasper, James M. *Protest: A Cultural Introduction to Social Movements*. Malden, MA: Polity Press, 2014.
Johnston, Josée, and Judith Taylor. "Feminist Consumerism and Fat Activists: A Comparative Study of Grassroots Activism and the Dove Real Beauty Campaign." *Signs: Journal of Women in Culture and Society* 33, no. 4 (June 2008): 941–66. https://doi.org/10.1086/528849.
Jones, Sarah. "The Turpins Won't Be the Last." *New Republic*, January 18, 2018. newrepublic.com.
Kessler, Luba. "Birtherism and the Deployment of the Trumpian Mind-Set." In *The Dangerous Case of Donald Trump: 37 Psychiatrists and Mental Health Experts Assess a President*, edited by Bandy X. Lee, 261–67. New York: St. Martin's, 2019.
Klein, Jessie. "An Invisible Problem: Everyday Violence against Girls in Schools." *Theoretical Criminology* 10, no. 2 (May 1, 2006): 147–77. https://doi.org/10.1177/1362480606063136.
———. *The Bully Society: School Shootings and the Crisis of Bullying in America's Schools*. New York: NYU Press, 2012.
Klicka, Christopher J. "HSLDA—Legal Memorandum on Homeschooling in Texas." Home School Legal Defense Association, 2011. /www.hslda.org.
Kohn, Alfie. *Punished by Rewards*. Boston: Houghton Mifflin, 1993.

———. *The Case against Standardized Testing: Raising the Scores, Ruining the Schools*, edited by Lois Bridges. Later printing edition. Portsmouth, NH: Heinemann, 2000.

Kolenc, Antony Barone. "Legal Issues in Homeschooling." In *The Wiley Handbook of Home Education*, edited by Milton Gaither, 59–85. New York: Wiley, 2016. ebookcentral.proquest.com.

Kopan, Tal. "Ben Carson Ends Campaign, Will Lead Christian Voter Group." *CNN Politics*, March 4, 2016. www.cnn.com.

Krause, Jean M. "Homeschooling: Constructing or Deconstructing Democracy." MA thesis, California State University–Long Beach, 2012. search.proquest.com.

Lareau, Annette. *Unequal Childhoods: Class, Race, and Family Life*. Berkeley: University of California Press, 2011.

Levy, Tal. "Homeschooling and Racism." *Journal of Black Studies* 39, no. 6 (July 1, 2009): 905–23. https://doi.org/10.1177%2F0021934707305393.

Light, Donald W. "Health-Care Professions, Markets, and Countervailing Powers." In *Handbook of Medical Sociology*, 6th ed., edited by Chloe Bird, 270–89. Nashville, TN: Vanderbilt University Press, 2010.

Lipka, Michael. "5 Facts about the Pledge of Allegiance." *Pew Research Center* (blog), September 4, 2013. https://www.pewresearch.org/fact-tank/2013/09/04/5-facts-about-the-pledge-of-allegiance/.

Lois, Jennifer. *Home Is Where the School Is: The Logic of Homeschooling and the Emotional Labor of Mothering*. New York: NYU Press, 2013.

Lubienski, Christopher, Tiffany Puckett, and T. Jameson Brewer. "Does Homeschooling 'Work'? A Critique of the Empirical Claims and Agenda of Advocacy Organizations." *Peabody Journal of Education* 88, no. 3 (July 1, 2013): 378–92. https://doi.org/10.1080/0161956X.2013.798516.

Maranto, Robert, Scott Milliman, Frederick Hess, and April Gresham, eds. *School Choice in the Real World: Lessons from Arizona Charter Schools*. Boulder, CO: Westview Press, 1999.

Martin, Karin A. "Normalizing Heterosexuality: Mothers' Assumptions, Talk, and Strategies with Young Children." *American Sociological Review* 74, no. 2 (April 1, 2009): 190–207. https://doi.org/10.1177/000312240907400202.

Martin, Karin A., and Emily Kazyak. "Hetero-Romantic Love and Heterosexiness in Children's G-Rated Films." *Gender & Society* 23, no. 3 (June 1, 2009): 315–36. https://doi.org/10.1177/0891243209335635.

Martin, Karin A., and Katherine Luke. "Gender Differences in the ABC's of the Birds and the Bees: What Mothers Teach Young Children about Sexuality and Reproduction." *Sex Roles* 62, no. 3–4 (January 12, 2010): 278–91. https://doi.org/10.1007/s11199-009-9731-4.

Massey, Douglas S. *Categorically Unequal: The American Stratification System*. New York: Russell Sage Foundation, 2008.

Mazama, Ama, and Garvey Lundy. "African American Homeschooling and the Quest for a Quality Education." *Education and Urban Society* 47, no. 2 (March 1, 2015): 160–81. https://doi.org/10.1177/0013124513495273.

———. "African American Homeschooling and the Question of Curricular Cultural Relevance." *Journal of Negro Education* 82, no. 2 (2013): 123–38. https://doi.org/10.7709/jnegroeducation.82.2.0123.

———. "African American Homeschooling as Racial Protectionism." *Journal of Black Studies* 43, no. 7 (October 1, 2012): 723–48. https://doi.org/10.1177/0021934712457042.

McQuiggan, Meghan, Mahi Megra, and Sarah Grady. "Parent and Family Involvement in Education: Results from the National Household Surveys Program of 2016." Washington, DC: National Center for Education Statistics, Institute of Education Sciences, US Department of Education, 2017. nces.ed.gov.

Messner, Michael A. *It's All for the Kids: Gender, Families, and Youth Sports*. Berkeley: University of California Press, 2009.

Michels, Patrick. "A House Divided." *Texas Observer*, April 2015. www.texasobserver.org.

Migliaccio, Todd, and Juliana Raskauskas. *Bullying as a Social Experience: Social Factors, Prevention, and Intervention*. Burlington, VT: Ashgate, 2015.

Mineo, Liz. "Law School Professor Says There May Be a Dark Side of Homeschooling." *Harvard Gazette*, May 15, 2020. news.harvard.edu.

Moloney, Kara. "Teaching to the Test." *International Journal of Learning* 13, no. 6 (2006): 19–25. https://doi.org/10.18848/1447-9494/CGP/v13i06/44973.

Moore, Mignon R. *Invisible Families: Gay Identities, Relationships, and Motherhood among Black Women*. Berkeley: University of California Press, 2011.

Murphy, Joseph. *Homeschooling in America: Capturing and Assessing the Movement*. Thousand Oaks, CA: Corwin Press, 2012.

———. "The Social and Educational Outcomes of Homeschooling." *Sociological Spectrum* 34, no. 3 (May 2014): 244–72. https://doi.org/10.1080/02732173.2014.895640.

Noel, Amber, Patrick Stark, and Jeremy Redford. "Parent and Family Involvement in Education, from the National Household Education Surveys Program of 2012 (NCES 2013–028)." Washington, DC: National Center for Education Statistics, Institute of Education Sciences, US Department of Education, 2013.

O'Donnell, Erin. "The Risks of Homeschooling." *Harvard Magazine*, April 10, 2020. www.harvardmagazine.com.

Olson, Kristina R., Lily Durwood, Madeleine DeMeules, and Katie A. McLaughlin. "Mental Health of Transgender Children Who Are Supported in Their Identities." *Pediatrics* 137, no. 3 (March 1, 2016): e20153223. https://doi.org/10.1542/peds.2015-3223.

Orso, Anna. "Philadelphia May Soon Require All Charter Schools, Youth Organizations to Accommodate Trans Kids." *Philadelphia Inquirer*, September 25, 2019. www.inquirer.com.

Ozga, Jenny. "Deskilling a Profession: Professionalism, Deprofessionalisation, and the New Managerialism." In *Managing Teachers as Professionals in Schools*, edited by Hugh Busher and Rene Saran, 21–37. London: Routledge, 1995.

Pace, Elizabeth. "Texas Home School Coalition Speaks Out against Regulation." *Everything Lubbock*, February 21, 2018. www.everythinglubbock.com.
Packer, George. "When the Culture War Comes for the Kids." *Atlantic*, October 2019. www.theatlantic.com.
Padilla, Mark. *Caribbean Pleasure Industry: Tourism, Sexuality, and AIDS in the Dominican Republic*. Chicago: University of Chicago Press, 2007.
Pascoe, C. J. *Dude, You're a Fag: Masculinity and Sexuality in High School*. Berkeley: University of California Press, 2007.
———. "Notes on a Sociology of Bullying: Young Men's Homophobia as Gender Socialization." *QED: A Journal in GLBTQ Worldmaking*, 2013, 87–104. https://doi.org/10.14321/qed.0087.
Payne, Elizabethe. "Sluts: Heteronormative Policing in the Stories of Lesbian Youth." *Educational Studies* 46, no. 3 (June 2, 2010): 317–36. https://doi.org/10.1080/00131941003614911.
Payne, Elizabethe, and Melissa Smith. "Gender Policing." In *Critical Concepts in Queer Studies and Education*, edited by Nelson M. Rodriguez, Wayne J. Martino, Jennifer C. Ingrey, and Edward Brockenbrough, 127–36. New York: Palgrave Macmillan, 2016. https://doi.org/10.1057/978-1-137-55425-3.
———. "LGBTQ Kids, School Safety, and Missing the Big Picture: How the Dominant Bullying Discourse Prevents School Professionals from Thinking about Systemic Marginalization or . . . Why We Need to Rethink LGBTQ Bullying." *QED: A Journal in GLBTQ Worldmaking*, 2013, 1–36. https://doi.org/10.14321/qed.0001.
Pevey, Carolyn, Christine L. Williams, and Christopher G. Ellison. "Male God Imagery and Female Submission: Lessons from a Southern Baptist Ladies' Bible Class." *Qualitative Sociology* 19, no. 2 (June 1996): 173–93. https://doi.org/10.1007/BF02393417.
Pew Research Center. "Public's Views on Human Evolution." Pew Research Center's Religion & Public Life Project, 2013. www.pewforum.org.
Phipps, Polly A., and Margaret K. Vernon. "Twenty-Four Hours: An Overview of the Recall Diary Method and Data Quality in the American Time Use Survey." In *Calendar and Time Diary: Methods in Life Course Research*, edited by Robert F. Belli, Frank P. Stafford, and Duane F. Alwin, 108–28. Thousand Oaks, CA: Sage, 2009.
Pugh, Allison J. *The Tumbleweed Society: Working and Caring in an Age of Insecurity*. New York: Oxford University Press, 2015.
Ray, Brian. "African American Homeschool Parents' Motivations for Homeschooling and Their Black Children's Academic Achievement." *Journal of School Choice* 9, no. 1 (January 2, 2015): 71–96. https://doi.org/10.1080/15582159.2015.998966.
Ray, Brian D. "Homeschooling Rising into the Twenty-first Century: Editor's Introduction." *Peabody Journal of Education* 88, no. 3 (2013): 261–64. https://doi.org/10.1080/0161956X.2013.796822.
Redford, Jeremy, Danielle Battle, and Stacey Bielick. "Homeschooling in the United States: 2012." Washington, DC: National Center for Education Statistics, Institute of Education Sciences, US Department of Education, 2017. nces.ed.gov.

Reich, Jennifer A. *Calling the Shots: Why Parents Reject Vaccines.* New York: NYU Press, 2016.

———. "Neoliberal Mothering and Vaccine Refusal: Imagined Gated Communities and the Privilege of Choice." *Gender & Society* 28, no. 5 (October 1, 2014): 679–704. https://doi.org/10.1177/0891243214532711.

Renold, Emma. "'Coming Out': Gender, (Hetero)Sexuality, and the Primary School." *Gender and Education* 12, no. 3 (September 1, 2000): 309–26. https://doi.org/10.1080/713668299.

———. "'If You Don't Kiss Me, You're Dumped': Boys, Boyfriends, and Heterosexualised Masculinities in the Primary School." *Educational Review* 55, no. 2 (June 1, 2003): 179–94. https://doi.org/10.1080/0013191032000072218.

———. "Learning the 'Hard' Way: Boys, Hegemonic Masculinity, and the Negotiation of Learner Identities in the Primary School." *British Journal of Sociology of Education* 22, no. 3 (September 1, 2001): 369–85. https://doi.org/10.1080/01425690120067980.

———. "Presumed Innocence: (Hetero)Sexual, Heterosexist, and Homophobic Harassment among Primary School Girls and Boys." *Childhood* 9, no. 4 (November 1, 2002): 415–34. https://doi.org/10.1177/0907568202009004004.

Rich, Adrienne. "Compulsory Heterosexuality and Lesbian Existence." *Signs* 5, no. 4 (July 1, 1980): 631–60. https://doi.org/10.1086/493756

Ridgeway, Cecilia L. *Framed by Gender: How Gender Inequality Persists in the Modern World.* New York: Oxford University Press, 2011.

Rios, Edwin. "A California Couple Abused Their 13 Kids—and Weak Homeschooling Rules Helped Them Do It." *Mother Jones*, February 7, 2018. www.motherjones.com.

Robelen, Erik. "Common Core: The Push for Common Standards." *Education Writers Association*, 2014. www.ewa.org.

Roberts, Dorothy. *Killing the Black Body: Race, Reproduction, and the Meaning of Liberty.* 2nd ed. New York: Vintage Books, 2016.

Robertson, Mary. *Growing Up Queer: Kids and the Remaking of LGBTQ Identity.* New York: NYU Press, 2019.

Rooks, Noliwe. *Cutting School: Privatization, Segregation, and the End of Public Education.* New York: New Press, 2017.

Rudolph, Thomas J., and Jillian Evans. "Political Trust, Ideology, and Public Support for Government Spending." *American Journal of Political Science* 49, no. 3 (2005): 660–71. https://doi.org/10.1111/j.1540-5907.2005.00148.x.

Rutherford, Markella B. *Adult Supervision Required: Private Freedom and Public Constraints for Parents and Children.* New Brunswick, NJ: Rutgers University Press, 2011.

Ryan, Caitlin, Stephen T. Russell, David Huebner, Rafael Diaz, and Jorge Sanchez. "Family Acceptance in Adolescence and the Health of LGBT Young Adults." *Journal of Child and Adolescent Psychiatric Nursing* 23, no. 4 (2010): 205–13. https://doi.org/10.1111/j.1744-6171.2010.00246.x.

Salmivalli, Christina. "Bullying and the Peer Group: A Review." *Aggression and Violent Behavior* 15, no. 2 (March 2010): 112–20. https://doi.org/10.1016/j.avb.2009.08.007.
Sanchez, Laura, and Elizabeth Thomson. "Becoming Mothers and Fathers: Parenthood, Gender, and the Division of Labor." *Gender & Society* 11, no. 6 (December 1, 1997): 747–72. https://doi.org/10.1177/089124397011006003.
Sarkisian, Natalia, and Naomi Gerstel. *Nuclear Family Values, Extended Family Lives.* New York: Routledge, 2012.
Schalet, Amy T. *Not under My Roof: Parents, Teens, and the Culture of Sex.* Chicago: University of Chicago Press, 2011.
Sears, William, and Martha Sears. *The Attachment Parenting Book: A Commonsense Guide to Understanding and Nurturing Your Baby.* New York: Little, Brown, 2001.
Sheingate, Adam. "Why Can't Americans See the State?" *Forum* 7, no. 4 (January 25, 2010). https://doi.org/10.2202/1540-8884.1336.
Shuffelton, Amy B. "How Mothers Divide the Apple Pie: Maternal and Civic Thinking in the Age of Neoliberalism." *Philosophy of Education Archive*, 2014: 328–36.
Simons, Lisa, Sheree M. Schrager, Leslie F. Clark, Marvin Belzer, and Johanna Olson. "Parental Support and Mental Health among Transgender Adolescents." *Journal of Adolescent Health* 53, no. 6 (December 1, 2013): 791–93. https://doi.org/10.1016/j.jadohealth.2013.07.019.
Smith, Kevin B. *The Ideology of Education: The Commonwealth, the Market, and America's Schools.* Albany: State University of New York Press, 2003.
Spring, Joel H. *The American School: From the Puritans to No Child Left Behind.* Boston: McGraw-Hill, 2008.
Stevens, Mitchell L. *Kingdom of Children: Culture and Controversy in the Homeschooling Movement.* Princeton Studies in Cultural Sociology. Princeton, NJ: Princeton University Press, 2001.
———. "The Normalisation of Homeschooling in the USA." *Evaluation & Research in Education* 17, no. 2–3 (2003): 90–100. https://doi.org/10.1080/09500790308668294.
Stone, Pamela. *Opting Out? Why Women Really Quit Careers and Head Home.* Berkeley: University of California Press, 2007.
Sullivan, Andrew. "When the Ideologues Come for the Kids." *New York Magazine: The Intelligencer* (blog), September 20, 2019. http://nymag.com/intelligencer/2019/09/andrew-sullivan-when-the-ideologues-come-for-the-kids.html.
Taylor, Tiffany. "Re-Examining Cultural Contradictions: Mothering Ideology and the Intersections of Class, Gender, and Race." *Sociology Compass* 5, no. 10 (October 1, 2011): 898–907. https://doi.org/10.1111/j.1751-9020.2011.00415.x.
Templeton, Rosalyn, and Celia E. Johnson. "Homeschool Learners." In *21st-Century Education: A Reference Handbook*, edited by Thomas L. Good, 297–308. Thousand Oaks, CA: Sage, 2008. https://doi.org/10.4135/9781412964012.
"The ANES Guide to Public Opinion and Electoral Behavior: Trust in Government Index, 1958–2016." American National Election Studies. Accessed September 28, 2019. electionstudies.org.

Thomas Jeremy N., and Daniel V. A. Olson. "Evangelical Elites' Changing Responses to Homosexuality, 1960–2009." *Sociology of Religion* 73, no. 3 (2012): 239–72. https://doi.org/10.1093/socrel/srs031.

Thorne, Barrie. *Gender Play: Girls and Boys in School.* New Brunswick, NJ: Rutgers University Press, 1993.

Thorne, Barrie, and Zella Luria. "Sexuality and Gender in Children's Daily Worlds." *Social Problems* 33, no. 3 (February 1, 1986): 176–90. https://doi.org/10.2307/800703.

THSC. "Leeper Case Decisions." *Texas Home School Coalition* (blog). Accessed February 1, 2014. http://www.thsc.org/homeschooling-in-texas/the-history-of-home-education-in-texas/leeper-case-decisions/.

Timmermans, Stefan, and Hyeyoung Oh. "The Continued Social Transformation of the Medical Profession." *Journal of Health and Social Behavior* 51, no. Extra Issue (2010): S94–106. https://doi.org/10.1177/0022146510383500.

Tolman, Deborah L. "Doing Desire: Adolescent Girls' Struggles for/with Sexuality." In *Sexualities: Identities, Behaviors, and Society*, edited by Michael S. Kimmel and Rebecca F. Plante. New York: Oxford University Press, 2004.

Truong, Debbie. "In a Virginia School, a Celebration of Transgender Students in a Kindergarten Class." *Washington Post*, March 3, 2019, sec. Education. www.washingtonpost.com.

US Bureau of Labor Statistics. "American Time Use Survey: Charts by Topic: Household Activities." 2016. Accessed May 15, 2020. www.bls.gov.

US Government Publishing Office. "Code of Federal Regulations: Title 34—Education." Accessed August 21, 2019. www.govinfo.gov.

Villalobos, Ana. *Motherload: Making It All Better in Insecure Times.* Berkeley: University of California Press, 2014. www.ucpress.edu.

Wade, Lisa. "The Invisible Worry Work of Mothering." *Sociological Images* (blog), May 9, 2016. https://thesocietypages.org/socimages/2016/05/09/the-invisible-worry-work-of-mothering/.

Walks, Michelle. "Chestfeeding as Gender Fluid Practice." In *Breastfeeding: New Anthropological Approaches*, edited by Cecilia Tomori, Aunchalee E. L. Palmquist, and EA Quinn, 151–63. New York: Routledge, 2017.

Walzer, Susan. "Thinking about the Baby: Gender and Divisions of Infant Care." *Social Problems* 43, no. 2 (1996): 219–34. https://doi.org/10.2307/3096999.

Weiner, Lois. "A Lethal Threat to U.S. Teacher Education." *Journal of Teacher Education* 58, no. 4 (September 2007): 274–86. https://doi.org/10.1177/0022487107305603.

Westover, Tara. *Educated: A Memoir.* New York: Random House, 2018.

"What Is FoSE." FoSE: Future of Sex Education. Accessed September 29, 2019. www.futureofsexed.org.

Wikipedia contributors. "Individualized Education Program." *Wikipedia, The Free Encyclopedia.* Accessed August 10, 2019. en.wikipedia.org.

———. "2008 United States Presidential Election." *Wikipedia, The Free Encyclopedia.* Accessed September 21, 2019. en.wikipedia.org.

Wilhelm, Gretchen M., and Michael W. Firmin. "Historical and Contemporary Developments in Home School Education." *Journal of Research on Christian Education* 18, no. 3 (2009): 303–15. https://doi.org/10.1080/10656210903333442.

Wilson, Julie Ann, and Emily Chivers Yochim. "Mothering through Precarity." *Cultural Studies* 29, no. 5–6 (September 3, 2015): 669–86. https://doi.org/10.1080/09502386.2015.1017139.

Wong, Jocelyn L. N. "Control and Professional Development: Are Teachers Being Deskilled or Reskilled within the Context of Decentralization?" *Educational Studies* 32, no. 1 (March 2006): 17–37. https://doi.org/10.1080/03055690500415910.

Yavorsky, Jill E., Claire M. Kamp Dush, and Sarah J. Schoppe-Sullivan. "The Production of Inequality: The Gender Division of Labor across the Transition to Parenthood." *Journal of Marriage and Family* 77, no. 3 (2015): 662–79. https://doi.org/10.1111/jomf.12189.

Zelizer, Viviana A. *Pricing the Priceless Child: The Changing Social Value of Children.* New York: Basic Books, 1985.

INDEX

agency, 7–8, 13, 33, 52–54, 56, 57, 110, 117, 170
ambivalence, 38, 72, 77, 91, 103, 108, 116, 164
Asperger syndrome, 79–80, 97. *See also* autism
attachment parenting, 14, 158–162, 168
Attention Deficit (Hyperactivity) Disorder (ADD/ADHD), 2, 59–61, 69, 78, 90
autism, 64, 69–70, 79–80, 89, 97, 133
autonomy: of children, 13, 29, 31–33, 52–54, 130, 180, 186, 188–189; of teachers, 94, 106, 109–110, 112

Bartholet, Elizabeth, 177–181, 187, 188, 233n5
"born this way" discourse, 57–58
boys: as future husbands/fathers, 40, 44–45; and gender messaging, 55, 165; and masculinity, 99
bullying, 4, 60, 63, 69–70, 90–91, 95–99, 144, 172–173, 180, 225n15

Carson, Ben, 139, 231n24
Charlotte Mason method, 23
character, 43–45, 47, 57, 130–131, 186–187
charter schools, 6, 25, 76–77, 228n40
child abuse, 21, 41, 53, 79, 177–179, 202, 222n26, 225n12, 233n5, 234n6
Child Protective Services (CPS), 115, 139
child training, 44, 54, 157, 179
childhood: beliefs about, 4, 5, 7–8, 12–13, 33–34, 42–47, 54–58, 146–147, 185–188, 225n11; gender and sexuality, 3–5, 7–8, 29–58, 64, 137, 185–188, 219n12, 224n1, 224n9; health and illness, 84–86; ideologies of, 13, 15, 33–35, 57–58, 62, 86–88, 130–131, 186–187; innocence, 4, 12, 34–35, 39–42, 46–47, 55–57, 64, 130, 224n9; as a life stage, 7, 33, 54, 131. *See also* children; children's rights; mental health: of children
children: and agency, 7–8, 13, 33, 52–54, 56, 57, 170; and autonomy, 13, 29, 31–33, 52–54, 130, 180, 186, 188–189; as belonging to the state, 122, 137; as belonging to their parents, 122, 137, 187–188; and dating, 29–31, 51–52, 64; as heterosexual, 29–31, 40, 44–46, 170; as natural learners, 61, 161; and personhood, 160–161, 180, 186, 188; respect for, 31–32, 49, 84, 186; as sexual beings, 48, 53, 54–56; temperament of, 59, 61, 63–67, 86; as unique (*see* unique child, the). *See also* childhood; children's rights; mental health: of children
children's rights, 33, 56, 178–180, 185–189, 233n5
Christianity: Catholic, 10, 45, 127, 149, 153, 169, 196, 200–201, 210–211; Christian homeschooling conferences, 40–41, 43–44, 52–53, 114–115, 126–127, 137, 139–140, 149–153, 161, 169, 187, 200–201, 231n23; conservative/Evangelical, 3, 18, 26, 119, 131, 170, 183, 187, 196, 203, 211, 222n19, 225n12, 230n13, 230n17, 235n35; fundamentalist, 1, 10, 17, 19, 27, 126–127, 149, 178–180, 187–188, 203, 205, 211, 221n11, 230n16, 235n35; and public schools, 36–37, 40, 79, 115, 120, 126–127, 131; United States as a Christian nation, 123–124, 234n12

251

Classical education, 23
Coalition for Responsible Home Education, 178, 222n25
common school model, 6, 92
compulsory education, 7, 17, 19, 132, 175
Common Core, 110, 125–126, 135–139, 202, 230n20
consent, 32, 48–49, 52–54, 170, 186
corporal punishment, 179, 234n11
creationism, 123, 126–127, 178, 230n13, 230n15

deskilling of the teaching profession, 108–11
disability, 69–76, 133–134, 226n13; accommodation for, 4, 71, 78, 226n11; behavioral, 69, 71; developmental, 69, 71, 79; learning, 1, 67–69, 73–74, 91, 226n5; and medication, 66, 71, 75, 90–91
Dobson, James, 18
Duggan, Lisa, 92, 181
Duggar, Michelle, 43–44, 151, 225n12

education reform, 6–7, 14, 17–18, 62, 91–95, 88, 105, 110, 118, 135–138, 141, 182–183, 185
educational neglect, 177–179, 222n25, 226n10, 233n5
evolution, 122–124, 126–127, 230n13, 230n17

fathers/fatherhood, 114; and accountability, 14, 152–153; authority of, 152–153, 186; as breadwinners, 157–158, 162–163; and childcare, 148; as head of household, 152; and homeschooling labor, 142, 162–163; role in/contributions to homeschooling, 44–45, 114–115, 144, 149, 152–155, 163, 169, 232n18
Focus on the Family, 18

gender: and childhood, 3, 4, 5, 7–8, 29–58; differences, 44–45; division of labor, 14, 142–176; essentialism, 14, 56, 148, 150, 159, 161–162, 164, 232n16; expression, 56;

identity/sense of self, 50, 54–56, 57–58, 186–187; inequality, 5, 8–9, 14–15, 148, 162–170, 182, 187, 188, 232n16, 232n19, 233n25–26; as innate, 55–56; and the institution of education, 7–8, 34–35, 219n12; and the institution of the family, 34–35; and methodology, 204–206; policing, 99; social constructionist view of, 47, 161–162. *See also* boys; fathers/fatherhood; girls; mothers/motherhood
giftedness, 4, 69, 76–79, 89–90, 95–97, 101, 133
girls: as future wives/mothers, 40, 44–45; and gender messaging, 187; and modesty, 45; and self-confidence, 2, 85, 98; and sexuality, 1–2, 30, 39, 42, 48–49, 50, 64, 99, 224n9, 225n14, 225n16;
government: anti-Christian bias of, 126, 231n23; as anti-education, 128–130; discourses about, 12; encroachment into family, 116, 120–122, 125–126, 139–140; federal, 116–118, 135–139, 231n22; local, 117, 136; state, 20, 115, 117, 136, 139; trust in, 116–118, 130–131, 146–148; views on, 14, 21, 87, 114–141, 147, 231n23. *See also* state, the
Great Homeschool Conventions, 139, 202

Harvey, David, 181, 235n19
Hays, Sharon, 8–9, 147–149
hegemonic masculinity, 99
Heritage Foundation, 181
heteronormativity, 225n19; and children, 31, 35–36, 40, 44, 57–58, 99, 137, 170, 187; of homeschooling community, 26, 149, 168–170; of public schools, 4, 13, 35, 40, 170
Holt, John, 17–18, 19, 221n5
Home School Legal Defense Association, 11, 19, 179, 222n23, 234n12
homeschooling: advantages of, 1–2, 10, 29–30, 32, 36, 59–88; co-ops, 22–23, 38, 82, 169, 222n19; critiques of, 15; curriculum/instruction, 12, 21–25, 65, 68,

79–84, 86, 114, 223n33; demographics of homeschoolers, 12, 26–27, 198; disadvantages of, 10, 36; and diversity, 4–5, 12, 131, 209; eclectic, 23, 38, 65, 80, 86; history of, 12, 17–20, 25, 220n11; laws, 115, 139, 152; legalization of, 19–20, 221n11; misconceptions about, 23–24, 208–209; normalization of, 92; outcomes, 12, 24–25; philosophies, 10, 21–25; prevalence of, 3, 5, 11, 12, 17, 25–27, 223n38; and race, 26–27, 182–185, 199, 221n11; regulation of, 11, 12, 15, 19–21, 22, 139–141, 177–179, 181–182, 185, 220n29, 222n21, 222n23–26, 226n10, 233n5; religious, 11, 18–19, 23, 35–47, 60, 83, 127, 178–179, 187, 204, 222n19, 235n35; as a social movement, 12, 17–20, 139, 151–152, 222n19; as under threat, 115, 139–140, 177, 231n23; as women's work, 14–15, 114, 142–176, 199, 204
homosexuality. *See* LGBTQ+

ideology, 117–118, 180, 220n19, 225n11, 234n14; of childhood, 13–14, 33–34, 57–58, 62, 88, 130–131, 137, 186–188; of education, 93; of gender and sexuality, 56–58; ideological sacrifice, 130–131; of motherhood, 8–9, 14–15, 87, 146–149, 168, 172, 176, 184; neoliberalism as, 9, 87–88, 175, 179, 184; of school choice, 88, 111–113, 180–184
individualism, 62, 170–176, 181, 185
Individualized Education Program (IEP), 78, 226n11. *See also* disability: accommodation for
intensive motherhood, 5, 8–9, 15, 87, 103, 146–150, 158–162, 168, 172, 182, 186

Jasper, James, 139, 152, 231n23

Kohn, Alfie, 171, 233n28

La Leche League, 143, 160
Lambert, Lyndsay, 114, 149

Lambert, Tim, 114–116, 139, 149
Leeper v. Arlington Independent School District, 20
LGBTQ+: anti-LGBTQ+ sentiment, 6, 36–37, 45–46, 119, 122–125, 136, 137, 139, 169–170, 203, 205, 230n13; and methodological concerns, 203–206; parents, 38, 166–167, 169–170, 211, 232n16; researcher identity, 203; youth, 3, 52, 57–58, 99, 187, 211, 224n1
Lois, Jennifer, 9, 148

mental health: of children, 71, 89–91, 96–98, 105, 173, 180, 187; of mothers, 74, 102–103; of teachers, 110
methodology: access, 202–204, 210–211; challenges, 204–211; data analysis, 200, 202; interviews, 9, 10, 12, 119, 195, 196–200, 207, 216–217; participant observation, 9, 10, 12, 14, 146, 195, 200–202; positionality, 202–204, 210–211; recruitment, 196, 198, 204; respondent characteristics, 10, 197–200, 212–215, 229n10; study design, 9, 11–12, 195–202, 236n2; survey, 9, 10, 146, 195–197, 199, 204, 205–210
Meyers v. Nebraska, 19
modesty, 45, 161, 204
Moore, Raymond and Dorothy, 18–19
mothers/motherhood, 5, 8–9, 13–15, 26, 142–176, 232n16; and accountability, 75–76, 147, 168; as advocates, 72, 74, 103, 150; depoliticization of, 15, 146, 170–176, 188–189; and disability, 71–72, 75–76, 180; as divinely ordained, 150–151; "good mother," 8, 75, 141, 148, 175, 183–184; as ideal educators, 108–111, 150; and invisible labor, 167–168; managerial role of, 71–72, 75, 77–78, 85–88, 95, 103, 188; and neoliberalism, 9, 15, 73, 78, 86–88, 92–93, 102–103, 108, 146–149, 168–176, 182, 184, 188; and paid labor force participation, 60, 74, 85, 87, 143–145, 147–148, 155–158, 161, 165, 166, 184;

mothers/motherhood (*cont.*)
and responsibility, 89, 94, 101, 113, 125, 147, 150–152, 156–158, 163, 168, 173–176, 181; and sacrifice, 142, 145, 158, 165, 184, 188, 233n32; and social change, 173–176. *See also* ideology: of motherhood; intensive motherhood; parenting

motivations for homeschooling, 3–4, 5, 10–12, 26–27, 195; bullying, 98–99; educational needs, 59–113; religion, 1, 5, 26, 208; peer environment, 2, 39, 50–52; peer influence, 4, 34, 35; school environment, 5, 26, 34–35; gender and sexuality related, 35–58

Murphy, Joseph, 204, 219n8, 220n1, 223n28

National Center for Education Statistics (NCES), 25–27, 207, 223n38

neoliberalism, 5–7, 15, 92–93, 148, 179, 181–182, 185–186, 235n19; and childhood, 186; and education, 62, 88, 91–95, 105–111 146, 181–183, 185, 188–189; and family life, 92–93, 182, 189; and motherhood, 9, 15, 73, 78, 86–88, 92–93, 102–103, 108, 146–149, 168–176, 182, 184, 188

No Child Left Behind, 110, 135, 138

Obama, President Barack, 119–122, 126, 132, 136, 229n11

obedience, 44, 76, 153, 186

parental rights, 11, 19, 56, 115, 126, 139, 187–188, 222n23, 222n25, 233n5

parenting: active parenting, 112; beliefs about, 5, 8–9, 12; and citizenship, 183–184; as gendered practice, 14, 103, 146–148, 161–162, 233n25; and intuition, 171–172; and mindfulness, 54; practices, 156–157, 171–172, 186; responsibilities of parents, 47, 56, 120–121, 125, 130–131, 175, 188. *See also* attachment parenting; fathers/fatherhood, mothers/motherhood

peer pressure, 2, 43, 50–52

Pesta, Duke, 137

Pierce v. Society of Seven Sisters, 19

private schools, 4, 6, 11, 20, 37, 66, 76, 78–79, 88, 92, 95–97, 100, 102–104, 107, 182–183

privatization, 5–7, 15, 92–94, 181, 219n8. *See also* neoliberalism

progressive education, 11, 17–19

public school(s): administrators, 73–74, 78, 93–94, 100–102, 104, 112, 134, 173; as anti-Christian, 1–2, 115, 122–127, 139, 231n23; as childcare, 74, 125, 129–130; and children's needs, 13, 18, 32; conflict with, 2–4, 69–76, 90, 99–102, 139, 180; as constraining gender/sexuality, 1, 4, 12–13, 33–34, 47–57, 180; curriculum/academic instruction, 4, 8, 13, 35–38, 48–50, 110, 185; funding, 14, 94–95, 118, 131–135, 180, 185, 188–189; as gendered institutions, 7–8, 35, 219n12; as inflexible, 67–68, 73–75, 80, 81, 112; metaphors for, 130, 143; and mothers, 13–14, 76–77, 170–176; as overly sexual spaces, 4–6, 12, 33, 35–47, 57, 123–124, 137, 180; and peers, 8, 34, 35–36, 38–39, 89–90; policies, 69–70, 73, 101; political bias of, 4, 118–131, 135; and politics/the state, 4, 14, 89, 109, 117–118; privatization of, 5–7, 15, 94, 219n8; as producing workers, 128–129; quality of, 24–25, 89, 91, 93, 95, 99–108, 119–120, 181; ratings of, 102, 104–105; relationship with families, 5, 7, 94–95, 125; school environment, 8; and sexuality, 1, 28–58, 89, 91, 123–125, 137; as a state institution, 5, 117–135, 128, 131, 148; student safety,

70, 77, 85, 89, 95–99, 188; support for, 1–2, 65–66, 85, 106
Pugh, Allison, 86, 148

race/racism, 18, 26–27, 34, 88, 121, 136, 147, 169, 182–185, 188–189, 198–199, 203–204, 235n29
Reich, Jennifer, 86, 103, 199, 233n29, 233n32
religious freedom, 19
religious Right, the, 18–19, 183, 221n11

sacred child, the, 7–8, 33–34, 62, 87–88
school choice, 5–7, 13–15, 62, 88, 91–95, 102, 104, 107–108, 112–113, 146, 180–189, 228n40
school prayer, 1, 10, 18, 195
secularism, 18, 126–127, 140, 187, 202, 231n23
segregation, 18, 182–185, 189, 221n11
segregation academies, 182–183
sex education, 1, 3, 5, 10, 34, 36–39, 48–49, 89, 91, 120, 137, 186, 195, 231n22
sexual harassment, 98–99
sexual violence, 49, 53, 225n16
sexuality, 30; abstinence, 3, 34, 45, 48–49, 89, 137, 224n9; and childhood, 3–5, 7–8, 29–58, 64, 137, 170, 180, 185–189, 195; and education/schools, 4, 8, 12–13, 33–38, 40, 47–52, 122–125, 137, 180, 186, 189, 219n12; essentialist view of, 56–58; and family, 34–35, 37–38, 49, 186, 219n12; as innate, 33, 54–58; and methodological concerns, 203–206; and morality, 36, 41, 42–47, 48–49, 57, 89, 91, 186; and religious beliefs/values, 1–2, 29–31, 36–37, 41, 45–46, 122–125, 230n13; sexual behavior, 42–47, 50–52, 57–58; sexual desire, 58, 225n14, 225n16; sexual identity, 33, 43, 46–47, 50, 52, 54–56, 57–58, 186–187; sexual knowledge, 34, 39, 40–42, 48–50, 57, 137 186;

sexual pleasure, 49, 53, 225n16; social constructionist view of, 47, 57–58. *See also* heteronormativity; LGBTQ+; sex education; sexual harassment; sexual violence
single parents, 73–75, 79–80, 169, 198–199
social class, 8, 15, 18, 26, 34, 57, 103, 147, 182–185, 188–189, 199–200, 204
socialization, 63, 128, 144, 170,
standardized tests/testing, 21, 24, 61, 77, 84, 90, 93–94, 104–110, 134, 171, 180
state, the, 5, 7, 12, 33, 14–15, 115–118, 148–149, 152, 234n14; critiques of, 118–141; and education, 109–110, 117–118, 128–130; and parents' rights, 115, 181–182, 187. *See also* government
Stevens, Mitchell L., 5, 62

Teach for America, 110, 228n40
teachers: and accountability, 93, 105, 110; agency/autonomy, 94, 106, 109–110, 112; conflict with, 2–3, 27, 59–60, 73–74, 77–78, 90–91, 100–101, 111; credentialing of, 110–111; efficacy of, 13, 67, 69–72, 76, 90, 93–95, 100–101, 110, 112, 132–134, 173, 180; praise for, 66, 69–70, 105; as state employees, 117–119; unions, 94. *See also* deskilling of the teaching profession
Texas, 11–12, 20–21, 115, 134, 139–140, 171, 178, 195–197, 206–207, 220n32, 222n21, 226n10, 230n20
Texas Home School Coalition (THSC), 20, 44, 114–115, 126, 139, 149–151, 202, 211, 222n25, 225n12
Texas Unschoolers, 52–54, 154, 200–201
transgender. *See* LGBTQ+
Turpin family, 177–178, 222n26, 234n6

unique child, the, 13, 59–88, 89, 95, 106, 112, 146, 180, 181, 185–186 unschooling, 10, 11, 22–23, 31–32, 35, 52–54, 65–67, 82–84, 86, 107, 130, 154, 160–162, 167–172, 175, 188, 200–201, 211, 233n28

vaccination, 9, 86, 171–172, 233n29, 233n32
virtues, 45, 187

vouchers, 6, 182–183

whiteness, 18, 26, 136, 169, 182–185, 198–199, 203–204, 235n29
Wisconsin v. Yoder, 19, 221n15

Zelizer, Viviana, 7, 33, 62, 86–88

ABOUT THE AUTHOR

KATE HENLEY AVERETT is Assistant Professor in the Department of Sociology and an affiliate of the Department of Women's, Gender, and Sexuality Studies at the University at Albany, SUNY. She studies gender and sexuality in the context of childhood, family, and education.

www.ingramcontent.com/pod-product-compliance
Lightning Source LLC
Chambersburg PA
CBHW020249030426
42336CB00010B/692